WILLIAM WORDSWORTH

THE MAN AND HIS WORKS

By E. Hershey Sneath, Ph.D., LL.D.

© COPYRIGHT 1969 AND PUBLISHED BY
FORUM HOUSE PUBLISHING COMPANY
TORONTO — LONDON — SYDNEY
AUCKLAND — CAPETOWN — SINGAPORE
PRINTED IN CANADA

CONTENTS

CHAPTER I

PAGE

BIRTH, HEREDITY, AND CHILDHOOD   1

CHAPTER II

YOUTH. DEVELOPMENT OF POETIC IMAGINATION. NATURE AND MAN .   15

CHAPTER III

IMAGINATION'S BROKEN SLUMBER. NATURE AND MAN IN THE ALPS. NATURE AND MAN IN THE CITY   32

CHAPTER IV

THE FRENCH REVOLUTION. A MENTAL AND MORAL CRISIS   55

CHAPTER V

DOROTHY WORDSWORTH. SPIRITUAL CONVALESCENCE   72

CHAPTER VI

COLERIDGE. THE "LYRICAL BALLADS." POETRY RELATING TO MAN . .   86

CHAPTER VII

THE "LYRICAL BALLADS" (CONTINUED). NATURE AND HER RELATION TO MAN   103

CHAPTER VIII

THE "LYRICAL BALLADS" (CONCLUDED). "LINES COMPOSED A FEW MILES ABOVE TINTERN ABBEY"   124

CHAPTER IX

GERMANY AND RETURN. POETRY OF NATURE   136

CHAPTER X

PAGE

GRASMERE. POEMS OF NATURE 151

CHAPTER XI

GRASMERE (CONTINUED). "THE BROTHERS." "MICHAEL." "RESOLUTION
AND INDEPENDENCE." "THE AFFLICTION OF MARGARET ——." POLITI-
CAL SONNETS 177

CHAPTER XII

GRASMERE (CONTINUED). "THE PRELUDE." "ODE TO DUTY." "CHAR-
ACTER OF THE HAPPY WARRIOR" 194

CHAPTER XIII

GRASMERE (CONCLUDED). "ODE. INTIMATIONS OF IMMORTALITY" . . 204

CHAPTER XIV

COLEORTON. STOCKTON-ON-TEES. ALLAN BANK 231

CHAPTER XV

THE EXCURSION 249

CHAPTER XVI

THE EXCURSION (CONTINUED) 264

CHAPTER XVII

THE EXCURSION (CONCLUDED) 279

CHAPTER XVIII

THE PERIOD OF WORDSWORTH'S BEST WORK. SUMMARY. WORDSWORTH'S
CONTRIBUTION TO POETRY 295

INDEX 317

WORDSWORTH

Of Nature's inner shrine thou art the priest
                          HARTLEY COLERIDGE

                              He sang
          A lofty song of lowly weal and dole
                          WILLIAM WATSON

WORDSWORTH

CHAPTER I

BIRTH, HEREDITY, AND CHILDHOOD

An acquaintance with the mental and spiritual development of a poet is necessary for the fullest understanding and appreciation of his work. This is doubtless true of all poets, but it is preëminently true of Wordsworth. No one familiar with his poetry will deny its peculiarly subjective character. Almost from beginning to end the personal note is struck. It is in a large measure the record of his own experiences and of the feelings, imaginings, and reflections occasioned by them. But Man is no mere microcosm, unfolding his mental life by an inner law of necessity altogether independent of relations to an outer world. He is part of a larger order,— a macrocosm, — in interaction with which he unfolds and develops, working out a personal history. Thus understood, a poet's art is an expression of himself, and all fundamental relations, both outer and inner, must be considered if we are to gain a true insight into his mental life and, through it, a true understanding of his poetry.

One of these fundamental relations is heredity. By virtue of his race connection the poet is related to a Past. His mental history, like the history of his bodily organism, does not begin with what is generally conceived of as birth. The ultimate origin of the mind is, and probably always will be, a debatable question. But if it be in some way an inheritance or derivation, then it seems probable that we derive our mental being, not only in its

essentiality but also, to a certain extent, in its particular disposi-
tions or tendencies. The poet, then, can hardly be regarded as an
exception to the rule. Although genius may be a perplexing problem
to the evolutionist, still the man possessed of it, as organically
connected with the species, is doubtless subject to the same biological and psychological laws which govern the derivation and
development of his fellows. If, then, we are to understand the
life of Wordsworth as a necessary condition to the fullest com-
prehension and highest appreciation of his art, we must study it
in relation to his birth and inheritance. It may be that the knowledge thus gained will aid us very little in endeavoring to account
for his poetic powers; but whether it does or not, it is part of the
obligation of his mental biographer to take into consideration the
Poet's ancestry — paternal and maternal, immediate and remote
— and determine, if possible, in these antecedents, the origin
of those unique powers, "the vision and the faculty divine,"
which, in their highest exercise, enabled him to "see into the
life of things."

Unfortunately, we find very little in Wordsworth's ancestry that
accounts for his peculiar gifts. On his father's side his descent
can be traced from a line of yeomen — a line of forceful men,
some of whom seem to have been active in private and public
affairs. His father was a lawyer of fair abilities. Of his mother's
antecedents very little is known beyond what is given in Wordsworth's "Autobiographical Memoranda." Christopher Wordsworth
informs us that one of William's maternal ancestors was Richard
Crackanthorpe, "one of the ablest and most learned divines in the
most erudite age of English theology, the reign of James I." [1]
Legouis suggests that "those interested in symbolism will doubtless find an instance of it in these antecedents of a man who
was destined so to weld together nature and theology as to form
from them the most complete and most orthodox scheme of

---

[1] Memoirs of William Wordsworth, edited by Henry Reed, I, 30,

natural religion." [1] But symbolism is not science and it is value-less in helping us to determine origins, so that we have little in what is known of Wordsworth's more immediate ancestors, paternal or maternal, that throws light on the subject of in-herited gifts.

The problem of hereditary obligation in Wordsworth's case becomes still more perplexing when we take into consideration the peculiar character of his genius. He was endowed with the mystic's consciousness, which was intimately associated with his poetic power ; indeed, much of his imaginative life was profoundly affected by it. When most truly a poet, he was a mystic poet — a seer, with the seer's mystical vision. The tendency toward a spiritual conception of the universe, which marks so much of his poetry, appears to have its roots in this form of consciousness, in which the spirit seems gradually to withdraw from sense and to gaze with a penetrating eye on the inner nature of Reality. " The vision and the faculty divine," " the light that never was, on sea or land," — these are the very soul of his poetic genius, when he is at his best as a poet. But it is this power of poetic vision, or insight, which is inseparably connected with a peculiar mysticism which often reaches its most pronounced form in a trance to which the Poet was subject not only in his childhood and youth but even in mature years. The more specific nature of this trance experience, and its relation to his genius, will be manifest as we proceed. So far as evidence is concerned, we can trace very little in his ancestry that adequately accounts for this peculiar phenomenon. In the present state of uncertainty concerning the explanation of *normal* consciousness from the point of view of heredity, it would certainly be unsafe to infer anything of a very specific character in regard to the explanation, from this standpoint, of that which seems so preëminently supernormal, especially in view of the very meager data at hand.

[1] Legouis, The Early Life of William Wordsworth, translated by J. W. Matthews, 21,

It may be said, however, in a general way, that Wordsworth's poetic genius, in its more spiritual aspects, may be due to an hereditary obligation which, as a Northman, he owed to a remote past. It does not require much straining of belief to accept the statement of Professor Veitch, who, in speaking of the Poet's emotional sense of the unseen, says it "had its source deep down in a certain heredity of feeling, due to the past, and nourished by circumstances of scenery and of race. In him it was sublimated. What had been but a dim working through the ages on the fears of the older Cymric and Scandinavian people became in him, as he lived and grew with open and fervid heart, a revelation of moral and spiritual truth, and thus an inspiration for mankind. And this was at the root of his moral and theistic feeling." [1]

On the whole, we can recognize only this very general and somewhat indefinite obligation to his ancestors on the part of Wordsworth as a poet. This seems still more singular when it is remembered that nearly all of the Wordsworth children were possessed of poetic temperament. Dorothy Wordsworth was in many respects as real a poet as her brother William. It will be evident, in the course of our study, to what extent he was indebted to her keen observation, imagination, and insight, and how truly he could say :

> She gave me eyes, she gave me ears;
> And humble cares, and delicate fears;
> A heart, the fountain of sweet tears;
> And love, and thought, and joy. [2]

Captain John Wordsworth, the brother whom William and Dorothy so dearly loved, was also a man of poetic sympathy and appreciation, as well as of poetic judgment. His brother speaks of him as "the silent Poet." He had the love for Nature so characteristic of this generation of Wordsworths; also the "practised eye," the "inevitable ear," and the "watchful heart" of a

---

[1] Wordsworthiana, edited by William Knight, 298.
[2] The Sparrow's Nest, 17-20.

poet. Furthermore, he read and understood the merit of his brother's poetry, and predicted for it a future, when many of his more eminent contemporaries were pointing out its real and supposed deficiencies, and consigning it to an inglorious oblivion. All this reveals the fact that he was, in a measure at least, the "silent Poet" his brother thought him to be.

There was, then, in this Wordsworth family a decided poetic strain, and the common possession of this endowment by the brothers and sister makes it still more difficult for the psychologist to account for Wordsworth's genius, except in a very general way, on the basis of inheritance.

Wordsworth, however, seems to have recognized a certain hereditary obligation to his mother. This recognition consists of conjecture only, and it is somewhat ambiguous in character. On the surface it seems to be merely an acknowledgment of what he considers to be a common indebtedness of infants to maternal parents. Indeed, we are left in doubt whether he refers to a peculiar maternal inheritance at all or merely to an acquisition, due to the intimate relation which the child sustains to his mother after birth, or to both. The more obvious interpretation of his words would indicate belief in an inherited "infant sensibility," which is "augmented and sustained" as the child drinks in "the feelings from his mother's eye," and "holds mute dialogues with his mother's heart." This infant sensibility links him to the external world, and irradiates, beautifies, and exalts objects of sense. It gives him "the first poetic view of our human life." It is thus that the otherwise prosaic world is transformed. The mysticism so characteristic of Wordsworth is quite manifest in this beautiful conception, which he clothes in equally beautiful words :

> Blest the infant Babe,
> (For with my best conjecture I would trace
> Our Being's earthly progress), blest the Babe,
> Nursed in his Mother's arms, who sinks to sleep,
> Rocked on his Mother's breast ; who with his soul

Drinks in the feelings of his Mother's eye!
For him, in one dear Presence, there exists
A virtue which irradiates and exalts
Objects through widest intercourse of sense.
No outcast he, bewildered and depressed:
Along his infant veins are interfused
The gravitation and the filial bond
Of nature that connect him with the world.
Is there a flower, to which he points with hand
Too weak to gather it, already love
Drawn from love's purest earthly fount for him
Hath beautified that flower; already shades
Of pity cast from inward tenderness
Do fall around him upon aught that bears
Unsightly marks of violence or harm.
Emphatically such a Being lives,
Frail creature as he is, helpless as frail,
An inmate of this active universe:
For feeling has to him imparted power
That through the growing faculties of sense
Doth like an agent of the one great Mind
Create, creator and receiver both,
Working but in alliance with the works
Which it beholds.— Such, verily, is the first
Poetic spirit of our human life,
By uniform control of after years,
In most, abated or suppressed; in some,
Through every change of growth and of decay,
Preëminent till death.[1]

But, beautiful as this conception is, it cannot be reckoned with seriously as a factor in the explanation of poetic genius. Science is too prosaic and matter-of-fact for that. It may do for the poet, but not for the inductive philosopher. It may satisfy æsthetic imagination and feeling, but of course it is not logical inference from established fact. This conception is inconsistent, also, with the conviction entertained by Wordsworth in his famous poem entitled " Ode. Intimations of Immortality from Recollections of Early Childhood." Here he inclines to belief in the preëxistence

---

[1] The Prelude, II, 233–264.

of the soul; its incarnation is a limitation of its power. The radiant vision of the child is due to its nearness to his former state of existence as compared with the remoteness of later years. His mental vision is a vision brought with him from another world, instead of a maternal inheritance nurtured by close communion with the maternal parent in the dawn of his earthly life; so that, disregarding the symbolism referred to by Legouis, and the mysticism of Wordsworth's conception, both of which belong to the sphere of imagination rather than to the sphere of science, we conclude that all that can be safely said in attempting to explain the poetic powers of Wordsworth on the basis of his antecedents is that, so far as his immediate ancestors are concerned, very little can be found that indicates obligation to them for his unusual gifts. He was, however, descended from a line of yeomen who were close to Nature, and as a Northman his peculiar feeling for Nature may be an inheritance from early ancestors who daily lived in Nature's presence, and whose emotional regard for her may have been transmitted by Nature herself, through a long line of generations, to him who was to become one of her most faithful devotees, worshiping humbly at her shrine and acknowledging her sovereignty in reverence and love.

Wordsworth seems to have possessed certain original aptitudes or predispositions which, whether received through inheritance or by immediate endowment on the part of the Creator, peculiarly fitted him for the poet's art. In the first place, he had an unusually keen organic sensibility; his powers of sense were very susceptible to Nature's stimuli. From earliest childhood, so far as his mental history can be traced, an exceptional sensitiveness of eye and ear are manifest. This keenness of perceptive faculty, added to another apparent predisposition,— a unique emotional regard for Nature,— preëminently fitted him to be a Nature poet. Their union resulted in an intensity and minuteness of observation that furnished the imagination with a wealth of images of " beauteous forms " with which to carry on its work of idealization and insight.

Furthermore, his imaginative life was, as we have seen, closely associated with a mystical consciousness which so warmed and colored it as greatly to enrich the fruits of its poetic activity. This, probably more than anything else, was responsible for " the gleam" that is such a distinguishing mark of his genius. It affected powerfully his apprehension of Nature and was largely accountable for the refined spiritual conception of things which is to be found in his poetry. This unique tendency of mind was unquestionably original; its manifestations are among his earliest recorded experiences.

There was, too, a constitutional moral sensitiveness which characterized Wordsworth and very early affected his imagination, notably in its æsthetic interpretation and insight. This element was a pronounced factor in his consciousness as a boy, and became more and more so throughout the history of his mental unfolding. Early in his career it impelled him to an ethical interpretation of nature, not only ascribing to her a moral life, but also investing her with a moral office in her relation to Man. How greatly this moral sensitiveness enriched his poetry will be manifest in the course of our study. Indeed, it was involved in his very birth as a poet. He was called and dedicated to be Nature's high priest, and it was his to accept the high office, "else sin greatly." It lies at the foundation of his conception of the poet's art, for with him poetry must have an ethical aim. The poet must be a teacher,—the bearer of a divine message to the race. He deals not with a dream but with things oracular, and is morally responsible for the right use of his gifts.

Another fundamental relation which must be kept in mind in studying the development of the inner life of Wordsworth is his relation to the social environment. The poet cannot, any more than ordinary men, be regarded as an isolated personal unit. He belongs to a race system, and from birth is surrounded by human beings with whom he is in interaction, and by whom he is greatly influenced. He is born into the family and is brought under its personal and organized life. Soon he is initiated into a community whose members are bound together by common interests, manners, institutions, sentiments, and ideals, and is in a large measure molded by its influence. He is born, also, into the state, the community organized under political government, with which he is in constant relation and by which his life of intelligence, feeling, and will is powerfully affected. The poet, by virtue of his genius, may be freer from the law of social environment than his fellows, but he cannot escape it. Even genius is subject to law, as the whole history of the arts testifies.

Wordsworth is certainly no exception among the poets in this respect. Throughout the major part of his poetical career he seems to have been especially sensitive to his human surroundings. Certain individuals proved to be powerful factors in his life and art. Then, too, the simplicity and sincerity of the humbler classes of society appealed to his heart, and the fundamental in Man, as he read it in these simple folk, inspired much of his song. The inequalities of society, the tyranny of the classes over the masses, the evils of the industrial organization, the weakness of the educational system, the oppression of the political order, and the tremendous social and political conflicts of his time affected him profoundly, awakening the great deeps of his nature, coloring his feeling and imagination, and making him preëminently a poet of Man. Remarkable poet of Nature that he was, the human within him was so powerfully affected by the human without and around him that, almost in the very beginning of his career as a poet, he resolved that his theme should be

> No other than the very heart of man,
> As found among the best of those who live.[1]

And although this resolve was by no means literally carried out,— Nature, also, occupying a conspicuous place in his affections and art,— still he attained the position where, under the influence

[1] The Prelude, XIII, 241–242.

of his human environment, he learned to look even upon Nature as hearing often "the still, sad music of humanity."

One of the more formal and direct influences of the social environment brought to bear upon the individual mind in its unfolding and development is education. This usually plays a large and important part, although in the case of Wordsworth it belonged to the category of minor influences. His early education was in a measure directed by his mother. She was not a woman of great attainments, nor possessed of much pedagogical skill, but she dealt wisely with her son. In after years, when reflecting on her method, or lack of method, he commended her judgment in guiding his mental development. An insight into her educational creed, which consisted chiefly in faith in Nature's beneficent instincts, may be gained from "The Prelude." He was permitted to unfold his physical and mental powers mainly under Nature's guidance and under the benign influence that flowed from his mother's heart. He grew up almost like the child of Rousseau's "Émile," Nature being allowed a comparatively free hand. Such liberty proved to be an important influence in molding and fashioning both his body and his mind, and was in a measure responsible for the development of that love for Nature which was so large a part of his life from youth even to manhood's prime.[1]

Wordsworth, however, received formal instruction also during this early period. Sometimes he was taught at Cockermouth by the Reverend Mr. Eillbanks; also at Penrith by Mrs. Anne Birkett. Writing of the latter to his friend, the Reverend Hugh James Rose, he says: "The old *Dame* did not affect to make theologians, or *logicians*, but she taught to read, and she practised the memory, often no doubt *by rote;* but still the faculty was improved."[2] His father too had a part in his early education. He was a man who evidently had some appreciation of poetry, as well as regard for it as a mental discipline, and required his boy to commit to memory certain selections from Spenser, Shakespeare, and Milton.

[1] The Prelude, V, 256–293.   [2] Memoirs, edited by Reed, I, 33.

This constituted the education of Wordsworth in these years of childhood. There is little here that has any special bearing on his future life except, as has already been suggested, the influence of his mother's method in dealing with him. Wordsworth, in the fifth book of "The Prelude," contrasts it with the artificial pedagogy in vogue in the schools at the time of his writing. His sympathies are undoubtedly with the more natural method of his mother. This is what might be expected of one born and nurtured so close to Nature's heart; he was too thoroughly a child of Nature to fail to appreciate later in life the advantages of such a method. He had too keen a regard for Nature's tutorial power to overlook the benefits that came to him during those first years of life, through the means adopted by maternal wisdom in the training of mind and body. And it may be that here, in these early experiences, we have the foundations laid for the educational views to which he gave expression later in "The Prelude" and "The Excursion." However this may be, it is certain that through the liberty granted to Nature by this simple Englishwoman in the training of her son, his susceptible soul early received impressions which gave direction to his future unfolding.

Again, the poet, like other human beings, is born into a physical environment, and this also has much to do with his mental and spiritual development. Not only is it a powerful influence in determining the general life of every soul but also in the determination of the particular quality and form of its functioning. It has much to do with what and how it perceives, imagines, thinks, feels, and wills, coloring its entire mental life and affecting both the quantity and quality of its content. Here again the poet is no exception to the rule; rather, because of his sensitiveness and susceptibility, does he most conclusively prove it. This was undoubtedly the case with Wordsworth. Born and brought up in the Lake country, far famed for its natural beauty, — of which no one has written more knowingly and eloquently than he, — from birth, through childhood and youth up to mature manhood, much of his life was spent in the presence of Nature — of Nature clothed with beauty as with a garment. Hills, mountains, valley, river, lake, and sea were his companions. From childhood he was conscious of Nature's influence, and owned her fashioning power. Nature is at work with his soul at Cockermouth, Penrith, Hawkshead, Racedown, Alfoxden, Sockburne, Grasmere, and other places of abode. When he is traveling among the Alps, or in the mountains of Scotland and Wales, or wandering over the hills or through the valleys, and around the lakes of his own country, Nature's presence is felt as the presence of a teacher, friend, and guide. Sometimes, indeed, her influence is so overpowering that the bodily sense falls asleep and he sees with a spiritual eye. Normal consciousness is lost in spiritual vision, and that which he beholds appears to be within himself, — "a dream, a prospect in the mind."

It is interesting to note Wordsworth's own conception of the influence of Nature upon his mental life during the first years spent in the place of his birth. Cockermouth is located on the western edge of the Lake country, and although not remarkable for its beauty, there was something in his natural environment here that led the Poet in later years to say :

> Fair seed-time had my soul, and I grew up
> Fostered alike by beauty and by fear :
> Much favoured in my birthplace.[1]

As a man he looks back and reflects upon his relation to his physical surroundings and sees in it a molding force. Especially does he call attention to the fact in "The Prelude." Reproaching himself, when in London, shortly after his graduation from Cambridge, for not having written a work really worthy of his powers, and feeling that he was a false and unprofitable steward, he turns to his infancy and childhood, and beholds what Nature has done for him in those early surroundings. There flowed the Derwent, "the fairest of all rivers," which, as the Poet says, loved

---

[1] The Prelude, I, 301–303.

> To blend his murmurs with my nurse's song,
> And, from his alder shades and rocky falls,
> And from his fords and shallows, sent a voice
> That flowed along my dreams.[1]

Again, noting the ministry of Nature through this river, he continues to reproach himself further :

> For this, didst thou,
> O Derwent! winding among grassy holms
> Where I was looking on, a babe in arms,
> Make ceaseless music that composed my thoughts
> To more than infant softness, giving me
> Amid the fretful dwellings of mankind
> A foretaste, a dim earnest, of the calm
> That Nature breathes among the hills and groves.[2]

Later he speaks of the sense of obligation to Nature experienced by him when living in London, as he reverted to the home of his childhood :

> With deep devotion, Nature, did I feel
> In that enormous City's turbulent world
> Of men and things, what benefit I owed
> To thee, and those domains of rural peace,
> Where to the sense of beauty first my heart
> Was opened.[3]

Exaggerated as may appear the belief of the Poet in regard to the extent of her influence thus early exerted, the general truth, at least, may be accepted, — that his natural surroundings were a molding force in the life of the child; and it is not improbable that here in Cockermouth we have the beginnings of that charm which Nature later exercised over him, and that profound regard and religious love with which in after years he worshiped her. It was a " seed-time " for his soul, and he grew up " fostered alike by beauty and by fear."

Studying, then, the mind of Wordsworth, as a poet of Nature and as a poet of Man, in the light of his birth and childhood, we

---

[1] The Prelude, I, 271–274.   [2] Ibid., 274–281.   [3] Ibid., VIII, 70–75.

find, in the first place, that, so far as his regard for Nature is concerned, he possessed a native keenness of sense perception which was closely associated with an imagination predisposed to spiritual interpretation and insight; also a native moral sensitiveness which soon led him to invest Nature with a moral life, and to apprehend her as a moral fashioner, teacher, and guide. Furthermore, he was possessed of an original mystical tendency of mind that powerfully affected his life of imagination. All of this may have been an obligation, of a more or less general character, to a remote ancestry. At any rate, these seem to have been original mental traits. In the second place, in regard to social environment, we recognize primarily an indebtedness to his mother's training, in which she delegated much of the teacher's task to Nature, — a more skillful pedagogue than herself. And finally, much is due to his physical environment for fostering his childish spirit by beauty and fear, for sowing, in this early springtime of his life, seed which later blossomed and bore fruit, yielding a rich harvest of reverence and love for a so-called physical world that, for him at least, lived and moved and had its being in an all-animating Spirit, and which long proved to be the soul of his religion and the inspiration of his art.

CHAPTER II

YOUTH. DEVELOPMENT OF POETIC IMAGINATION. NATURE AND MAN

The years spent at school at Hawkshead, in Lancashire, are a much more important period in the history of Wordsworth's development as a poet, and especially as a poet of Nature and of Man, than the years of his childhood. Wordsworth, with his brother Richard, left home to attend this school in 1778, shortly after his mother's death. He was then nine years of age. We find nothing in the instruction here that seems to have had much bearing on Wordsworth's future as a poet. The few poems composed during this period are not remarkable in any respect, and do not point toward " a career." But in the life that he led, amid his natural surroundings, we find the significance of this part of his personal history. At this time he came in close touch with Nature. His keen sense of sight and sound, and the unusual power of imagery associated with it, were called into activity in an environment such as the Lake district afforded in the neighborhood of Hawkshead, and by the freedom of his school life, which permitted many excursions into Nature's domains; so that contact with Nature became the most significant feature of this period.

The Poet often refers to these early years spent in Esthwaite Vale as most important in their relation to his mental and spiritual unfolding. Here, as at Cockermouth, Nature is at work with him, and Wordsworth as poet, and especially as poet of Nature, is really born. It is in the midst of these beautiful surroundings that a poetic vision dawns and an insight into the life of things is gradually gained.

His experience during these years must be carefully examined, for his ultimate conception of Nature had its roots in it. Indeed, we can hardly exaggerate the importance of this period in our efforts to understand the future poet of Nature. In his autobiographical poem Wordsworth has recorded the powerful influence of his physical surroundings upon his mind at this time. He recites a number of experiences which evidence it and furnish interesting material for the student of the psychology of the Poet. There is an account of how, when snaring woodcock on the mountain slopes, he yielded to the temptation to take a bird trapped by another, and then, influenced undoubtedly by his boyish conscience, heard, amid the solitary hills, "low breathings" following him,

> and sounds
> Of undistinguishable motion, steps
> Almost as silent as the turf they trod.[1]

That is, there is a crude recognition of Nature either as haunted by or possessed of Spirit. Influenced by his moral sense, as well as by his physical environment, he conjures up a retributive spirit of Nature which avenges wrongdoing.

Again, when hunting the raven's eggs on a mountain crag, he has another unique experience, which leads him to conceive of Nature as invested with a kind of spirit life.[2] Conscience seems to have been active here also. We have something more than a boy's ordinary conception of Nature. There is a vague consciousness of a spiritual being in things, that sustains a moral relation to man. The wind utters a strange speech in his ears; the sky wears an unearthly aspect, and the clouds have a peculiar motion. Nature speaks to him through an awakened ethical sense.

The Poet records still another incident in the life of this period which reveals how susceptible his sensibility, imagination, and conscience were to Nature's influence, and the tendency on the part of his mind to invest things with life. Once, on a moonlight

---

[1] The Prelude, I, 323–325. [2] Ibid., 329–339.

night on Esthwaite Lake, while rowing a boat secured by stealth, he saw the huge black peak of Wetherham raise its head from behind a craggy steep which, till then, had appeared to constitute the horizon's bound. This great peak seemed to be "with voluntary power instinct." The grim form appeared to grow in stature as he rowed along, and to stride after him

> with purpose of its own,
> And measured motion like a living thing.[1]

Trembling with fear, he stole back to the place where he had secured the boat, and walked homeward in sober mood. This, however, was not the end of the matter, for he adds:

> After I had seen
> That spectacle, for many days, my brain
> Worked with a dim and undetermined sense
> Of unknown modes of being; o'er my thoughts
> There hung a darkness, call it solitude
> Or blank desertion. No familiar shapes
> Remained, no pleasant images of trees,
> Of sea or sky, no colours of green fields;
> But huge and mighty forms, that do not live
> Like living men, moved slowly through the mind
> By day, and were a trouble to my dreams.[2]

Again we have compunctions of conscience; again Nature is invested with Spirit; once more there is a retributive Power or Powers dealing with the boy and making a profound impression on his sensitive soul.

It is well to note that in all of the experiences mentioned above there was a moral offense committed; an "act of stealth" was involved. In the first case, he had stolen a woodcock trapped by another; in the second, he was endeavoring to rob a raven's nest; and in the third, he was rowing a boat taken without permission of the owner. The conscience of the boy was active. Remorse and fear of punishment had taken possession of him. The

---

[1] The Prelude, I, 383-384.   [2] Ibid., 390-400.

character of the punishment which he feared, at least vaguely, was determined for his consciousness by his peculiar susceptibility to the influence of Nature. It is doubtless the conscience of a remote inheritance working in him, — the conscience of primitive ancestors emerging in this late descendant, who, by a native predisposition, seems in some respects to be almost as closely linked to Nature as they were. He approaches close to the conception of Nature spirits found among uncivilized peoples. His soul seems to hark back to early man.[1] The important fact is that Nature, as something other than brute matter or lifeless reality, has arrested his attention. There are "low breathings" among the solitary hills; the wind utters a strange speech in his ears; the clouds move with a peculiar motion; the huge peak appears to him as if "with voluntary power instinct," — it seems to pursue him "like a living thing"; and in the last instance the impression is so powerful as to cause, for many days, a vague consciousness of "unknown modes of being" that sustain a moral relation to the human spirit. There are here, undoubtedly, the crude beginnings of that spiritual apprehension of Nature which was Wordsworth's rich possession in after years, and which lies at the foundations of his philosophy of Nature.

But Nature does not always appear to him as an avenging or punishing spirit or spirits, inspiring him with fear. Sometimes, even in these early years, she brings joy to his heart, — such joy, indeed, that in after life he recognizes it to be a salutary influence. The Poet records in "The Prelude" still another experience of this period which illustrates the point. There appears to be a difference, in intensity at least, in the feelings of joy which Nature awakens in him as compared with those of his companions. In the experience which he recites, — that of a skating party on a beautiful starlit night, — we have a time that is a happy time for all, but for him "a time of rapture." The freshness and vigor of the boy's spirits are noticeable. The alertness of sense and feeling

[1] Cf. Tylor, Anthropology, 356–358.

is very marked, and his responsiveness to Nature's influence is quite manifest. He wheels about, "proud and exulting like an untired horse" to enter upon the sport. For him the precipices ring aloud, and the bare trees and mountain crags "tinkle like iron." He glides with such swiftness over the ice that, when he is brought to a sudden halt, the solitary cliffs seem to wheel by him "as if the earth had rolled with visible motion her diurnal round." But there is also a softer side to the boy's nature. He retires every now and then into a silent bay; he moves away from the noisy throng

> To cut across the reflex of a star
> That fled, and, flying still before me [him], gleamed
> Upon the glassy plain.[1]

Not unnoticed amid the din and sounds from precipices and crags was "the alien sound of melancholy" sent into the tumult from the distant hills. After his sudden stop he stands and watches the solemn train of receding cliffs until all is absolutely tranquil. Thus early the contemplative side of his nature begins to manifest itself.

Now what construction does the Poet put upon these unique experiences? How, in later years, after he had mingled with the world, far away from these haunts of his boyhood, and far removed from them by the tenor of his life, does he interpret them? There can be no doubt that in his judgment they have more than ordinary significance for the evolution of his mental and moral life. In these singular states of consciousness he recognizes Nature engaged in laying the foundations of his mind. She is ministering to him through her visitations, whether they occasion soft alarm, or whether she makes use of severer interventions, or, on the other hand, inspires him with joy. Nature and he are not strangers. She is close to him, with an important duty to perform. This is manifest in the impressive words of the Poet which follow his descriptions of snaring woodcock and seeking the raven's nest, referred to above:

[1] The Prelude, I, 450–452.

Dust as we are, the immortal spirit grows
Like harmony in music; there is a dark
Inscrutable workmanship that reconciles
Discordant elements, makes them cling together
In one society. How strange that all
The terrors, pains, and early miseries,
Regrets, vexations, lassitudes interfused
Within my mind, should e'er have borne a part,
And that a needful part, in making up
The calm existence that is mine when I
Am worthy of myself! Praise to the end!
Thanks to the means which Nature deigned to employ;
Whether her fearless visitings, or those
That came with soft alarm, like hurtless light
Opening the peaceful clouds; or she may use
Severer interventions, ministry
More palpable, as best might suit her aim.[1]

The "low breathings" heard coming after him, the "sounds of undistinguishable motion," "the strange utterance" of the wind, and the sky that seemed not of earth, — these were Nature's visitations. This heterogeneous complex of painful conscious states was gradually, under the "inscrutable workmanship" of Nature, being welded into a harmony which was to play a very important part in the building up of his real selfhood.

Again, immediately following his description of stealing a boat on Esthwaite Lake, and the troubled consciousness which was the result, he interprets the mental states then experienced as due to the presence of the Spirit of the Universe. This is apparently one of the "severer interventions" of Nature in his own behalf. It was a "ministry more palpable," purifying and sanctifying through pain and fear. Nature here, as well as in experiences from the dawn of childhood, he affirms, was intertwining passions that build up the human soul:

Wisdom and Spirit of the universe!
Thou Soul that art the eternity of thought,
That givest to forms and images a breath

[1] The Prelude, I, 340–356.

And everlasting motion, not in vain
By day or star-light thus from my first dawn
Of childhood didst thou intertwine for me
The passions that build up our human soul;
Not with the mean and vulgar works of man,
But with high objects, with enduring things —
With life and nature — purifying thus
The elements of feeling and of thought,
And sanctifying, by such discipline,
Both pain and fear, until we recognize
A grandeur in the beatings of the heart.[1]

The Poet here teaches what a true psychology and a true philosophy of mind always emphasize, — the important part that moral
experiences play in the development of personality. They, more
than any other class of conscious states, make Man aware of
himself. They, more than other experiences, reveal, indeed constitute, the uniqueness and individuality of personal being. The
consciousness of selfhood is preëminently associated with that of
responsibility, — with the feelings of moral obligation, and of ap-
proval and disapproval. It is in such experiences that Man feels
his conduct his own, — that he is a *self*-directing agent. From
childhood they have, as our Poet affirms, "borne a part, and that
a needful part, in making up the calm existence" that is ours when
we are worthy of ourselves; and it is through them, often awakened
by worthy objects, that Nature intertwines "the passions that build
up our human soul."[2]

Again, referring to his feelings when skating one starlit night
on Esthwaite Lake, he declares the ministry of Nature. For years
she haunts him in his boyish sports, impressing on all forms "the
characters of danger or desire." This is her educational method.
Is this not the import of the following apostrophe?

Ye Presences of Nature in the sky
And on the earth! Ye Visions of the hills!
And Souls of lonely places! can I think
A vulgar hope was yours when ye employed

[1] The Prelude, I, 401–414.   [2] Ibid., 407.

> Such ministry, when ye through many a year
> Haunting me thus among my boyish sports
> On caves and trees, upon the woods and hills,
> Impressed upon all forms the characters
> Of danger or desire; and thus did make
> The surface of the universal earth
> With triumph and delight, with hope and fear,
> Work like a sea?[1]

There can be no question, then, as to the interpretation which Wordsworth himself puts on these early experiences. They are fraught with meaning. The boy is not an alien in the physical world. It is his home. Nature and he do not live apart as absolutely unrelated beings; rather does she sustain an intimate and vital relation to him, as the molder and fashioner of his conscious life during these early years. She is a moral teacher, enforcing her lessons through pains and fears and by means of inspirations in the presence of high and enduring things. This is the plain meaning of the Poet, and we shall find it becomes more and more an essential article in his poetic and philosophic creed.

If we pursue the further development of Wordsworth under the direction of Nature, we find it exceedingly interesting to follow the Poet as he traces her influence upon him through fear, hope, and joy, to love. Gradually she appeals to him through the sense of pleasure awakened by her beautiful and sublime aspects. Gradually, too, the pleasures awakened seem to be "of subtler origin." Sensations are experienced that seem to own

> An intellectual charm; that calm delight
> Which, if I err not, surely must belong
> To those first-born affinities that fit
> Our new existence to existing things.[2]

Occasionally, even thus early in his relation to natural objects, amid his joys the mystical poetic vision dimly dawns, and he is conscious of "gleams like the flashing of a shield," and the physical universe speaks "rememberable things."[3] There is, too, a gradual

---

[1] The Prelude, I, 464–475.　　[2] Ibid., 553–556.　　[3] Ibid., 583–588.

transition to a more active intercourse with her. The passion, as he calls it, sustained by nourishment unsought is by degrees sustained by experiences which he himself seeks. As he grows older, more and more he consciously pursues the pleasures which Nature affords, and plans his sports with reference to them. She soon becomes so much of a minister to his desires, that he is

> taught to feel, perhaps too much,
> The self-sufficing power of Solitude.[1]

The psychology of his development during the later years of this school period is very interesting indeed. The gradual sovereignty which Nature gains over his affections is apparent. He becomes more sensitive to her subtler power. The incidental charms which first fastened his heart to her objects grow weaker in their influence day by day, until at last Nature is no longer intervenient and secondary, but is actually sought for her own sake. There is a closer communion with the physical world, resulting in increase of knowledge and in depth of insight. He walks with Nature in a spirit of religious love, and love leads not only to a better acquaintance with her but also to a sublimer joy in her presence. When night is blackened by an approaching storm, he stands and listens

> to notes that are
> The ghostly language of the ancient earth.[2]

Amid fair and tranquil scenes, as well as 'mid gloom and tumult, he says,

> that universal power
> And fitness in the latent qualities
> And essences of things, by which the mind
> Is moved with feelings of delight, to me
> Came strengthened with a superadded soul,
> A virtue not its own.[3]

No longer is he a mere passive, receptive soul. His spirit, in its interaction with Nature, asserts itself, making its own contribution

---

[1] The Prelude, II, 76–77. [2] Ibid., 308–309. [3] Ibid., 324–329.

to things perceived. The creative faculty has been awakened; a plastic power is with him; a spiritual hand molds and fashions; an "auxiliar light" sheds its radiance upon objects; and the soul becomes conscious of a transforming and transfiguring power.[1]

Then, too, so wonderful were his mystical experiences at this time that, later in life, when trying to describe them, he doubted whether faith in the marvelous things he felt could be found. At times there were extreme moments of calm, when normal consciousness was almost wholly submerged in a trance. The world of bodily sense receded from his sight, and another world, apparently emerging from his own inmost consciousness, took its place. Poetic intuition now manifested itself in a most pronounced and mystical form. His view of Nature was gradually transformed; the analytic conception yielded to the synthetic. He observed affinities in things which had no reality for duller and more passive minds. He recognized a brotherhood among natural objects. Through sympathy he transferred his own pleasures to inorganic things. Nature was instinct with life and happiness; truth was revealed to his soul, and blessings seemed to abound on every hand, — they spread around him like a sea.[2]

In short, the mystical Poet is born, and to him this new birth is as mysterious as the new birth of Holy Writ. All of his thoughts are "steeped in feeling," and a nonspiritual conception of things will no longer suffice. A world of isolated individual objects without intimate, sympathetic relations fails to satisfy him. He grasps the essential unity of Nature, and is contented only when, with ineffable bliss, he can feel the "sentiment of Being" spread o'er all things, and can recognize, with a rapturous joy, a spirit life as the very heart of all Reality, the very Soul of things. The world for him is a real cosmos. Such unity and harmony is there among things that, as his mystical soul listens, it hears them all singing the same song. So ravishing is the melody and so rich the harmony, that the fleshly ear is overcome, and the music is audible only to the

[1] The Prelude, II, 362–376.   [2] Ibid., 382–395.

spiritual sense. Sense consciousness is lost in the deeps of a mystical trance, in which he hears the soul-ravishing strains of the song of a spiritual universe:

> Thus while the days flew by, and years passed on,
> From Nature and her overflowing soul
> I had received so much, that all my thoughts
> Were steeped in feeling; I was only then
> Contented, when with bliss ineffable
> I felt the sentiment of Being spread
> O'er all that moves and all that seemeth still;
> O'er all that, lost beyond the reach of thought
> And human knowledge, to the human eye
> Invisible, yet liveth to the heart;
> O'er all that leaps and runs, and shouts and sings
> Or beats the gladsome air; o'er all that glides
> Beneath the wave, yea, in the wave itself,
> And mighty depth of waters. Wonder not
> If high the transport, great the joy I felt
> Communing in this sort through earth and heaven
> With every form of creature, as it looked
> Towards the Uncreated with a countenance
> Of adoration, with an eye of love.
> One song they sang, and it was audible,
> Most audible, then, when the fleshly ear,
> O'ercome by humblest prelude of that strain,
> Forgot her functions, and slept undisturbed.[1]

What an intuition of Nature! — a brotherhood in things, unity in variety, one in many, harmony in difference, spirit in matter, ideality in reality. That which the philosopher gains by the slow and toilsome processes of induction, and by inference from so-called self-evident principles, the Poet seizes in this spiritual intuition.

A more minute analysis of Wordsworth's account of his mystical apprehension of the world at this time reveals the fact that in his judgment it was due to Nature. He tells us that he had received so much from "Nature and her overflowing soul" that all his

---

[1] The Prelude, II, 396–418.

thoughts were steeped in feeling. As a result he could feel with indescribable happiness "the sentiment of Being" spread o'er all things. But not only was this mystical apprehension *due to* Nature; it also *concerned* Nature. There was a synthetic functioning of consciousness, largely dominated by feeling, that canceled the ordinary perception of Nature by the senses as a world of independent entities bound together only by space relations, and substituted for it a world of objects invested with spirit life and existing in spiritual relations, all constituting a harmonious system, and all adoring and loving the one Uncreated Source of Reality. Here, at least, Wordsworth's mysticism does not abolish the reality of things as philosophical mysticism usually does. It does not swamp their being in the immeasurable Being of the Infinite. It destroys merely the world of uncritical sense perception, which is a mere manifold or multiplicity of corporeal objects, and by a spiritual intuition lays hold of the spiritual reality of things, with their mutual spiritual relations and their relations to a spiritual Absolute.

Furthermore, he too is part of the world and is in communion with things, whether earthly or heavenly. And as he listens to the song of a spiritual universe, and his own soul is enraptured with the music, his mystical communion, though ecstatic, is not so profound as to submerge his own self-consciousness, as is so often the case with religious mystics. The "mortal limits of the self," to use Tennyson's expression, are not unloosed. The boundary lines of finite personality are not wiped out. Therefore there is no Pantheism here. The distinct reality of "the Uncreated," the reality of things, and the reality of self are preserved. Wordsworth has simply through his mystical mind apprehended the spiritual nature of *all* Reality.

It must not be forgotten, however, that this new birth, which yielded this world vision, was not instantaneous but rather the result of a gradual process, a stage in the mental evolution we have been tracing. This poetic birth of Wordsworth, with all that it involved, was the result of a gradual unfolding, under the direction of Nature, of a richly endowed, mystical mind. An insight into the life of reality is gained during these years, which constitutes the rosy dawn of that larger and saner vision of the Poet, when he reaches the very height of his power. And if, later, he gives us in verse a poetic and philosophic insight into the heart of things, it is largely due to the fact that in this early period, under the leadings of Nature, he had gained a vision which, if it grew less radiant as he advanced in years, at least grew less ethereal and more truly spiritual, unto the perfect day of his genius.

And now let us turn to another aspect of his mental development during this period. Thus far we have been engaged chiefly in tracing the influence of heredity, education, and physical environment in the genesis and development of Wordsworth as a Poet of Nature. There is, however, another subject of importance pertaining to these years spent at Hawkshead, and to the latter part of his early life at Cockermouth. It relates to his views of Man formed at this time under the direction of Nature. For it must be kept in mind that Wordsworth aimed to be a poet of Man as well as a poet of Nature. Indeed, he claimed that Man was the chief object of his consideration. Although at this time Nature was, of course, preëminent in his mind and heart, nevertheless

> the common haunts of the green earth,
> And ordinary interests of man,
> Which they embosom,[1]

were gradually fastening on his attention. Slowly but surely, under the leadings of Nature, he was learning to love Man, and to love him for his own sake. He soon learned that kindliness of heart abounded most where Nature dictated the tasks of men, — where the complexity of social, industrial, and commercial conditions had not entered to destroy the simplicity of life. Among such vocations was that of the shepherd, and this class of men early appealed to his imagination. They were close to Nature, — so close, indeed, as

[1] The Prelude, VIII, 116–118.

to hear her very heart beat. Their life was natural, simple, artless.
These shepherds, however, were not those of whom we read in
ancient lore, nor those of whom Shakespeare sang and Spenser
fabled, nor such, indeed, as Wordsworth himself had seen living
in a veritable pleasure ground on the vast plains at the foot of the
Harz mountains. These were neither heroic nor hardy enough.
Their tasks were too easy — too free from exposure and daring.
Theirs was not really a contest with the elements nor a struggle
with ferocious beasts. Fit subjects they were for song, but could
not serve as an ideal of Man. Wordsworth's shepherd was of
different mold, — a more hardy and heroic type, the shepherd
of his native hills and mountains. He followed his vocation under
far different conditions, enduring the rigors of a hostile climate,
braving terrifying winds, plodding through deep snows, and ford-
ing swollen streams. He traversed a rough country, caring for
his flocks amid rude conditions, and companionless amid "awful
solitudes." This man, with his giant frame and simple mien,
with his consciousness of freedom in his vast domain, appealed
to Wordsworth. He felt his presence

> As of a lord and master, or a power,
> Or genius, under Nature, under God,
> Presiding.[1]

Nature had given to him a sanctity. He had seen him glorified "by
the deep radiance of the setting sun." He had descried him, as it
were, in the distant sky, "a solitary object and sublime, above all
height!" Thus outwardly man was ennobled before his sight, and
thus early he was led "to an unconscious love and reverence of
human nature." The human form became to him "an index of
delight, of grace and honour, power and worthiness." This type
of man later served as an ideal which accompanied him, and was
present with him in forming his judgments of Man under far different conditions, when he came in contact with the coarseness,

---

[1] The Prelude, VIII, 258-260.

vulgarity, and bodily and spiritual degradation of the world. This
will be manifest as we follow him to London and note the effect
as he beheld the vast, heterogeneous, and depressing throng, —
the sick and crippled, the ignorant and vicious, the downtrodden
and overworked, the idle and beggarly. Nature, through the Poet's
imagination, saved his judgment then, and over all that throng he
could discern a presiding Spirit. In it all he recognized the essential unity of Man, and perceived a noble destiny for him under
God. He had learned his lesson concerning Man so well among the
hills and mountains, through the ministry of Nature, that he was
able to carry it with him into life, and his spirit did not fail as he
beheld the sorrowful human spectacle which the great city presents.[1]

Thus early Nature led Wordsworth to contemplate Man. It is
not meant, of course, that at this time he was supreme in his thought.
During this period not even Nature was prized for her own sake.
In what has just been said the Poet undoubtedly refers to an early
period of his life, — the later years of Cockermouth and Penrith
and the earlier years spent at Hawkshead. Indeed, in his autobiographical poem he confesses that at least during his first twenty-
two years Man was subordinate to Nature in his affections.[2] But
the point to be emphasized is that, through boyhood and youth
up to young manhood, Nature was leading him gradually to a love
of Man for his own sake. Under her guidance he was furnished
with a type of Man on the basis of which, under her inspiration,
he was prompted to idealization; and the ideal thus formed in
these early years became a saving grace to him later in life, —
when he met men in all conditions of physical and moral deform-
ity, — transforming the offensive and depressing picture of sense
into a glorious vision of the spiritual imagination.

But a complete story of the Poet's inner life must consider another influence at work, molding him during childhood and early
youth, even though it be of minor character. Books were not
without effect at this time; they furnished food especially for

[1] The Prelude, VIII, 293-322.   [2] Ibid., 340-364.

fancy. Early in life he read a volume of the Arabian Nights. He learned from companions that this book contained only a portion of these fascinating stories, — that there were four volumes of similar character. This information was to him "a promise scarcely earthly." He arranged with a friend to save enough money to purchase them. Their purpose, however, was never realized. Wordsworth's estimate of the value of such literature is interesting. Contrasting his education as a child with the more modern methods in vogue when he was writing "The Prelude," he states what he regards to be the real merit of books of this character. Indeed, there is hardly anything more delightful in his entire autobiographical poem than the tribute paid to these dreamers and writers of tales. What a ministry they perform! What a benediction to childhood! They minister to the child's self-forgetfulness, transforming the dull world of actuality into the enchanting world of fancy and daydream. But more than this, they prepare the mind for the larger and more serious life of imagination, and this especially is the obligation which Wordsworth himself felt to these "forgers of tales." The words embodying his tribute present a splendid description and, to a large extent, an accurate measure of the influence of the spirit of romance on the mind of the child. That this spirit powerfully affected his own mind when a boy can hardly be doubted.[1] His early days were made happy largely because he was left free to read whatever books he liked. These included all of Fielding's works, "Don Quixote," "Gil Blas," portions of Swift's works, — "Gulliver's Travels" and "A Tale of a Tub," — the last two books being especially to his taste. During holidays, on returning to his father's house, it gave him great joy to find these books again. He calls attention to the fact that often, when fishing, he would abandon his sport, though conditions were favorable to its pursuit, to lie down by the side of his favorite river to read them, and then awake to a consciousness of idling, and experience the "smart reproach" of conscience for thus "defrauding

[1] The Prelude, V, 491–533.

the day's glory." Nevertheless, he feels that these books were performing a very gracious and important ministry, inferior, indeed, to that of Nature, but nevertheless sufficiently potent to call forth in later years a profoundly grateful acknowledgment on the part of the Poet. In his address to Coleridge he asks, "Where had been the Man, the Poet where," had the child not been allowed to range at will these blessed pastures? What would have become of both of them, not only as *men* but as *poets*, if this life of fancy had been curbed? The imagination of the Poet might have died with the death of the fancy of the child. The daydream of childhood and early youth was the precursor and, in the Poet's judgment, the precondition of the poetic vision and insight of maturer years which disclosed to him a world alive with spiritual beauty and meaning.

Thus it is seen that these years spent at Hawkshead constitute an important period in the evolution of Wordsworth as a poet of Nature and a poet of Man. They witnessed the birth of his poetic imagination, whose idealization, vision, and intuition were for many years to be immediately concerned with these two great subjects. They show how, very early in life, Nature arrested his attention, and how he attributed to her a spiritual life and conceived of her in close relations to his soul, ministering to him through moral admonition as well as through joy. They reveal also how even thus early Man engaged his interest, awakening in him an unusual reverence for human nature, and how his boyish imagination formed an ideal of his species that proved a safeguard to him when later he beheld humanity under most discouraging and forbidding aspects, so that his regard for human nature was increased rather than diminished by virtue of the contrast. Here, in these early years, we see the dawn of a day that is destined to grow to a noontide brightness, revealing to us a physical world pulsating with conscious life and disclosing the native dignity and splendor of Man as well as his glorious destiny under God.

CHAPTER III

IMAGINATION'S BROKEN SLUMBER. NATURE AND MAN IN THE ALPS. NATURE AND MAN IN THE CITY

In October, 1787, when seventeen and a half years old, Wordsworth entered St. John's College, Cambridge, as an undergraduate. In "The Prelude" he does not speak very enthusiastically of the benefits derived from his college life. He evidently was not in sympathy with much of the formal instruction there, nor did he have great reverence for those in authority. The general life of the college also failed to appeal to him to any considerable extent. He felt that, by temperament and training, he was not fitted for such an environment. Still, with all of his misgivings, he had his solaces. These came from a consciousness of "holy powers and faculties" with which Nature had endowed him.[1] Often he withdrew from his comrades and the ordinary scenes and experiences of the day, and as he walked alone through the fields his mind would return into herself and be refreshed. At times, "as if awakened, summoned, roused, constrained," he says:

> I looked for universal things; perused
> The common countenance of earth and sky:
>
> .   .   .   .
>
> I called on both to teach me what they might;
> Or turning the mind in upon herself,
> Pored, watched, expected, listened, spread my thoughts
> And spread them with a wider creeping; felt
> Incumbencies more awful, visitings
> Of the Upholder of the tranquil soul,
> That tolerates the indignities of Time,
> And, from the centre of Eternity
> All finite motions overruling, lives
> In glory immutable.[2]

[1] The Prelude, III, 88 f.   [2] Ibid., 106–121.

32

Here, too, as in the Hawkshead days, he invested Nature with spirit, attributing to things not only life but moral life. His mystical soul was functioning. Everything had meaning, even the loose stones lying in the road. Exceedingly sensitive and obedient to Nature's various aspects, he lived in a world of his own creation and was happy in its conscious possession. The description of his riches amid the poverty of his other experiences is very interesting, and relieves the somewhat melancholy account of his Cambridge life:

> I was mounting now
> To such community with highest truth —
> A track pursuing, not untrod before,
> From strict analogies by thought supplied
> Or consciousnesses not to be subdued.
> To every natural form, rock, fruit, or flower,
> Even the loose stones that cover the highway,
> I gave a moral life: I saw them feel,
> Or linked them to some feeling: the great mass
> Lay bedded in a quickening soul, and all
> That I beheld respired with inward meaning.
> Add that whate'er of Terror or of Love
> Or Beauty, Nature's daily face put on
> From transitory passion, unto this
> I was as sensitive as waters are
> To the sky's influence in a kindred mood
> Of passion; was obedient as a lute
> That waits upon the touches of the wind.
> Unknown, unthought of, yet I was most rich —
> I had a world about me — 't was my own;
> I made it, for it only lived to me,
> And to the God who sees into the heart.[1]

Here his mysticism seems even more pronounced than before. He attributes not only life but *moral* life to things — even to loose stones covering the highway. For him the whole world of so-called corporeal things lies embedded "in a quickening soul." We see at a glance how far removed this is from the ordinary view of the material world. An apprehension of corporeal reality

[1] The Prelude, III, 122–143.

that invests with moral life the stones lying in the road indicates a nature endowed with profound mystical insight, and the student of Wordsworth's Nature poetry will fail utterly to understand his spiritual conception and interpretation of things if he does not study them in their relation to his mystical nature. Wherever we find the gleam in his Nature poetry, it is the mystical gleam. Wherever we find the vision, it is the mystical vision. And the meaning that things have is a meaning for Man, and it is an ethical and spiritual meaning. They impart lessons to Man's moral and spiritual nature. Things themselves are possessed of spirit, and live and move and have their being in an omnipresent Spirit, and their office is to minister unto spirit.

Wordsworth manifested his feelings and sympathies, sometimes in gestures and looks, in such a manner that those observing him thought him afflicted with a kind of madness, but he understood it and was not disturbed. It was a heavenly endowment that acquainted him with the spirit of things and enabled him to commune with them. If "steady moods of thoughtfulness matured to inspiration," if prophecy, if poetic vision, or the vision of primeval man may be called madness, then indeed was Wordsworth mad. This was not madness, however, but merely a unique spiritual sympathy with, and mystical insight into, Reality. These exalted moods, with their illuminating visions, were the " god-like hours " of his life at Cambridge.

Still he was not insensible to university life. Often such moods gave way to the pastimes incident to such a place. The sight of so many young men, gathered from different quarters, at this renowned institution, had its influence upon him. It was a scene good to behold. There was also a social side to his nature. Often he went with the throng, loving the idleness and joy of good fellowship. Then, too, Wordsworth was not utterly devoid of sentiment, — indifferent to the memories of the place. He could not walk the ground trod by generations of illustrious poets and philosophers without being stirred in spirit. It was not a matter of indifference

to him that Newton, Chaucer, Spenser, Milton, and other immortals
had lived and learned here. Although imagination slept, it did not
sleep utterly. The subtle influences of his surroundings penetrated
his soul. He "laughed with Chaucer in the hawthorn shade, beside
the pleasant Mill of Trompington," and "heard him, while birds
were warbling, tell his tales of amorous passion." He called

> Sweet Spenser, moving through his clouded heaven
> With the moon's beauty and the moon's soft pace,[1]

"Brother, Englishman, and Friend!" And he continues:

> Yea, our blind Poet, who, in his later day,
> Stood almost single; uttering odious truth —
> Darkness before, and danger's voice behind,
> Soul awful — if the earth has ever lodged
> An awful soul — I seemed to see him here
> Familiarly, and in his scholar's dress
> Bounding before me, yet a stripling youth —
> A boy, no better, with his rosy cheeks
> Angelical, keen eye, courageous look,
> And conscious step of purity and pride.[2]

Once, indeed, he drank to Milton's memory

>   till pride
> And gratitude grew dizzy in a brain
> Never excited by the fumes of wine
> Before that hour, or since.[3]

On the whole, however, the first months of life at Cambridge
were disappointing, and imagination was comparatively inactive.
They were characterized largely by indifference, low aims, and a
dismissal of duty. His memory was languid, his heart "reposed
in a noontide rest," and "the inner pulse of contemplation almost
failed to beat." The exalted emotion which the place excited in
others was not bred in him, nor were the influences of the place
sufficiently potent to shame him out of an easy life or to arouse
him to worthy resolve and earnest endeavor.

[1] The Prelude, III, 280–281.   [2] Ibid., 283–292.   [3] Ibid., 299–302.

Wordsworth left Cambridge to enjoy his summer vacation at Hawkshead. On his return he began at once to renew his acquaintance with things, places, and persons, and his spirit was refreshed. And now his peculiar mystical consciousness asserts itself again. He makes the circuit of the little lake, and a quiet thoughtfulness reigns within him. An exalted mood is his, in which his soul unveils herself and stands as in the presence of God. He has an intuition, or at least "glimmering views," of the immortal life, and of the dignity and strength of high endeavor.

It is interesting to note that here his mysticism, as compared with its description in the previous chapter, takes on the nature of vision. There it was predominantly emotional and in its most pronounced form is described in terms of spiritual *hearing* rather than of spiritual *seeing*. But during the Cambridge period it is pre-eminently a consciousness that assumes the form of vision. This is evident in the account of the trance already given, where he attributed a moral life to all things and *saw* all things embedded "in a quickening soul." Indeed, he says, "I saw them feel." The noetic element is more conspicuous too. The mystical consciousness becomes more articulate in its functioning, and the eternal verities of God, Immortality, and Duty are disclosed to his spiritual eye.

There is, too, a change in his mental attitude toward his surroundings. There is a freshness in the daily life of those whose occupations he loved. The peace and simplicity of these rural folk greatly charm him. Furthermore, he notes a human-heartedness in his love for things. A "pensive feeling" reigns within him. The emotional reactions to the great objects of Nature, and their suggestions of import, are now more subdued, and a calm and semimelancholy thoughtfulness, with its corresponding life of feeling, is his as he contemplates them.[1]

Despite these visions and pensive moods, however, when later he reviewed this period of his history, Wordsworth felt that he had

---

[1] The Prelude, IV, 160–255.

lost ground spiritually, as he compared it with the life of his school days. There was an "inner falling off." He was not as close to Nature now as then. Although conscious that he loved deeply all he had loved before, still there was not that devotion to Nature which characterized the earlier times. A multitude of trivial schemes, of social gayeties and pleasures, seemed to lure him away from a life of solitary and happy communion with her, which meant so much to him in the former days. Yet, in the midst of these social pleasures and pastimes, we are brought to an exceedingly important event in the history of the inner life of the youth, — an event which marks his dedication to the poet's art. He awakes to a sublime consciousness of his poetic endowment. He makes no vows, but vows are made for him, that henceforth, unless sinning greatly, he is to be "a dedicated Spirit." The young man receives a " call " to a high vocation. He will sin grievously if he fails to respond. This call is a profoundly interesting fact in the psychology of the poet. The account of it given to his friend Coleridge must be reproduced here to fully appreciate it :

> 'Mid a throng
> Of maids and youths, old men, and matrons staid,
> A medley of all tempers, I had passed
> The night in dancing, gaiety, and mirth,
> With din of instruments and shuffling feet,
> And glancing forms, and tapers glittering,
> And unaimed prattle flying up and down;
> Spirits upon the stretch, and here and there
> Slight shocks of young love-liking interspersed,
> Whose transient pleasure mounted to the head,
> And tingled through the veins. Ere we retired,
> The cock had crowed, and now the eastern sky
> Was kindling, not unseen, from humble copse
> And open field, through which the pathway wound,
> And homeward led my steps. Magnificent
> The morning rose, in memorable pomp,
> Glorious as e'er I had beheld — in front,
> The sea lay laughing at a distance; near,
> The solid mountains shone, bright as the clouds,

Grain-tinctured, drenched in empyrean light;
And in the meadows and the lower grounds
Was all the sweetness of a common dawn —
Dews, vapours, and the melody of birds,
And labourers going forth to till the fields.
Ah! need I say, dear Friend! that to the brim
My heart was full; I made no vows, but vows
Were then made for me; bond unknown to me
Was given, that I should be, else sinning greatly,
A dedicated Spirit. On I walked
In thankful blessedness, which yet survives.[1]

Here we see Nature speaking to him again, making an appeal to his conscience. The beauty and sublimity of the morning scene awaken in him a consciousness of rare powers, and a moral obligation to make a noble use of them. He seems to be in the control of a higher Spirit, — the Spirit already recognized by him in Nature, — which so lays hold upon him as to dedicate him to her service. He is to be her high priest. It is imposed upon his conscience, and he cannot without grievous sin refuse to accept the call. There is here another instance, more pronounced than any previously referred to, of a sublime consciousness of a moral relationship existing between him and Nature, — that she morally influences and leads him. Later this becomes a fundamental position in his creed.

Furthermore, this consciousness of a " call " sustains some relation to the conception which Wordsworth afterwards held concerning the nature of his art. He never viewed poetry from the standpoint of art for art's sake. Poetry for him is a means for the realization of an ethical end. As a poet he is not merely a painter, nor an artist merely dealing with metrical language and form, but a *seer*, possessed of intuitive powers and vision, beholding the heart of Reality. Hence, like the prophet, he has a message for men. He is responsible for the proper use of the gift of insight. Verse is primarily a medium through which to convey the message. It embodies the vision, which is the reality, the inspired truth. In

[1] The Prelude, IV, 309–338.

this morning hour Nature brought home to him the sacred obligations of his gifts, — of his power of more than ordinary spiritual
insight. His was "the vision and the faculty divine," the power
"to see into the life of things." He was called to be Nature's
oracle, to speak in song the vision she vouchsafes. Thus far
he was merely trifling with rare possessions, an ingrate, ignoring
Nature's beneficence. He must awake and go forth in the strength
and plenitude of his powers, and proclaim what he had seen and
heard, and what he might still see and hear.

This unique experience is for him not merely a *subjective* one.
It is not simply the realization of compunctions of conscience for
trifling with exceptional endowments. The call does not seem to
him to come from within, in the form of the moral self rebuking
or giving command to itself. It is more objective than that, for it
appears to him to come from without. Another Spirit seems to
talk with him, to rebuke and to command. It is the Spirit of
Nature speaking to his soul through the beauty of the dawn. *He*
does not make vows, but *vows are made for him*. A bond unknown to him is given, that he should be "a dedicated Spirit," else
be morally recreant to his trust. To his own consciousness he
undoubtedly seemed to be in the mighty grip of a moral Spirit,
seeking to snatch him away from a life of triviality and indifference
to higher things, and to dedicate him to her lofty service. In this
unique experience we have another manifestation of Wordsworth's
mystical nature.

Wordsworth returned to Cambridge in October, 1788, to enjoy
a life of comparative freedom. It seems, however, to have been a
life of progress. Though free from much of the formal routine,
his time was spent in acquainting himself with literature, and in
quiet meditation. "The Poet's soul," he tells us, was with him, and
ambitions began to stir. He had sufficient confidence in his own
powers to trust that he might produce a work which would endure,
— a work worthy of the reverence of pure hearts. The instinctive
humility which he felt in regard to books and authorship seemed

to pass away, and he no longer stood in awe of mighty names. In other words, he was becoming more and more conscious of his own poetic power, and worthy, and even immortal, achievement did not seem a thing impossible to him. The immortals were men and did not appear so far removed.

One cannot study carefully the history of Wordsworth at this time without being impressed by the fact that even here his regard for Nature seems ever present. Throughout the winter, whenever he could, he was accustomed to visit the college groves and walks, "lingering there through hours of silence" until summoned to his room by the porter's bell. The spell of the place was on him, and the poetic imagination, with its visions, was his. He was accustomed at this time to measure the truth of what he read by the standard established by him through his own previous careful observation of Nature, her forms and laws. He did not value highly the study of the classics. Geometric science, however, yielded him both elevation and delight, and it is interesting to note that the relation of these mathematical abstractions to the laws of Nature — their application to the study of star, sphere, and system — had a great fascination for him. They are the mind's own creation, — created by and out of herself, — and therein, doubtless, in a large measure, lay the ground of the poetic mind's affinity for them. He also derived quiet and profound pleasure, and a sense of permanence and immortality, as well as of certainty, from the study of this science.

During this period Wordsworth had also his moods of mild melancholy "that loved a pensive sky, sad days, and piping winds," "the twilight more than dawn," and autumn more than spring. Many hours, too, were spent in indolence. On the whole, these two winters at Cambridge record comparatively little development, and show merely ambitions and hopes of doing something worthy of his poetic gifts, but with no definite, earnest resolve.

We come now to the second summer after he had begun his life at Cambridge. Evidently Nature is still uppermost in his mind. This vacation was spent chiefly in visiting scenes noted for their beauty. He explored a stream that flowed through Dovedale, and pried into the dales of Yorkshire, and also into less exposed tracts of his native place. He was joined by his sister Dorothy and Mary Hutchinson, later Mrs. Wordsworth. Together they wandered through the Penrith district, visiting the banks of the Emont and exploring Brougham castle. There is little more to note concerning this holiday season except the completion of a poem, begun the previous autumn vacation, entitled "An Evening Walk."

It is apparent from a perusal of the poem that Wordsworth was a careful observer of Nature. One can easily believe his statement, " There is not an image in it which I have not observed." Still he did not deal with Nature literally. His poem, although descriptive, is idealized description. Imagination improvised on Nature. Indeed, he himself bears testimony to this fact. In a prefatory note he says : " I will conclude my notice of this poem by observing that the plan of it has not been confined to a particular walk, or an individual place ; a proof (of which I was unconscious at the time) of my unwillingness to submit the poetic spirit to the chains of fact and real circumstance. The country is idealized rather than described in any one of its local aspects." [1] Intense and accurate observer of Nature that he was, even thus early in his poetic career we notice, what will be more and more evident as we proceed, how far removed Wordsworth as a poet of Nature is from the mere landscape artist in verse. He is something more than a realist in his art. He impresses his ideals upon reality as it is presented to the senses. He himself contributes something to the formation of the poetic product. Later this personal contribution becomes very pronounced and results in an idealization which practically transforms the materials of sense. Then vision and insight become the dominant factors in his apprehension of Nature.

A note of melancholy is struck in this work of his early years, especially in the first two verses. It seems almost feigned when we compare it with the joyous note struck in his later works.

[1] Poetical Works, I, edited by Knight, 5 n.

Nevertheless the melancholy is in a certain sense real. It is characteristic of his early poetry. Legouis says : " Wordsworth, who, at a later time asserted, in opposition to Beattie, that poetry is identical with joy, bore much resemblance, as a lad, to Edwin in ' The Minstrel.' In this light he appeared to his sister, and thus, no doubt, he loved to regard himself. Melancholy casts its shadow over his early compositions ; it emanates from him and diffuses itself over Nature, in which he delights to find its chastened reflection. Profoundly happy as he was in youth, so that in manhood the mere recollection of those blissful years would raise a blush for his momentary bondage to dejection, he nevertheless expresses, in the midst of his delight, no sentiments but those of grief or pain." [1] It is evident from a careful reading of the poem " An Evening Walk " that he was influenced by Collins, Gray, and Beattie, and Legouis is doubtless right in affirming that " Wordsworth contracted the cherished complaint chiefly from others ; from Collins and Gray, but most of all from Beattie's ' Minstrel.' " [2] Melancholy seems to have pervaded the verse of these poets. In the case of Wordsworth it was, at this time of life, his own contribution to Nature rather than Nature's contribution to him.

Wordsworth returned to college in October, to spend an uneventful year. He decided to spend his third summer vacation in a visit to the Alps, accompanied by a young friend, Robert Jones, a fellow student at St. John's. This project was entered upon with misgivings. It was the custom of students at St. John's to devote the third summer vacation to preparation for the competitive examination of the senior year. But Nature had more of charm for Wordsworth than books, and he resolved to slight tradition, and face the disapproval of friends, that he might take this pedestrian tour.

Of course, a tour to the very heart of Nature's beauty and sublimity could not fail to make a deep impression on such a soul as Wordsworth's. Confessedly it was undertaken because at this time Nature was supreme in his mind. He was on the alert, with an

---

[1] Legouis, The Early Life of William Wordsworth, 155–156.   [2] Ibid., 155.

eye natively keen, and carefully trained for observation, and a soul peculiarly sensitive to all that Nature afforded in the way of beauty and grandeur. Not only the account given in " The Prelude," but a long letter to his sister Dorothy,[1] expressive of his great appreciation of the glorious beauty of the Alps, as well as his poem entitled " Descriptive Sketches," published in 1793, reveal a spirit close to Nature, intoxicated by her loveliness and charm, and in preparation to be her high priest and oracle. It is doubtless true that in " Descriptive Sketches " he is influenced by Raymond, with whose account of the Alps he was acquainted, and also by Rousseau, so that there is a lack of spontaneous and original feeling aroused by the memory of his visit. But if the poem is wanting in these respects, in the long letter to his sister there is enough of spontaneity and originality in the enthusiastic account of his visit to convince the reader that Nature, as seen in the Alps, made a deep and lasting impression upon him.

This summer tour had interest for him not only from the standpoint of Nature but also from the point of view of Man. As he journeyed from France to Switzerland he was greatly impressed by the peaceful homes of the peasants. To what extent the simplicity and contentment of their lives appealed to him is made known to us in his own words :

> Oh! sorrow for the youth who could have seen
> Unchastened, unsubdued, unawed, unraised
> To patriarchal dignity of mind,
> And pure simplicity of wish and will,
> Those sanctified abodes of peaceful man,
> Pleased (though to hardship born, and compassed round
> With danger, varying as the seasons change),
> Pleased with his daily task, or, if not pleased,
> Contented, from the moment that the dawn
> (Ah! surely not without attendant gleams
> Of soul-illumination) calls him forth
> To industry, by glistenings flung on rocks,
> Whose evening shadows lead him to repose.[2]

[1] Memoirs, I, 57–65.   [2] The Prelude, VI, 504–516.

In " Descriptive Sketches," also, he speaks of these peaceful abodes. These accounts are all in harmony with what seems to be fundamental in Wordsworth's thinking — that Man and Nature are not far apart. The nearer that social conditions approach those of primitive or patriarchal man, the more accurately does Man hear Nature's voice, and the more fully does she reveal herself to him. This simple life is not "without attendant gleams of soul-illumination." After Wordsworth reaches the Alps, the same peacefulness and simplicity of domestic scene arrest his attention. The pastoral life everywhere has a fascination for him. He is impressed by the simplicity and strength of the natives. He reads

> Lessons of genuine brotherhood, the plain
> And universal reason of mankind,
> The truths of young and old.[1]

In " Descriptive Sketches " he speaks of him who was born and dwelt among the Alps as one who

> all superior but his God disdained,
> Walked none restraining, and by none restrained:
> Confessed no law but what his reason taught,
> Did all he wished, and wished but what he ought.[2]

From a psychological point of view it is well to note Wordsworth's account of the relation between the world without, which he beheld as he journeyed throughout this summer vacation, and the world within himself. There was an inner life that responded to the outer, especially to the life of Nature as he beheld it clothed in beauty and majesty. As of old, she ministered to him, and his soul profited by her service. All that he saw, heard, or felt, he declares,

> was but a stream
> That flowed into a kindred stream; a gale,
> Confederate with the current of the soul,
> To speed my voyage; every sound or sight,
> In its degree of power, administered
> To grandeur or to tenderness,— to the one

---

[1] The Prelude, VI, 545–547.   [2] Descriptive Sketches, 434–438.

Directly, but to tender thoughts by means
Less often instantaneous in effect;
Led me to these by paths that, in the main,
Were more circuitous, but not less sure
Duly to reach the point marked out by Heaven.[1]

And, notwithstanding it was a time when great social and political changes were expected, when triumphant looks were "the
language of all eyes," and "the Nations hailed their great expectancy," and although on their way home they crossed the Brabant
armies on the fret for battle in the cause of liberty, still all of this
had merely a superficial and passing interest for him. This was
not the joy he wanted. He needed no such help, for his soul had
other interests. Nature was his joy and support. The ever-living
universe, he says,

Turn where I might, was opening out its glories,
And the independent spirit of pure youth
Called forth, at every season, new delights
Spread round my steps like sunshine o'er green fields.[2]

His heart was with Nature, and his mind, conscious of her happy
and helpful ministry, was open to her instruction, inspiration, and
delight.

It was natural, of course, that such a journey should increase his
awe of, and strengthen his love for, Nature. He wrote to his sister:
"Among the more awful scenes of the Alps, I had not a thought
of man, or a single created being; my whole soul was turned to
Him who produced the terrible majesty before me." [3]

Many places, for example Lake Lugano and Lake Como, impressed him by their beauty and loveliness, and afforded him much
delight. In the letter just referred to he says: "Ten thousand
times in the course of this tour have I regretted the inability of
my memory to retain a more strong impression of the beautiful
forms before me; and again and again, in quitting a fortunate
station, have I returned to it with the most eager avidity, in the

[1] The Prelude, VI, 743-753.   [2] Ibid., 774-778.   [3] Memoirs, I, 60.

hope of bearing away a more lively picture. At this moment, when many of these landscapes are floating before my mind, I feel a high enjoyment in reflecting that perhaps scarcely a day of my life will pass in which I shall not derive some happiness from these images." [1]

A mind so closely observant, so sensitive to beauty, so eager to drink in the full measure of loveliness afforded by Nature in the Alps, could not fail to undergo a development. A lively and susceptible imagination must have been molded by such an environment. The mind feasted daily on scenes of beauty, which were probably as rich in suggestion as in actual content. It is doubtless true, as Legouis says, that " except when he wrote the Sketches, he was not, and had no ambition to be, the poet of the Alps. But when once he had seen them, however hastily, there remained ever after in his mind a lofty exaltation with which the lakes and mountains of his own country alone could never have inspired him. From this time forward there arose, in the background, as it were, of his thought, forms of more majestic grandeur than those of Helvellyn. His imagination dilated that it might embrace a horizon wider and more fascinating than those of Hawkshead and of Grasmere. And lastly, although he afterwards protested unceasingly against the practice of comparing the scenery of one country with that of another, his travels in Switzerland enabled him to understand better the peculiar charm of Cumberland." [2] The sixth book of " The Prelude," composed in the spring of 1804, and " Descriptive Sketches," written 1791 and 1792, and published 1793, are largely fruits of this journey to the Alps. Wordsworth returned to St. John's College in October, 1790, to complete his course. In January, 1791, he received the degree of Bachelor of Arts, and left Cambridge.

At the time of graduation Wordsworth had not come to a decision concerning his life work. Neither the ministry nor the law seems to have had attractions for him. Thus far the poet's

[1] Memoirs, I, 62.   [2] Legouis, The Early Life of William Wordsworth, 118.

vocation was really the only one that appealed to him. Possibly for pecuniary reasons, the vows that were made for him during the first college vacation did not seem to bind him to the poet's calling. So, possessed of a little money, he decided to spend several months in London, and went up to the great metropolis in February, 1791. Here the social environment becomes more and more a factor in his development, although Nature continues a powerful influence.

The impressions and observations of his visit, recorded in " The Prelude," disclose his mental life during a three months' stay in an environment entirely different from that to which he had been accustomed at Hawkshead and Cambridge. This new world was almost unconsciously viewed with a poet's eye. True, we are told the imaginative power slept at this time, when " pressed by tragic suffering," but it was not an unbroken slumber ; at intervals it was wide awake. Here, too, the Spirit of Nature was upon him, and the city became a source of poetic inspiration and vision. " The place was thronged with impregnations like the Wilds " in which his " early feelings had been nursed." His imagination transfigured what the eye of flesh saw ; his feeling dignified and ennobled it ; his intuition grasped the unity and meaning of it all. Indeed, no previous English poet has given us such a unique description and, at the same time, such a profound interpretation of the life of the great city as Wordsworth. It bears the stamp of a mind of singular and intense individuality.

This individuality is manifest especially in Wordsworth's interpretation of the variety of scene and life that greets his eyes in the mighty city. Different things and events are not regarded merely in their isolation and particularity, but as parts of a whole. All objects are reduced by his poetic intuition into an identity under law, and the vast multiplicity which a great city presents is apprehended as having rational meaning and end. In a striking passage in " The Prelude," Wordsworth contrasts his own view of the city with that of the multitude who live within its limits. To them its manifoldness presents a kind of identity, but its differences are lawless, meaningless, and point to no rational goal. To him, on the other hand, they present a unity and ennobling harmony. This, he informs us, was due to the Spirit of Nature that was upon him, revealing its essential oneness and interpreting its hidden meaning.

However, the vision vouchsafed was primarily a vision of Man. To one having had little experience with the world, with lofty conceptions of the dignity of human nature, and its essential divineness, the revelations of a sojourn in the heart of such a great center as London, presenting all forms of physical and moral evil, might cause a violent shock; his preconceptions and ideals might require decided alteration. But this was not the case with Wordsworth. Under the guidance of Nature he had formed his ideal of Man long ago among his native hills, and it did not fail when he beheld him under less pleasing and less promising aspects. When he came in contact with human ignorance and vice, with crime and misery, although they weighed heavily on his soul, his confidence in Man and in his destiny was not shaken. Neither was he induced to believe that all his preconceptions were wrong; that he had merely been dreaming the solitary's dream; that, far away from the busy haunts of men, he had framed an ideal in ignorance of the real nature of the being he was dealing with, as he manifests himself in the complexity of relations, and under the repulsive conditions, which obtain in the great city. Heart-sick though he was at times, he could gaze upon the dark and dismal human picture and see in it touches of the divine, and its divinity shone all the brighter by virtue of its striking contrast with the earthliness of the human. This is idealism of the most wholesome type. It is optimism born of a healthy poetic imagination. It is poetic power that penetrates outward conditions, and sees into the life of Man as it sees into the life of things.

Furthermore, here in the city he beholds men not merely as personal units. His poetic eye sees *Man* in men. More than heretofore the Poet discerns the essential oneness of the race. In Man's moral endowment, whether manifesting itself in good or in evil, he discerns the common element of our nature. Men are all subject to the same moral law and to the same moral ideal. Over all moral conditions the same spirit presides. In the ethical sphere the individual transcends his individuality. He becomes universalized — a member of a great spiritual system. The real unity of the race is a spiritual unity.

In Wordsworth's apprehension of the city we again note his mysticism. It will be recalled how, in the development of his poetic imagination, he attained the power of observing affinities in things "where no brotherhood exists to passive minds"; how he was able, by one supreme mystical poetic intuition, to grasp all material Reality in its essential unity, feeling the sentiment of "Being spread o'er all things." The philosopher's conclusion became the poet's vision. And so it is when he reaches the city. Here, too, he sees a diversity of objects, but it is not "blank confusion" for him, as it is for the multitudes that live within its borders, for whom things are

> melted and reduced
> To one identity, by differences
> That have no law, no meaning, and no end.[1]

The Spirit of Nature was upon him, and

> The soul of Beauty and enduring Life
> Vouchsafed her inspiration, and diffused,
> Through meagre lines and colours, and the press
> Of self-destroying, transitory things,
> Composure, and ennobling Harmony.[2]

And he sees men too, multitudes of them, under divers conditions and in divers states — a vast, heterogeneous, motley, and often repulsive throng; but his mystical mind looks beyond all individual peculiarities, all personal conditions, all differentiating physical and moral shapes, and sees the essential, the universal in Man — the

---

[1] The Prelude, VII, 726–728.   [2] Ibid., 767–771.

tie that binds all human beings into one great system or brotherhood. The mystical synthetic vision is his once more, and he
beholds

> the unity of man,
> One spirit over ignorance and vice
> Predominant in good and evil hearts;
> One sense for moral judgments, as one eye
> For the sun's light.[1]

Now this view of the city, with unity and meaning in its manifoldness of things and life, is no ordinary view. How essentially
striking and unique it is in literature may be learned by comparing it with views of previous writers in English prose and verse.
Legouis has made an interesting comparison of Wordsworth's
treatment of the city with that of other poets and literary men,
without, however, emphasizing sufficiently those features of Wordsworth's conception which make it fundamentally unique, and in
which its great superiority lies. So far as the prose writers are
concerned, their treatment of London relates largely to its varied
interests and material greatness, or it deals with detailed pictures
of different sections of the city, or descriptions of the feelings of
provincial folk on viewing the great metropolis. There is nothing
specially interesting in all this, and certainly very little that is inspiring. The poets, on the other hand, made the city an object of
attack. " Juvenal's third satire had served as a model for a series
of invectives against the capital, beginning with a direct imitation
by Oldham, in 1682, and continued in 'The City Shower' of
Swift, 'Trivia, or the Art of Walking the Streets of London,'
by John Gay, down to Samuel Johnson's 'Satire on London.'
Johnson is the most pronounced type of the eighteenth-century
poets, who were for the most part inveterate townspeople, and
would not have exchanged the shops of Fleet Street for all the
delights of Arcadia. Faithful, nevertheless, to classical tradition,
they held themselves bound to celebrate the charms of the country,

---

[1] The Prelude, VIII, 668–672.

and to heap execrations upon city life." [1] Legouis further remarks
that "up to that time the only poet whose work had reflected
something of the grandeur of London, was the very one who had
turned from it in horror as a hot-bed of vice and corruption. For
Cowper, towns were the work of man, or, in other words, of the
devil, while the country was created by God. He had succeeded
in suggesting a powerful image of the dreadful city, which appeared
to him, as Satan appeared to Milton, the majestic personification
of evil. It was the seat of the arts, of eloquence, philosophy, and
knowledge; the market of the earth; 'the fairest capital of all
the world.'

> Babylon of old
> Not more the glory of the earth than she,
> A more accomplished world's chief glory now.

These utterances, however, escaped him, to some extent, in spite
of himself, and the pious poet's indignation too soon completed
his unfinished picture with a sermon :

> O thou, resort and mart of all the 'earth,
> Chequered with all complexions of mankind,
> And spotted with all crimes; in which I see
> Much that I love, and more that I admire,
> And all that I abhor; thou freckled fair,
> That pleases and yet shocks me, I can laugh
> And I can weep, can hope, and can despond,
> Feel wrath and pity, when I think on thee !
> Ten righteous would have saved a city once,
> And thou hast many righteous. — Well for thee
> That salt preserves thee; more corrupted else,
> And therefore more obnoxious at this hour,
> Than Sodom in her day had power to be,
> For whom God heard his Abraham plead in vain. [2]

Here, as in other cases, the moral quickly ruined the picturesque
effect. Left almost untouched, therefore, by Cowper, this magnificent theme was appropriated by Wordsworth. The future poet of

---

[1] Legouis, The Early Life of William Wordsworth, 168.
[2] Cowper, The Task, III, 835–848.

the lakes was really the first, if not to feel, at any rate to attempt to render in verse worthy of the theme, and without satirical design, the grandeur of London and the intensity of its life. Strange as this fact appears at first sight, it is less surprising when we reflect that the requisite striking impression could only be felt by a man fresh from the world outside of London, capable of new and vivid sensations, and sufficiently open in mind and independent of classical authorities to venture on a frank description of his novel impressions. This was the new departure taken by Wordsworth. The man who is usually regarded as imbued with rustic prejudices was able to understand the strange and powerful attraction of the capital, and deemed it worthy of poetic treatment." [1]

This is undoubtedly true, and it reveals the individuality of Wordsworth's attitude toward the city. However, the uniqueness and real merit of his poetic treatment of the great city does not lie in his descriptions of its everyday appearance and life — its streets and lanes, its private courts and quiet suburbs, its museums, theaters, and homes of justice, its halls of parliament, with their great debates — nor of the intensity of its life, nor of its solitudes. It lies rather in his mystical poetic intuition, by which he discovers in its brick and mortar, its dirty streets and lanes, its deafening din, its busy life, and its motley crowds "impregnations like the Wilds" in which his early feelings had been nursed, as in the feelings suggested by "that huge fermenting mass of humankind" that served "as a solemn background, or relief, to single forms and objects" [2] — in the vision of the dignity, grandeur, and unity of Man, and in the sublime faith (inspired by the checkered human throng) in what he may become under divine guidance. Contrast the exalted views of the essential nature of Man which the city brings to him, confirming and enriching a lofty ideal formed under the influence of a less corrupting environment, with the observations of the writers referred to by Legouis. Note

[1] Legouis, The Early Life of William Wordsworth, 169-170.
[2] The Prelude, VII, 622-623.

Wordsworth's optimism as he beholds Man under the unwhole-
some, depressing, and diverse conditions of crowded city life, and
proclaims his true greatness and grandeur, apprehending his soli-
darity and unity under moral law; note his profound insight into human nature, and his sublime confidence in its dignity and destiny,
and contrast them with the quasi-cynicism and pessimism involved
in the irony and satire of previous poets, and observe how immeasurably superior the inspiration which the city brought to Wordsworth!
In one case we have superficial observation, ironical description,
and more or less of skeptical interpretation; in the other we have
poetic insight, profound faith, and hopeful outlook. They deal
with *Men;* he deals with *Man.* They deal with the *individual;*
he deals with the *universal.* They deal with the *incidental;* he
deals with the *essential.* Their imagination is burdened with the
weight of sense; his mounts on the wings of spirit. They see
largely outward aspects; he sees into the life of things and men.
In short, we have in Wordsworth the vision and prophecy of the
seer — the truest and sublimest poet, the idealist and optimist.
And if we are to determine his historical position or significance
with reference to the treatment of the city in literature, we shall
find it in these lofty visions and conceptions of things and men
which the city brought to him, and which he has embodied in
noble and inspiring verse.

We are apt to miss the real significance of Wordsworth's second
visit to London unless we carefully note his *personal* attitude
toward Man during this brief sojourn. The eighth book of "The
Prelude" is entitled "Retrospect"; but it also bears the subtitle,
"Love of Nature leading to Love of Man." Many writers on
Wordsworth are so occupied with his views of Nature that they
apparently fail to recognize the fact that Wordsworth, during the
best years of his career as a poet, was primarily interested in Man.
Man was the supreme object of his thought and affections — the
chief source and end of his poetical inspiration. Nature is recognized as a teacher leading to a proper attitude toward Man.

Of course, in his early years, and here also, in London, Nature is still sovereign in his heart; but all along, "by slow gradations," she has been leading his thoughts to human-kind, and we shall fail of the real import of this London visit unless we see in it how, under her inspiration and guidance, Man becomes more and more an object of affectionate regard, a source of poetic contemplation and feeling, resulting in enlarged and exalted views of his essential dignity and greatness, his noble destiny, and the oneness of the race under moral law. Addressing Coleridge on this subject, the Poet says:

> Thus from a very early age, O Friend!
> My thoughts by slow gradations had been drawn
> To human-kind, and to the good and ill
> Of human life: Nature had led me on;
> And oft amid the "busy hum" I seemed
> To travel independent of her help,
> As if I had forgotten her; but no,
> The world of human-kind outweighed not hers
> In my habitual thoughts; the scale of love,
> Though filling daily, still was light, compared
> With that in which *her* mighty objects lay.[1]

But the "scale of love" was filling somewhat rapidly here in the city, and though still light compared with the scale of love for Nature, it was daily growing heavier, and we shall see in the next chapter that "the world of human-kind" was destined soon to outweigh the world of Nature in the Poet's affections. At present, Man is only an occasional delight, "an accidental grace," whereas Nature is "a passion," indeed "a rapture often," and an "immediate love ever at hand." But Man's hour is not far distant. Only one more summer must be told before he too shall become not only a passion but a rapture, and ever afterwards the supreme object of Wordsworth's love and art.[2]

[1] The Prelude, VIII, 676–686.   [2] Ibid., 346–356.

CHAPTER IV

THE FRENCH REVOLUTION. A MENTAL AND MORAL CRISIS

Wordsworth was more or less prepared, by his previous life and training, to sympathize with the aims and underlying principles of the great social and political conflict raging across the channel. In his boyhood and youth his social environment was such that he had rarely come in contact with men who were accustomed to receive attention because of their wealth or blood. He lived where these artificial social relations did not abound. Furthermore, in his college career he shared in the democratic life which usually prevails in academic circles — a democracy which recognizes the members of such circles as "brothers all in honour, as in one community, scholars and gentlemen," where distinction was open to all, and talents, worth, and successful industry counted for more than wealth and titles. Again, he had been prepared for this hour by the fact that he had learned from the beginning subservience "to presences of God's mysterious power," which were made manifest in the sovereignty of Nature; also by "fellowship with venerable books" that sanctioned the consciousness of the dignity and lofty powers of the soul and its freedom. Hence, he says,

> it could not be
> But that one tutored thus should look with awe
> Upon the faculties of man, receive
> Gladly the highest promises, and hail
> As best, the government of equal rights
> And individual worth.[1]

So that, when he visited France in the summer of 1791, he soon became deeply interested in the course of events; and it was not

[1] The Prelude, IX, 238–243.

long before he was identified in sympathy with what he deemed to be the sacred cause of the people. As he came into closer contact with the momentous situation he was profoundly impressed with its significance. In his enthusiasm he saw it loom large with promise, not only for France, but for the whole world, and he followed its varying fortunes with anxious interest. It was soon evident that under the influence of political events he was rapidly reaching a crisis in his career, for they were intimately related to his mental and spiritual life. It was primarily through the French Revolution that he became specially interested in Man. For him, as we have seen, the Revolution was not merely a local movement; it had meaning also for humanity at large. It was a movement in the interest of a greater liberty for the race, which would prove a tremendous advantage to human progress. It carried with it larger rights for the masses, and less authority for the classes. The essential rights of Man were to be gained and maintained. Wordsworth was borne along by his enthusiasm and hopes for the cause to such an extent that soon he was steeped in republicanism, despite his natural conservatism and the form of government under which he was born and reared. However, his republicanism was not the blind enthusiasm of a fanatic. It was not a faith without at least some rational foundation. The French Revolution had its intellectual side. Indeed, one of the things that prepared the way for this great crisis was French philosophy of the eighteenth century. Many of the most ardent revolutionists were affected by the philosophy of Rousseau and the Encyclopædists. The Revolution, of course, involved certain fundamental conceptions and principles concerning Man — his nature, dignity, and rights, both natural and political — and the nature, functions, forms, and ends of political government. These were questions which appealed to reason for solution, and many of the principles laid down for practical adoption were proclaimed in the name of this exalted faculty. Tradition in politics and religion was thrown aside, and both were brought before the bar of man's rational nature. Indeed, with many of the patriots reason was deified. Even with the *sansculotte* the Goddess of Reason was enthroned in Paris in 1793.

Wordsworth was affected by the saner rationalistic spirit of the age. In the eleventh book of " The Prelude " he traces, with the hand of a skilled psychologist, his mental unfolding under the influence of the times — a mental evolution along the lines of reflective thought, which begins with great joy and hopefulness, with naïve confidence in the conformity of the world of fact to the world of reason, and with a corresponding optimism, and ends in the temporary wreck of his poetic imagination, in his despiritualization of Nature, in loss of faith in Man, and in moral skepticism and despair. This is one of the most interesting as well as one of the most pathetic chapters in the personal history of the poet.

Early in life (as early, indeed, as his twentieth year) Wordsworth became interested in political questions. He approached such questions with the optimism of youth, believing in the essential goodness of human nature and in the supreme worth and might of the principles of moral reason; and he was willing, if need be, to fight and die for his faith. What is best in the individual, "wise in passion," "sublime in power," "benevolent in small societies, and great in large ones " — these were questions which were often considered by him, and concerning which he felt deeply, although he did not clearly understand them. But with a general insight into the nature of evil, and its distinction from good, he soon began to devote himself earnestly to a more formal and systematic consideration of the problems of government. His political reflection was not the academic reflection of the student; it was born of a deep interest in current political and social conditions. He found great hope and pleasure in his reasoning. Indeed, Reason seemed to be a veritable enchantress, assisting the work that was being done in her name. She seemed to be on the side of what he deemed to be socially and politically right. The earth wore a cheerful aspect, it was clothed in the beauty of promise, and at this time he found it bliss to be alive, and very heaven to be young.

Under the stimulus of events Wordsworth had been forming his social and political ideal. He dreamed a dream of social good, but it was not merely a dream — no mere Utopia. It was a dream in the form of a rationalized social ideal, formed by meditation and reflection. Having its foundations in Eternal Reason, its might and right could not be doubted. According to his belief, events were soon to conform to what it sanctioned and demanded. In this serene ethical faith he moved about, "an active partisan," making things suit his ends, and entertaining genial feelings toward those who differed from him in their political views.

Now with all the changes that had taken place since he had first become interested in the cause of the Revolution — the fortunes and misfortunes, the successes and failures — this really was his general state of mind until his own country entered into war with France. This action proved a great moral shock to Wordsworth. It affected him so seriously not merely because he was a partisan of the cause, but because he was a *rational* partisan. How was Britain's action to be reconciled with his ethical faith? What rational justification had England for this step? In his judgment she had none. Nevertheless her action was a fact, and a tremendously real fact, and it shattered his confidence in the essential harmony between the world of reality and the world of rationality. His faith was too highly colored by emotion — by personal wish and desire. Reason may be justified in its conclusion as to what ought to be done in a given situation, or under certain conditions, but it does not follow that what *ought to be* necessarily *is*, or *will be*, at least in the near future. Ethical faith, based upon calm reflection, may be justified in affirming that, sooner or later, truth and righteousness will prevail, but the mystery and tragedy of the moral world is just this awful lack of conformity of fact to the Right. Here faith must have a wide horizon and a large perspective. What is more common than to see right at least temporarily defeated, and wrong victorious? This is the case with individuals; why should it not be with nations? Here is where Wordsworth's

faith, though in a measure well grounded, failed him. And he suf-
fered a terrible shock, the mental and spiritual reaction being
most unfortunate.

In the eleventh book of "The Prelude" Wordsworth treats
more specifically of the nature of this shock to his moral being
caused by England's behavior. It stands in striking contrast to the
mental state which he describes as having been his up to the time
of the sorrowful event. It was this action that first threw him " out
of the pale of love," souring and corrupting his sentiments at their
very source. He was no longer enabled to see in such actions a
case of lesser things being swallowed up in greater, but rather a
contrariety in things, which led him to serious mistakes and false
and dangerous conclusions. A feeling of pride in his own country
was changed into a sense of shame ; his likes and loves were directed into a new channel, and the old ones ran dry. An event
which in later years would only have affected his judgment now
struck deep into his emotional nature. It was a blow at his heart,
the very center of his moral being. This moral shock is a significant
fact in Wordsworth's history, for it had much to do in bringing
about a crisis which proved to be one of the most potent factors in
determining his future career as a poet, ultimately humanizing his
affections still more, and thus directly and indirectly affecting both
the form and the content of his poetry.

Wordsworth gradually began to feel the necessity of grounding
his sentiments on surer evidence than that afforded by mere
" inward consciousness." Things were going from bad to worse in
France. Events did not seem capable of interpretation from the
standpoint of moral reason. And, as his mind was gradually matur-
ing, the criterion by which he was wont to judge of events no longer
satisfied him. He was therefore compelled to cast about for something better. Under these circumstances he fell back upon tenets
having at least the authority of age. Still he did not abandon reflective or speculative thought. Rather did he pursue it farther than
ever before — so far, indeed, that it led him into rational and moral

chaos and despair. Because of the condition of the times, speculation became more abstract — farther removed from the current
of events. It was more and more lifted from the realm of passion
into the realm of pure reason. Man, in the conscious possession of
the lordly powers of reason and will, destined sooner or later to shake
off the tyranny of custom and law, and to build up social liberty on
personal freedom, guided by the light of circumstances, constituted
a delightful object for the reflective mind to consider. Man, thus
regarded, appealed to Wordsworth. He contemplated him with
great satisfaction — all the greater, indeed, by virtue of the marked
contrast presented by men as he had observed them during the
stormy period of the Revolution. The result was that he again
took heart.

But to take refuge in pure reason is not always a safe course for
certain minds to pursue. The rationalistic spirit lives largely by
proof, which is often far from possible, and then skepticism is
likely to follow. This spirit carries its methods into spheres of life
in which strict logical proof is not the way of approach to Reality.
Barrenness, and often worse, is the outcome. It proved to be so
in Wordsworth's case. He had forsaken the light by which his
sentiments had been

> by faith maintained
> Of inward consciousness, and hope that laid
> Her hand upon her object.[1]

He wanted a safer guide, and, finding tradition and ancient tenets
insufficient, he finally accepted pure reason, free from instinct, passion, and sentiment, with the melancholy result that he was led into
utter darkness. All things — "all precepts, judgments, maxims,
creeds " — were dragged to the bar of Reason. They were treated
like culprits. The mind herself was viewed with suspicion, and was
called upon to vindicate her own veracity, dignity, and honor.
Reason sat in judgment even upon herself, often attended by
grave suspicion. Wordsworth was now in a state of vacillation.

---

[1] The Prelude, XI, 201–203.

Sometimes he believed; sometimes he doubted. The great problems of motive, the nature of right and wrong, the ground of moral obligation, its rule and source of authority, were questions that perplexed him beyond measure. So critical and suspicious did he become that ultimately nothing could be accepted without proof. This, indeed, was demanded and sought, and, not finding it, he finally gave up in skepticism and despair the consideration of moral problems.[1] His philosophizing ended ignominiously. It resulted in complete failure, bringing disaster to his spiritual life. It led him into deepest darkness — into a night apparently devoid of any star of hope.

It is well to note that it was *moral* skepticism and despair which were the outcome of his reflective thinking — the most serious kind of doubt and dejection that can lay hold upon the human spirit, because of the vital relation which morality sustains to life. Morality is the fact of supreme worth for human nature; it, above all things, unifies, dignifies, and exalts the human soul. It has the same value for society, which, indeed, is based upon it, is held together by it, and progresses only when dominated by its ideals and imperatives. How essential, then, that its commands should be clear, unmistakable, categorical! Why should there be any question about them; why any doubt? And yet Wordsworth did find grounds for serious doubt. Inquiring into the ultimate source of their authority, the ultimate ground of ethical obligation, the reality of free will, and the nature of the moral ideal, he found human opinion so divided, indeed so contradictory, and the moral nature itself apparently so at variance with itself, that it became exceedingly difficult to attain to a definite and abiding conviction. As a consequence, moral skepticism was the outcome:

> This was the crisis of that strong disease,
> This the soul's last and lowest ebb; I drooped,
> Deeming our blessèd reason of least use
> Where wanted most: " The lordly attributes

[1] The Prelude, XI, 293-305.

> Of will and choice," I bitterly exclaimed,
> "What are they but a mockery of a Being
> Who hath in no concerns of his a test
> Of good and evil; knows not what to fear
> Or hope for, what to covet or to shun;
> And who, if those could be discerned, would yet
> Be little profited, would see, and ask
> Where is the obligation to enforce?
> And, to acknowledged law rebellious, still,
> As selfish passion urged, would act amiss;
> The dupe of folly, or the slave of crime." [1]

There was, too, another loss, of a very serious nature, that Wordsworth sustained because of this rationalistic spirit. His mind had degenerated into a logic-machine. It could

> unsoul
> As readily by syllogistic words
> Those mysteries of being which have made,
> And shall continue evermore to make,
> Of the whole human race one brotherhood, [2]

as, by a mere wave of the hand, a wizard dissolves a palace or a grove. Such a mind was bound to suffer deterioration of imaginative power — of poetic vision and insight. This was the case with Wordsworth, and this serious loss added to the pathos of his condition. With faith in the integrity of moral reason gone, there might be some consolation in the visions and illuminations of the poetic imagination. But this faculty had apparently been destroyed by the critical spirit, and, as a result, Wordsworth was robbed of his poetic conception both of Man and of Nature. As to Man, what a sorry spectacle he presented compared with the being that youthful imagination had transfigured and idealized, when as a boy he roamed over his native hills, and saw the rude shepherd, with his heroic mien, "glorified by the deep radiance of the setting sun," and his young heart was "introduced to an unconscious love and reverence of human nature." [3] Nature then gave a sanctity to Man that appealed to

[1] The Prelude, XI, 306–320.   [2] Ibid., XII, 83–87.   [3] Ibid., VIII, 256 f.

the boy's imagination, and he formed an ideal of human-kind that
later proved

> a sure safeguard and defence
> Against the weight of meanness, selfish cares,
> Coarse manners, vulgar passions, that beat in
> On all sides from the ordinary world
> In which we traffic. [1]

Compare the picture of Man which an arid, rational skepticism
portrayed for him to the glorious picture that was presented to his
poetic eye even under the depressing conditions of city life. There
in London he saw the divineness of human nature shining through
the portentous gloom, and shining more brightly because of the
contrast. There, where he saw man at his worst, he also saw him
at his best, and beheld the dignity of his rational and moral invest-
iture, as well as the glory of a noble destiny. But now he beholds
Man with the eye of reason; and the pity of it all is that, when
it presents a distorted picture, he finds the eye of imagination
apparently destroyed, and there is no power within to sketch a true
likeness of him who was the cherished object of his love.

Alas! this, too, is the case concerning Nature. Nature, his early
love, who ministered to him in his childhood and youth; who,
by her visitations, warned, counseled, and sustained him; who refreshed him with her beauty, and gave him vision and insight —
she, too, is now viewed with a critical eye. The vision once vouchsafed, by which he saw all things bound together in a brotherhood
and animated by one living Spirit, gave way to an analytical scrutiny.
Now he scanned Nature just as he had scanned the moral world.
He looked at her through a microscope, going from part to part,
from scene to scene, losing sight of her unity, her wholeness. As
a result he lost that sense of intimacy which was one of the dearest
possessions of his boyhood and youth. He was lost, also, to her
moral power. The senses gained dominion over his soul as he
came in contact with her, and they ruled with the scepter of tyranny.

[1] The Prelude, VIII, 318–322.

They laid the inner powers asleep. How different this from his
relation to Nature in the earlier years! Then he waited on her,
not only with eye and ear awake, but also with a heart ready to
worship and receive. Then he loved intensely whatever he saw.
He "felt, observed and pondered" as he stood in her presence.
Never did he think of judging her. He was filled and satisfied
with her glory. So also was it in the Alps. There he was intoxicated with her beauty, overcome by her majesty, and he loved and
worshiped her with a grateful and reverent heart. But how is it
now? He looks at her with sense apart from soul. He sees her
outward aspect, but fails to see into her inner life. The beautiful
vision is gone. Imagination seems dead, and sensibility dulled.
Nature is robbed of her spiritual charm and power. For him she
no longer has a heart and utters no consoling message; she no
longer ministers through beauty and æsthetic 'joy. The mystic
sense of kinship has vanished. He has unsouled her, and stands, a
spiritual orphan, in the midst of a dead universe. In short, the poet
is lost in the skeptical philosopher. He stands not only in a world
of moral chaos and darkness, but also in a soulless universe, that
once was alive with the transcendent beauty and grace of an all-
pervading Spirit.

This picture is not overdrawn if we are to accept the Poet's own
account of his mental condition during this period. It is a tragic
tale that he tells, as he contrasts his relations to Nature at this
time with those of former years.

> What wonder, then, if, to a mind so far
> Perverted, even the visible Universe
> Fell under the dominion of a taste
> Less spiritual, with microscopic view
> Was scanned, as I had scanned the moral world? [1]

The result of thus scanning "the visible Universe" is manifest in
his address to the Soul of Nature.

[1] The Prelude, XII, 88–92.

O Soul of Nature! excellent and fair!
Thou didst rejoice with me, with whom I, too,
Rejoiced through early youth, before the winds
And roaring waters, and in lights and shades
That marched and countermarched about the hills
In glorious apparition, Powers on whom
I daily waited, now all eye and now
All ear; but never long without the heart
Employed, and man's unfolding intellect:
O Soul of Nature! that, by laws divine
Sustained and governed, still dost overflow
With an impassioned life, what feeble ones
Walk on this earth! how feeble have I been
When thou wert in thy strength! Nor this through stroke
Of human suffering, such as justifies
Remissness and inaptitude of mind,
But through presumption; even in pleasure pleased
Unworthily, disliking here, and there
Liking; by rules of mimic art transferred
To things above all art; but more, — for this,
Although a strong infection of the age,
Was never much my habit — giving way
To a comparison of scene with scene,
Bent overmuch on superficial things,
Pampering myself with meagre novelties
Of colour and proportion; to the moods
Of time and season, to the moral power,
The affections and the spirit of the place,
Insensible.[1]

This certainly represents a tremendous change in mental attitude
and feeling. It reveals the world-wide difference between the analytic and the synthetic, the critical and the poetic view of Nature
and Man. He has unsouled the objects of his love, robbing one
of spiritual life, and the other of the integrity of his essential constitution as a moral being, and the former lover of Nature and
Man is now a spiritual wreck in the midst of a lifeless world.

This rationalistic speculation and criticism, which resulted so
unfortunately to Wordsworth's mental and spiritual life, received,

1 The Prelude, XII, 93-121.

to a certain extent, its bent or direction from another mind than Wordsworth's. Just as many of the active partisans of the revolutionary cause had their intellectual leaders in Rousseau and the Encyclopædists, so a number of English sympathizers with the republican tendencies of the age had their intellectual leader. This leader was William Godwin. He seems to have attracted the attention of a number of poets, for he was on friendly terms with Coleridge, Lamb, Wordsworth, and Shelley — the latter marrying his daughter. Coleridge has a sonnet dedicated to him, crediting him with much virtue and power, although later he was far removed from him in sentiment and thought. Shelley, with his radical social ideas and his susceptible nature, was enthusiastic in his admiration for him. In 1793 Godwin published his political treatise "Enquiry Concerning Political Justice." Wordsworth was familiar with his political philosophy, and was greatly influenced by it. In view of the radical, if not, indeed, revolutionary character of his treatise, one cannot help wondering how such a mind as Wordsworth's came to be dominated by the principles therein advocated. In it a bald individualism is taught, which makes the individual superior to all organized social restraints, whether they be of the nature of conventionalities, customs, institutions, or laws. According to Godwin, reason is the great faculty of the mind, and the end of education is to develop the individual in the rational exercise of freedom.[1]

But there are certain things which stand in the way of a proper development and exercise of the individual's rational judgment. These are the institutions and customs of society — political, moral, and religious. These mislead him, restrain him, and often enslave him. They are a prolific source of social evils, and, as such, ought to be abolished. How, then, shall man be governed in his social relations, since he exists in a society of beings constituted like himself? According to Godwin, justice is a natural law, and it is the great law that governs social interaction, its end being human

---

[1] Godwin, Enquiry, I, i, v; also II, vi.

welfare, the highest good of all, the welfare of an aggregate of individuals, for this is what constitutes society in the final analysis. If there be political government at all, its authority ultimately rests with these individuals, and in such political government they are not to be bound together by social contract, but by open deliberation with reference to common concerns. " The true and only adequate apology of government is necessity,; the office of common deliberation is solely to supply the most eligible means of meeting that necessity." [1] We see here the emphasis laid on the individual. Indeed, the less political government the better. The ideal state of society would be a state in which each man should govern himself in the light of human reason, under the universal law of justice. Even the general rules of morality, while in a measure useful because of our imperfection and indolence, are not the best guides for man's government. Rather ought we to view each case of conduct in the light of its own evidence, and decide it on its own merits. [2]

We see in Godwin's political philosophy merely the philosophy of a dreamer or visionary. He is dealing with hypothetical and not with real men — with men practically removed from the sphere of passion, and living in the realm of pure reason. Such beings are easily regulated by reason, and make rapid progress in the rational exercise of freedom. They need no restraint of custom and law, and, to a certain extent, only the restraints of the general rules of morality. Godwin's " society " is simply an unrealizable Utopia, but it had its influence in its day. Being rooted in the most radical kind of democracy, it was acceptable doctrine in an age full of the spirit of social revolution. Wordsworth was captivated by this spirit, and, guided by Godwin, he proceeded " to anatomise the frame of social life," and to search " the whole body of society " to its very heart. Even his master's utopianism was converted into the Poet's visionary and impracticable social dream.

[1] Godwin, Enquiry, I, ii, ii; also iv.   [2] Op. cit. I, iv, vi.

What delight!
How glorious! in self-knowledge and self-rule,
To look through all the frailties of the world,
And, with a resolute mastery shaking off
Infirmities of nature, time, and place,
Build social upon personal Liberty,
Which, to the blind restraints of general laws
Superior, magisterially adopts
One guide, the light of circumstances, flashed
Upon an independent intellect.[1]

And, as we have seen, this spirit of rationalism, so characteristic of the age and so manifest in Godwin's political philosophy, was applied by Wordsworth not only to the study of social and political institutions but to the study of Man himself in his essential constitution, as well as to Nature. The poet who beholds things with the eye of the imagination was converted into the philosopher who views them with the eye of reason, with the disastrous results recorded above.

With his hopes and dreams of social good vanished, with his confidence in the integrity of moral reason shattered, with his poetic vision of Nature gone, little wonder was it that he sank into the abysmal depths of moral despair — a veritable slough of despond. Only time and careful nursing could enable him to rise from such an apparent spiritual death into a renewed life — the life of a larger faith, a saner hope, and a more lasting joy — that should witness a rebirth of the poetic soul, and turn again to Nature and Man in confidence and tender love, finding in them once more generous sources of inspiration and power.

The experiences of Wordsworth during the years of which we have been writing undoubtedly had a marked significance for his art. They had made an impression which was bound to influence more or less permanently his life of imagination, thought, and feeling, as these found expression in his poetry. In the first place, they were instrumental in bringing about, by the aid of his sister,

[1] The Prelude, XI, 235-244.

a definite decision with reference to his pursuit of the high vocation. The extremity of soul to which they had led him afforded Dorothy Wordsworth an opportunity to turn his attention again to poetry, and to make him seek beneath the poet's name his earthly office. But secondly, they were responsible for more than this. In a large measure they determined the direction of his mind with reference to the content and form of his poetry. So far as its subject-matter was concerned, Wordsworth, after his convalescence, turned again to Nature, the old-time source of his inspiration. But we find his mental attitude changed and colored by his sorrowful experience. In the former days, despite occasional moments of soul-illumination, when he saw into the life of things — apprehending Nature as invested with a spiritual Presence — he was often lost in the sense-vision. Henceforth, however, his vision became more spiritual. Nature for him was alive with feeling, thought, and sympathetic love. Henceforth he finds her touched with a feeling of Man's infirmities. There is a human note in her voice, and she breathes consolation, calmness, and peace to his spirit. She becomes the anchor of his purest thoughts, the nurse, guide, and guardian of his heart, and the very soul of his moral being — all of which is manifest in the Nature-poetry which was the fruit of his labors during the years immediately following.

Again, the experience of these momentous years brought about the birth of the poet of Man. Through it Nature led him gradually from love of herself to love of his own kind. At first this had most unfortunate results. It destroyed his faith in men and Man, and left him in gross spiritual darkness. But after he had emerged from the gloom of the skeptic's night, Man became more than ever the object of his regard, and he approached him with a mind and heart profoundly affected by his tragic experience — with a soul chastened and subdued. He now understood Man better than before. He had entered into his universal life in a manner that was previously impossible. He understood his basal needs, and beheld his intrinsic worth as only great suffering could reveal them.

He became the lover of men, championing and defending human rights, exploiting and extolling human virtue. The "Lyrical Ballads," many of the "Poems dedicated to National Independence and Liberty," "The Excursion," the intensely human poems of the Grasmere period, and still others to be considered will make this evident.

In view of all this the careful student of Wordsworth's life and poetry is amazed to read, in an interesting essay by Professor Masson, that "he [Wordsworth] appears to have passed through the battle of life all but unwounded. . . . Passing through the world as a pilgrim, pure-minded, and even sad with the sense of the mysterious future, nothing occurred in his journey to strike him down as a dead man, and agonize him into a full knowledge of the whole mystery of the present. Hence, we believe, the want of that intensity in his poetry which we find in the writings, not only of the so-called subjective poets, such as Byron and Dante, but also of the greatest objective poets, as Goethe and Shakespeare. The ink of Wordsworth is rarely his own blood." [1] This, assuredly, is a mistaken view of our Poet. He *was* struck down as a dead man. When England took up arms against France he sustained a shock so sudden and so severe that it affected his entire moral being. The awful tragedies of the French Revolution — the indescribable suffering, the wild passion, the infidelity of its leaders, the crimes committed in the name of liberty — made him stand in blank amazement at the weakness and wickedness of men. The mad course of events, its contradiction of all that right reason would lead him to expect, his gradual loss of faith in men and Man, brought on a mental and spiritual suffering that seemed even worse than death. All of this was a shock — a sustained mental and moral shock — that paralyzed his spiritual being. If ever a man had reason to sink beneath "the burthen of the mystery," "of all this unintelligible world," with its heavy and weary weight,

[1] Masson's Wordsworth, Shelley, Keats, and other Essays, 69-70

Wordsworth was that man during these eventful years. And he did sink. What worse fate could attend a man "passing through the world as a pilgrim" than that which attended Wordsworth's life at this time? The pain was not less intense because long sustained, nor was the shock less sudden and severe when it came with its full force upon him. The effects are manifest in the humanizing influence it had upon him and his art. It is manifest in the actual presence of that very intensity which Professor Masson finds absent in his poetry. There is intense passion, as well as a "calm and almost terrible strength," to use Professor Raleigh's phrase, in many of Wordsworth's poems. It is evident in such poems as "Ruth," "The Brothers," "Michael," "The Affliction of Margaret ———," "The White Doe of Rylstone," in certain portions of "The Excursion," and in many of the political sonnets. In writing these poems, and others like them, "the ink of Wordsworth" is "his own blood." Such intensity of passion and, on the other hand, such "calm and almost terrible strength" were possible to him, and to his art, because he had passed through these terrible fires of suffering. He was able to become the poet of Man because his sensitive soul was called upon to bear the human burden, with its tremendous stress of unintelligible experience, before he had yet been fairly initiated into the poet's life. He underwent "Love's sorrow," if not thus early for a specific individual, certainly for mankind, and he was awakened not only to "the melancholy side of things" but to the mysterious darkness that shrouds the world both of things and of men. The inevitable logic of it all is seen in poetry that is the product of an imagination warmed by a heart which, through suffering, got closer than ever to the great, consoling, calming, resourceful heart of Nature, and gained a deeper insight into, and throbbed with a profounder love for, the burthened heart of Man.

CHAPTER V

DOROTHY WORDSWORTH. SPIRITUAL CONVALESCENCE

Wordsworth did not emerge at once from the depths of moral despair into which he had been plunged by the course of political events and by his loss of faith in moral reason. The human soul does not behave in that way. It requires time to recover from such a moral disease. However, the strength and nobility of his character are manifest in the manner in which he bore himself in this crisis of his life. He gave a remarkable exhibition of sanity and self-control under the circumstances. In " The Prelude " he hints at the temptations of such a mental state. On the one hand, without faith in men and in the essential integrity of Man's rational and moral constitution, there is danger of growing spiritually callous and cynical — of scoffing at truth and virtue. On the other hand, there is also a temptation to idleness and waste of powers, especially those having to do with the pursuit of truth and the acquisition of knowledge. If Man's intellectual endeavor ends in defeat and moral despair, because of his constitutional impotency of mind, why make any further effort? If the tempter approached Wordsworth in either of these ways, or in both, he found him invulnerable. Depressed and bewildered though he was, he did not permit himself to yield to hardness and cynicism. Perplexed almost to distraction, and skeptical in regard to men and Man, he did not choose to " walk with scoffers," " seeking light and gay revenge from indiscriminate laughter." He still loved too much the life of serious thought, and the truth which is its own reward, to be reconciled to a life of mental idleness and waste. In this time of disappointment and despair he turned to an abstract world — the world of mathematics and physics. Here reason could find employment in a sphere free from disturbances of space and time occasioned by material objects or by human action. But this resort to abstract reasoning proved to be only a partial and temporary relief to his mind. He was suffering from a severe mental and spiritual malady — a "strong disease." He needed a physician to effect a complete and permanent cure, or some one to nurse him back to health. He could not do this for himself. Fortunately for him, and also for the world, such a one was at hand. It was chiefly to his sister, Dorothy Wordsworth, that he owed his gradual but complete recovery, and was saved from himself and to the poet's art.

Dorothy Wordsworth was in some respects an unusual personality, endowed with exceptional powers of mind and heart. Hers was a mind gifted with keen powers of observation, delicate and tender sensibility, and a refined and lively imagination. Her nature was essentially poetic. To these qualities of mind were added rare qualities of heart. She was generous and affectionate, absolutely unselfish in her devotion to others, and especially to her brother William, which made her an invaluable aid to him both as a man and as a poet. She was not merely his sister by virtue of being the child of his parents, but in a higher and truer sense — in spiritual endowment and affinity. She was, as he called her, the sister of his soul.

There seems to be an essential agreement of opinion and sentiment, among those who knew her best, in regard to the admirable qualities possessed by this simple, unique woman. Coleridge, in a letter to Cottle, says : " W. and his exquisite sister are with me. She is a woman indeed ! in mind I mean, and heart ; for her person is such that if you expected to see a pretty woman, you would think her rather ordinary ; if you expected to see an ordinary woman, you would think her pretty ! but her manners are simple, ardent, impressive. In every motion her most innocent soul outbeams so brightly, that who saw would say —

' Guilt was a thing impossible with her.'

Her information various. Her eye watchful in minutest observation of Nature; and her taste a perfect electrometer. It bends, protrudes, and draws in at subtlest beauties and most recondite faults."[1] De Quincey was long an intimate friend of the Wordsworths, and had excellent opportunities to study the personality and character of Dorothy. Later the friendly relations existing between them were broken, and the Poet and his sister did not escape the criticism of his caustic and gossipy pen. But long after he had been alienated from them, he wrote of Miss Wordsworth: "She was a person of very remarkable endowments intellectually; and, in addition to other great services which she rendered to her brother, this I may mention, as greater than all the rest, and it was one which equally operated to the benefit of every casual companion in a walk — viz. the exceeding sympathy, always ready and always profound, by which she made all that one could tell her, all that one could describe, all that one could quote from a foreign author, reverberate as it were *à plusieurs reprises*, to one's own feelings, by the manifest impression it made upon her. The pulses of light are not more quick or more inevitable in their flow and undulation, than were the answering and echoing movements of her sympathizing attention. Her knowledge of literature was irregular, and not systematically built up. She was content to be ignorant of many things; but what she knew and had really mastered, lay where it could not be disturbed, in the temper of her own most fervid heart."[2]

Such were the qualities, mental and spiritual, possessed by Wordsworth's sister. From childhood William and Dorothy had been very close in sympathy and interests. Together they roamed the fields, hills, and mountains of their native region. Endowed with unusual perceptive powers, imagination, and poetic feeling, they were keenly alive to the natural beauty of their surroundings. And when the force of circumstances — Wordsworth's school and university

[1] Knight, The Life of William Wordsworth, I, 112-113.
[2] De Quincey, Literary Reminiscences, 277-278,

life, his travels and wanderings — interrupted this pleasant companionship, their correspondence breathed tender and sweet affection. In her letters to others, also, Dorothy seldom failed to put on record her great happiness when more fortunate circumstances brought them together again. Her poetic temperament enabled her to understand her brother's moods, and sympathize with his aims and interests. From boyhood on through mature manhood he found in her a great source of comfort, strength, and inspiration. That he fully appreciated her worth and real helpfulness is manifest in his verse. In "The Sparrow's Nest" she is not only the blessing of his later years but also a gracious influence in his early life:

> The Blessing of my later years
> Was with me when a boy:
> She gave me eyes, she gave me ears;
> And humble cares, and delicate fears;
> A heart, the fountain of sweet tears;
>   And love, and thought, and joy.[1]

In "The Prelude" he tells us how, by her tenderness and love, she led him to a less austere view of Nature than he was wont to take; how she called him away from a too exclusive regard for the sterner, more severe, and even terrible aspects of the physical world to an appreciation of those of a softer and more peaceful character; and this was no small service to a mind such as Wordsworth's. How much he was indebted to her for the refined and spiritual conception of Nature which characterizes his maturest views, and which lies at the basis of his conception of the world, it is impossible to say. That he was thus under obligation to her is manifest in his own generous acknowledgment:

> Child of my parents! Sister of my soul!
> Thanks in sincerest verse have been elsewhere
> Poured out for all the early tenderness
> Which I from thee imbibed: and 't is most true
> That later seasons owed to thee no less;

[1] The Sparrow's Nest, 15-20.

> For, spite of thy sweet influence and the touch
> Of kindred hands that opened out the springs
> Of genial thought in childhood, and in spite
> Of all that unassisted I had marked
> In life or nature of those charms minute
> That win their way into the heart by stealth,
> (Still to the very going-out of youth)
> I too exclusively esteemed *that* love,
> And sought *that* beauty, which, as Milton sings,
> Hath terror in it. Thou didst soften down
> This over-sternness; but for thee, dear Friend!
> My soul, too reckless of mild grace, had stood
> In her original self too confident,
> Retained too long a countenance severe;
> A rock with torrents roaring, with the clouds
> Familiar, and a favourite of the stars:
> But thou didst plant its crevices with flowers,
> Hang it with shrubs that twinkle in the breeze,
> And teach the little birds to build their nests
> And warble in its chambers.[1]

Again, in that mental transition, when Nature, so long foremost in his affections and regard, finally yielded the supremacy to Man, Wordsworth acknowledges that it was his sister who, in a sense, led the way. Her breath was a "kind of gentler spring" that went before his steps, so that in his conception of and regard for Man we also find him indebted to her for a certain measure of help. He says:

> At a time
> When Nature, destined to remain so long
> Foremost in my affections, had fallen back
> Into a second place, pleased to become
> A handmaid to a nobler than herself,
> When every day brought with it some new sense
> Of exquisite regard for common things,
> And all the earth was budding with these gifts
> Of more refined humanity, thy breath,
> Dear Sister! was a kind of gentler spring
> That went before my steps.[2]

[1] The Prelude, XIV, 232-256.   [2] Ibid., XIV, 256-266.

A student of the mental and spiritual development of a poet must, of course, take cognizance of the influence of particular individuals as an important factor in his human or social environment, if he is to reckon with all the forces that were at work with his soul. There were a number of persons who exerted a marked influence on Wordsworth; among them his mother, Captain Beaupuy, William Godwin, his sister Dorothy, and Coleridge may be mentioned. But of all these none affected his life in general, nor his poetic life in particular, as powerfully as Dorothy Wordsworth. And one of the greatest of all her valuable services to him was rendered at this particular time of his life when he was lost in the darkness of an apparently hopeless skepticism. She it was who, understanding him in some respects better than he understood himself, called him away from the things "disturbing his peace"; who maintained for him "a saving intercourse" with his true self; who, in the hour of deepest gloom, whispered that brightness would come again. And after he had wandered here and there, unsettled in mind and perturbed in spirit, incapable of forming any definite purpose as to what course in life to pursue, in danger of drifting into some vocation where his poetic powers might be lost to him and therefore to the world, it was she who preserved him "still a poet" and made him "seek beneath that name, and that alone," his "office upon earth." She knew his powers. She saw the poet in him. She saw also that the poet's world must be his world, and it was her influence that largely compelled him to live in it. Henceforth she became a greater power in his life than ever — almost living for him — so constant and unselfish was her devotion. "Properly, and in a spirit of prophecy," says De Quincey, "was she named *Dorothy;* for, as that name apparently predestines her who bears it to figure rather in the character of aunt than of mother (insomuch that I have rarely happened to hear this name, except, indeed, in Germany, without the prefix of aunt), so, also, in its Greek meaning, *gift of God*, well did this name prefigure the relation in which she stood to Wordsworth, the mission with

which she was charged — to wait upon him as the tenderest and
most faithful of domestics ; to love him as a sister ; to sympathize
with him as a confidante, to counsel him as one gifted with a power
of judging that stretched as far as his own for producing ; to
cheer him and sustain him by the natural expression of her feelings — so quick, so ardent, so unaffected — upon the probable effect
of whatever thoughts, plans, images he might conceive ; finally,
and above all other ministrations, to ingraft, by her sexual sense
of beauty, upon his masculine austerity that delicacy and those
graces, which else (according to the grateful acknowledgement of
his own maturest retrospect) it would not have had." [1] All her
fine qualities of mind and heart were placed at his service, and
thus much of his art was made possible.[2]

Some of Wordsworth's biographers, while admitting the invaluable service rendered to Wordsworth by his sister, call attention
also to unfortunate results of her influence both on him personally
and on his poetry. It is said that her keen and superabundant
sensibility, uncontrolled by the higher mental powers, made her
and, through her, him also too susceptible to the ordinary in life
and Nature. It led to an exaggeration of the value of the commonplace, and to a marked indifference at times to the things of larger
and more vital import. It may be true that such devotion as
Dorothy gave to her brother was not an unmixed blessing. It may
have been fraught with a kind of hurtful influence to his poetry as
well as to his character. She may have been responsible, in a measure, for his selection of ordinary subjects and themes. This tendency, which was to a certain extent characteristic of Wordsworth
himself, was possibly encouraged by her. But were the larger hori-
zons of thought and the themes of vaster moment ever really in
danger ? Is the large number of small poems written by him conclusive evidence of this ? It is true that Wordsworth sometimes

[1] De Quincey, Literary Reminiscences, 364-365.
[2] Cf. Journals of Dorothy Wordsworth, edited by William Knight,

clothes ordinary subjects with an exaggerated interest, and treats them with unusual emotion. But even though Dorothy may be responsible in a measure for this, still both he and the world are under lasting obligations to her for the inestimable service rendered in the crisis of his life, which was so full of import concerning his future; also for the service rendered through long years of faithful devotion, in which she ministered to his bodily, mental, and spiritual needs.

It was fortunate that in the midst of this moral crisis the apparently aimless wanderings of Wordsworth were to come to an end — that he was to settle down to the comforts of a home, and to some definite work, both of which are powerful forces in unifying and steadying man's life. For many years he had been without a home, which added to his discontent and certainly was not conducive to productive effort. But now the dream of his sister and himself was about to be realized; they were to live together under the same roof. They began their new home life at Racedown in the autumn of 1795. From a letter written by Dorothy to Mrs. Marshall, shortly after they had settled there, we learn something of their physical environment, which here, as in their early home, was to have its influence on Wordsworth. She says: "We walk about two hours every morning. We have very pleasant walks about us; and what is a great advantage, the roads are of a sandy kind, and are almost always dry. We can see the sea, one hundred fifty or two hundred yards from the door; and at a little distance we have a very extensive view terminated by the sea, seen through different openings of the unequal hills. We have not the warmth and luxuriance of Devonshire, though there is no want either of wood, or of cultivation; but the trees appear to suffer from the sea-blasts. We have hills which, seen from a distance, almost take the character of mountains, some cultivated nearly to their summits; others in their wild state, covered with furze and broom. These delight me most, as they remind me of our native wilds." [1] Again,

[1] Knight, The Life of William Wordsworth, I, 108.

writing to another friend, she speaks of the "lovely meadows above the tops of the combs, and the scenery on Pilsden, Lewisden, and Blackdown-hill, and the view of the sea from Lambert's Castle."[1]

Wordsworth spent much of his time reading, writing, walking, and gardening. He was, according to his sister, very dexterous with the spade. He soon resumed his poetical work. He began to experiment with satire, adapting or paraphrasing certain parts of Juvenal, which he sent to his friend Wrangham. He and his friend contemplated publishing jointly a volume of satirical poems. In his productions Wordsworth satirized prevailing abuses, governmental vices, and corruptions of high society, revealing thus his continued interest in Man. Later, however, he came to the wise conclusion that this was not his work.[2]

It is to be regretted that at this time he did not exclude tragedy also from his poetical attempts. It too proved to be a kind of composition for which his gifts did not qualify him. This was soon to be made manifest in a tragedy entitled "The Borderers," which was begun by him in 1795 and completed in 1796. It has very little merit as a dramatic poem, but is of interest from a biographical point of view. Though rejected as a drama by the critics— by some of them almost in a spirit of contempt — to the student of Wordsworth's mental unfolding it is an important composition. It reveals the Poet, far removed from the ferment of society, under the beneficent influences of a quiet life with his faithful sister and an intimate association with Nature, subjecting the life of reason, which had brought him only moral disaster, to a careful scrutiny. Critics of "The Borderers" often fail to apprehend its real significance. They do not consider it sufficiently in the light of the terrible political events which immediately preceded its composition, and of the philosophy which had more or less tried to justify them, and of Wordsworth's relation to both.

In the philosophical bearing of the drama we may note the powerful influence of Godwin's philosophy. It seems to be the Poet's

---

[1] Dorothy Wordsworth, Memoirs, I, 94.   [2] Ibid., I, 95-96.

aim to reveal, in Oswald's character, conduct, and influence, the consequences of Godwinian principles when applied to life. The attainment of a spiritual freedom that flouts the "tyranny" of human opinion, custom, and law leads Oswald to be grateful to men who led him to commit the heinous crime of murder. Then, prompted by ambition and a desire for companionship in this lone freedom, he induces a noble man to commit a similar crime. He induces him to murder the father of the girl he loved by raising false suspicions concerning his honor and his daughter's purity, justifying the murder in the name of an exalted liberty. The outcome of running counter to established opinion and law, and following simply the guidance of unfettered individual nature, acting in the light of circumstances, is seen in the melancholy end of poor Marmaduke, the man whom Oswald thus betrayed. In him Oswald's philosophical faith is productive of fearful results, and issues in despair and moral ruin. It is evident that Wordsworth is pointing out the practical consequences of Godwin's political creed, with its naked individualism, and it is quite probable that the Poet is trying in this tragedy, as Legouis suggests, to purge himself of his own skepticism, for which this superficial but dangerous philosophy was in a large measure responsible.

In the case of earnest men moral skepticism is usually short-lived. They do not wander forever bewildered and distracted in the gloom of the skeptic's night. Sooner or later the darkened spirit sees the morning dawn. The normal attitude of the soul is not doubt, but belief; not denial, but affirmation. There is no "everlasting nay" for a healthy spirit. However confused and confounded by circumstances — by disappointed hopes, wrecked ambitions, the failure of ideals — however bewildered by the contrarieties and apparent antinomies of reason, ultimately, under wholesome conditions, the soul, as a rule, finds its way back to faith. The great truths which condition its life and progress finally compel acceptance. Their rightful home is the human spirit, whose development they shape and control, and although inhospitable

circumstances may occasionally drive them out, they return again
to find ready welcome and permanent lodgment. So it proved with
Wordsworth.

Here in Racedown, under most favorable conditions, the mental
situation was gradually changing. What was gone was slowly returning. Far from the noisy and fretful life of the world remedial
agencies were at work to restore his soul. The faithful ministries
of a devoted sister, the daily intercourse with Nature in peaceful
haunts, the lessons he had learned from her in years gone by,
his conversation with men of humble spirit and open manners,
the silent communion with wholesome books, the restoring power
of definite and daily occupation, the hours of meditation and calm
reflection, remote from the mad course of political events — these
were the forces at work to restore Wordsworth to his normal self.
It is impossible, of course, to determine definitely just when a full
recovery was effected. As in the case of bodily disease, it was
gradual. However, it is safe to say that, by the time he and his
sister left Racedown to take up their abode in Alfoxden, Wordsworth was mentally and spiritually in the advanced stages of convalescence. How complete the restoration was when it did come is
indicated in the thirteenth book of " The Prelude." The Poet's
account of the marvelous change that took place is both interesting
and instructive, revealing as it does Wordsworth's conception of
Nature's part in the work of his recovery. She did not desert the
heart that loved her. She calmed him, and gently led him back to
the recognition of great truths, and forward to the acceptance of
others, concerning both herself and Man. " Long time," he says,

> "in search of knowledge did I range
> The field of human life, in heart and mind
> Benighted; but, the dawn beginning now
> To re-appear, 't was proved that not in vain
> I had been taught to reverence a Power
> That is the visible quality and shape
> And image of right reason; that matures
> Her processes by steadfast laws; gives birth

> To no impatient or fallacious hopes,
> No heat of passion or excessive zeal,
> No vain conceits; provokes to no quick turns
> Of self-applauding intellect; but trains
> To meekness, and exalts by humble faith;
> Holds up before the mind intoxicate
> With present objects, and the busy dance
> Of things that pass away, a temperate show
> Of objects that endure; and by this course
> Disposes her, when over-fondly set
> On throwing off incumbrances, to seek
> In man, and in the frame of social life,
> Whate'er there is desirable and good
> Of kindred permanence, unchanged in form
> And function, or, through strict vicissitude
> Of life and death, revolving." [1]

"Above all," he adds,

> " Were re-established now those watchful thoughts
> Which, seeing little worthy or sublime
> In what the Historian's pen so much delights
> To blazon — power and energy detached
> From moral purpose — early tutored me
> To look with feelings of fraternal love
> Upon the unassuming things that hold
> A silent station in this beauteous world." [2]

One of the most interesting features of his recovery is the re-establishment, by degrees, under the guidance of Nature, of his faith in Man. He begins to study him not as an abstract creature — a mere mental creation — but as a real being clothed in flesh and blood. Having gained more judicious views of the worth of individual man, he inquires with more interest than heretofore why we find this glorious creature in such small numbers — " one in ten thousand." Why may not millions be what one is? If the obstructions of animal appetites and daily wants be not insuperable, then all others vanish. So he exhorts himself:

[1] The Prelude, XIII, 16–39.   [2] Ibid., 39–47.

> " Inspect the basis of the social pile:
> Enquire . . . how much of mental power
> And genuine virtue they possess who live
> By bodily toil, labour exceeding far
> Their due proportion, under all the weight
> Of that injustice which upon ourselves
> Ourselves entail." [1]

He turned to men as he found them in his daily walks — humble, unassuming, simple folk. He loved to

> Converse with men, where if we meet a face
> We almost meet a friend, on naked heaths
> With long long ways before, by cottage bench,
> Or well-spring where the weary traveller rests.[2]

He began to talk with strangers whom he met in his wanderings, and to learn of them important lessons. His intercourse with these lowly people began in Racedown, and was continued in Alfoxden. It proved to be a revelation to him. He was both astonished and gratified at the amount of native intelligence and virtuous sentiment his conversations with such men revealed, and it brought peace and steadiness, healing and repose, to his ruffled passions. These men were a direct contradiction of his Godwinian philosophy, which maintained that virtue belonged to the wise, and vice was the offspring of ignorance. Godwin taught that we owe everything to education. Here Wordsworth feels how little we are indebted, at least to formal education — how little it has to do with genuine feeling and just sentiment.[3] The outcome of all this subsequently had a most vital bearing on his poetry, for he was led to a firm determination to make Man the chief subject of his song. Furthermore, he would sing of Man not as judged by externals, but as he really is within himself. He would sing, too, of Man as found not in high places but in " the walks of homely life," for it is here, according to Wordsworth, that we find the fundamentally human. He would deal with men in the simplicity of their being, and in

---

[1] The Prelude, XIII, 94–100.   [2] Ibid., 138–141.   [3] Ibid., 168–185.

simple everyday circumstances and situations, and in the ordinary language of men instead of in a diction foreign to common life and belonging to a particular class of men whom we call poets. This determination is the key to much of his poetry.

In this gradual recovery of Wordsworth his former convictions concerning Nature were also strengthened. He was convinced that she

> for all conditions wants not power
> To consecrate, if we have eyes to see,
> The outside of her creatures, and to breathe
> Grandeur upon the very humblest face
> Of human life.[1]

He began to see an intimate relation existing between the works of Nature and those of Man ; to note that the passion which animates Nature's various forms intermingles with the work of Man to which she calls him. Again, he is convinced that the poet stands side by side with the prophet " in a mighty scheme of truth," each having his own peculiar gift, heaven-born, that enables him to perceive things never seen before. In other words, he is again conscious of the powers of the poet, the source from which they spring, the obligations they entail upon the possessor, and cherishes a hope that, thus endowed, he may be able to produce an enduring work.

Thus, gradually, a restoration to moral and spiritual health was taking place. Slowly faith and hope, and with them peace and joy, were returning. The soul of Nature and the soul of Man were again realities for him. The lost vision was beginning to dawn once more on the renewed spirit. He began, as of old, " to see into the life of things," to be conscious of heaven-born powers and sacred obligations. The process of recovery begun in Racedown was continued and completed at Alfoxden, where we shall soon find him standing again in Nature's presence,

> A sensitive being, a creative soul.

[1] The Prelude, XIII, 283-287.

CHAPTER VI

COLERIDGE. THE "LYRICAL BALLADS." POETRY RELATING TO MAN

Wordsworth and his sister moved from Racedown to Alfoxden July 13, 1797. This was a fortunate change, and was productive of one of the most fruitful chapters in the Poet's history. It was here, under the healing influence of his natural surroundings and the society of congenial friends, that he progressed rapidly to a complete restoration of his mental and spiritual health. It was here, also, that his brief acquaintance with Coleridge ripened into a warm friendship to the mutual advantage of both — a friendship that was destined to leave a permanent impression upon their work and greatly to enrich the pages of English poetry. Here, too, the "Lyrical Ballads" were written, inspired chiefly by what he learned from lowly folk, and by the beauty and charm with which Nature in the Quantock Hills greets the eye of sense and speaks to the spirit of man.

Nature has invested Alfoxden with a cheerful beauty which did not fail to have a salutary effect upon Wordsworth. The "Journals of Dorothy Wordsworth" abound in descriptions of the scenery. On her first visit she writes : " There is everything there, sea, woods wild as fancy ever painted, brooks clear and pebbly as in Cumberland, villages so romantic ; and William and I, in a wander by ourselves, found out a sequestered waterfall in a dell formed by steep hills covered with full-grown timber-trees. The woods are as fine as those at Lowther, and the country more romantic ; it has the character of the less grand parts of the neighborhood of the lakes."[1] Again, in a letter bearing the date of August 14, 1797, she writes :

---

[1] Dorothy Wordsworth, Memoirs, I, 102.

"Wherever we turn we have woods, smooth downs, and valleys with small brooks running down them, through green meadows, hardly ever intersected with hedgerows, but scattered over with trees. The hills that cradle these valleys are either covered with fern and bilberries, or oak woods, which are cut for charcoal. . . . Walks extend for miles over the hill-tops; the great beauty of which is their wild simplicity: they are perfectly smooth, without rocks.

"The Tor of Glastonbury is before our eyes during more than half of our walk to Stowey; and in the park wherever we go, keeping about fifteen yards above the house, it makes a part of our prospect." [1] Dorothy's "Journals" record numerous walks with her brother through this beautiful country, which daily ministered to his convalescing mind and gradually brought to it peace and joy. Child of Nature that he was, Wordsworth was very susceptible to her healing power. That he was alive to the rare beauty and charm of his new surroundings will be evident when we come to consider the nature of his work as we find it manifest in the "Lyrical Ballads."

According to Miss Wordsworth the primary motive for leaving Racedown to settle here was a desire to have the society of Coleridge. On first thought it seems rather singular that two men so unlike in many respects should become intimate friends and prove to be so mutually helpful. However, there were affinities which drew these two men together and made each a power in the other's life. In the first place, both were in sympathy with the political movements of the time in behalf of a larger liberty for Man, and against the artificial and tyrannical class distinctions and privileges which then obtained. They were in sympathy with the fundamental principles which underlay the French Revolution, and more or less out of harmony with the governmental policy of their own country at this early period in their career. In other words, both were decidedly republican in their political views. This probably

[1] Dorothy Wordsworth, Memoirs, I, 103-104.

constituted a bond of sympathy, although Wordsworth refused to engage in political discussion with his friends at Alfoxden.

In the next place, both were poets. Coleridge had read Wordsworth's "Descriptive Sketches" while at Cambridge, and was greatly pleased with the work. He saw in it the promise of a great poet. Later he met him at Bristol, and again at Racedown. He was not disappointed when, at the latter place, he heard him read "The Ruined Cottage" and "The Borderers," for at this time he wrote to Cottle, "I speak with heartfelt sincerity, and, I think, unblinded judgment, when I tell you that I feel myself a little man by his side."

Furthermore, far apart as they were in some respects because of temperamental differences, and in the peculiarities of their genius, nevertheless there was a similarity in their regard for and appreciation of Nature. The poetic sympathy that Coleridge felt and manifested for Wordsworth and his work, and his poetic way of apprehending Nature, which was so in harmony with Wordsworth's mental attitude, proved to be a source of encouragement and inspiration, and was responsible for much of Wordsworth's mental and spiritual progress as well as the progress of his art.

Again, another bond of affinity was a certain philosophical predisposition of mind. Much as Wordsworth was inclined at times to deal with small and commonplace themes, he had, nevertheless, the larger mental horizon which is characteristic of the philosopher. While living at Racedown and Alfoxden he planned an elaborate philosophical poem, "The Recluse," which should have as its subject "Man, Nature, and Society." This was probably the outgrowth of his experience with the French Revolution, and of his reflective tendencies, stimulated by his conversations with Coleridge. His mental life, in its philosophical moods, was affected to a considerable degree by Coleridge, whose mind, on the whole, was more speculatively disposed than Wordsworth's, and whose abilities in reflective thinking were certainly greater than those of his friend. That Wordsworth was conscious of his indebtedness in this respect is manifest in the Preface to "The Excursion," where he states, in explaining the original plan of his philosophical poem, that his intellect was greatly indebted " to a dear friend, most distinguished for his knowledge and genius." It is also manifest in his tribute to him, to be found in Book XIV of " The Prelude," where he points out, more or less specifically, the nature of this obligation:

> With such a theme,
> Coleridge ! with this my argument, of thee
> Shall I be silent? O capacious Soul !
> Placed on this earth to love and understand,
> And from thy presence shed the light of love,
> Shall I be mute, ere thou be spoken of ?
> Thy kindred influence to my heart of hearts
> Did also find its way. Thus fear relaxed
> Her overweening grasp ; thus thoughts and things
> In the self-haunting spirit learned to take
> More rational proportions ; mystery,
> The incumbent mystery of sense and soul,
> Of life and death, time and eternity,
> Admitted more habitually a mild
> Interposition — a serene delight
> In closelier gathering cares, such as become
> A human creature, howsoe'er endowed,
> Poet, or destined for a humbler name ;
> And so the deep enthusiastic joy,
> The rapture of the hallelujah sent
> From all that breathes and is, was chastened, stemmed
> And balanced by pathetic truth, by trust
> In hopeful reason, leaning on the stay
> Of Providence ; and in reverence for duty,
> Here, if need be, struggling with storms, and there
> Strewing in peace life's humblest ground with herbs,
> At every season green, sweet at all hours.[1]

It was probably in his reflective thinking, and in the rational interpretation of things and life, more than in any other way, that Coleridge influenced our Poet. Coleridge's large way of looking at things, the comprehensive sweep of his vision and thought, had

[1] The Prelude, XIV, 275-301.

a tendency not only to wean Wordsworth away from what too often seemed to be mere pettiness of theme and an exaggerated interest in the commonplace, but also to arouse him to a consideration of the larger and deeper problems of human life and thought.

Furthermore, there was a tendency toward mysticism in Coleridge's poetical functioning, as well as in his philosophizing, which of course made his thinking especially congenial to Wordsworth. In his reflection he was early influenced by Neoplatonism. His translation of the hymns of Synesius, his fondness for Taylor's translations of Plato and Plotinus, his poems entitled "Time, Real and Imaginary: An Allegory," "Monody on the Death of Chatterton," "Religious Musings," "The Æolian Harp," and the "Destiny of Nations," all indicate a mystical and more or less pantheistic trend. Later he reveals the influence of the mystical and pantheistic German philosopher Jakob Böhme. He even manifested a sympathy with the Quakerism of Fox. Still later the influence of Schelling's transcendental philosophy, with its idealistic pantheism, is quite marked. Now Wordsworth himself was a mystic of a pronounced type, and minds of this order must of necessity have proved congenial and mutually helpful. Certain it is that Coleridge did materially influence Wordsworth, and not the least part of the influence exerted by him was due to his philosophical mind, with its large perspective, its mystical vision, and its spiritual interpretation of Reality.

The volume of "Lyrical Ballads" was composed in Alfoxden. Wordsworth's account of its origin is given in a note preceding the poem entitled "We are Seven." Here we are told that he, Dorothy, and Coleridge decided to visit Linton and the Valley of Stones. Their funds were somewhat limited, so Wordsworth and Coleridge agreed to write a poem, to be sent to the *New Monthly Magazine*, to defray the expense of the trip. "The Ancient Mariner" was planned as they journeyed along the Quantock Hills. Wordsworth's contribution to it was small. He found that Coleridge and he differed so much in their "respective

manners " that he withdrew from the project. But later they resolved to publish jointly a volume of verse. The "Lyrical Ballads"
was the result.

As to the nature of this volume, it was agreed that it should
consist " of Poems chiefly on natural subjects taken from common
life, but looked at, as much as might be, through an imaginative
medium." [1] Wordsworth's contribution to the volume was far
greater in quantity than that of Coleridge. This is not a matter
of surprise, as he was a man more steady in his moods and more
industrious in his habits than his friend.

We are here interested simply in Wordsworth's contribution.
The poems written at Alfoxden are characteristic. They deal
with Man, Nature, and Man's relation to Nature. He illustrates
his own conception of poetry as " the image of Man and Nature."
Sometimes he is primarily engaged with Man, dealing with him
in his essential being, exploiting his general passions, and describing him in his fundamental relations to life. Then again
he is more especially engaged with Nature, investing her with
conscious spirit, seeing into the life of things, positing or intuit-
ing a relation between her and Man, and attributing to her the
functions of a ministering agent and teacher to the human soul.

A definite purpose lies at the foundations of the " Lyrical
Ballads," and an interesting history behind them, with both of
which one must be acquainted if one would properly understand
them. Two sources especially throw light on Wordsworth's object
in writing poetry of this character. One is the Preface to the
second volume of the " Lyrical Ballads, with Other Poems," published in the year 1800, and the additions made in the edition
of 1802.[2] This is an explanation and defense of his poetry. The
other is Book XIII of "The Prelude," in which we find the

[1] Poetical Works, edited by William Knight, I, 230 n.

[2] Cf. Prose Works, edited by William Knight, I, 45–82

personal history leading up to the composition of the Ballads. In the Preface he says concerning his purpose: " The principal object, then, proposed in these Poems was to choose incidents and situations from common life, and to relate or describe them, throughout, as far as was possible, in a selection of language really used by men, and, at the same time, to throw over them a certain colouring of imagination, whereby ordinary things should be presented to the mind in an unusual aspect; and, further, and above all, to make these incidents and situations interesting by tracing in them, truly though not ostentatiously, the primary laws of our nature: chiefly as far as regards the manner in which we associate ideas in a state of excitement. Humble and rustic life was generally chosen, because, in that condition, the essential passions of the heart find a better soil in which they can attain their maturity, are less under restraint, and speak a plainer and more emphatic language; because in that condition of life our elementary feelings co-exist in a state of greater simplicity, and, consequently, may be more accurately contemplated, and more forcibly communicated; because the manners of rural life germinate from those elementary feelings; and, from the necessary character of rural occupations, are more easily comprehended, and are more durable; and lastly, because in that condition the passions of men are incorporated with the beautiful and permanent forms of nature. The language, too, of these men is adopted (purified indeed from what appear to be its real defects, from all lasting and rational causes of dislike or disgust) because such men hourly communicate with the best objects from which the best part of language is originally derived; and, because, from their rank in society and the sameness and narrow circle of their intercourse, being less under the influence of social vanity, they convey their feelings and notions in simple and unelaborated expressions. Accordingly, such a language, arising out of repeated experience and regular feelings, is a more permanent and a far more philosophical language than that which is frequently substituted for it by Poets, who think that they are conferring honour upon themselves and their art, in proportion as they separate themselves from the sympathies of men, and indulge in arbitrary and capricious habits of expression, in order to furnish food for fickle tastes, and fickle appetites, of their own creation." [1]

We see in these words that Wordsworth wrote the "Lyrical Ballads" with a specific object in view, and also what that object was. A little later in the Preface he states, in a somewhat different way, the nature of his purpose and how it is illustrated in particular poems. He aims "to follow the fluxes and refluxes of the mind when agitated by the great and simple affections of our nature. This object I have endeavoured in these short essays to attain by various means; by tracing the maternal passion through many of its more subtle windings, as in the Poems of 'The Idiot Boy' and 'The Mad Mother';[2] by accompanying the last struggles of a human being, at the approach of death, cleaving in solitude to life and society, as in the Poem of 'The Forsaken Indian'; by showing, as in the stanzas entitled 'We are Seven,' the perplexity and obscurity which in childhood attend our notion of death, or rather our utter inability to admit that notion; or by displaying the strength of fraternal, or to speak more philosophically, of moral attachment when early associated with the great and beautiful objects of nature, as in 'The Brothers'; or, as in the incident of Simon Lee, by placing my reader in the way of receiving from ordinary moral sensations another and more salutary impression than we are accustomed to receive from them. It has also been part of my general purpose to attempt to sketch characters under the influence of less impassioned feelings, as in 'The Two April Mornings,' 'The Fountain,' 'The Old Man Travelling,' 'The Two Thieves,' etc., characters of which the elements are simple, belonging rather to nature than to manners,

[1] Prose Works, I, 48–49.
[2] In the editions of 1836–1843 Wordsworth added the words: "And the one beginning 'Her eyes are wild,' etc."

such as exist now, and will probably always exist, and which from
their constitution may be distinctly and profitably contemplated."[1]

Now if we turn to Book XIII of "The Prelude," we find
information that throws further light on the "Lyrical Ballads,"
especially on the history back of them. Here the Poet emphasizes
more particularly the ethical motive which lies at the basis of his
art. We learn how and why he was led to sing of Man free from
the corrupting influences of social artifice and conventionality —
to sing of him treading lowly paths and shadowing forth our
common life. This has already been remarked upon in the last
chapter, but it requires further amplification if we are fully to
understand the mental and spiritual history which constitutes the
background of the "Lyrical Ballads," and of which they are so
largely the product and expression. This will not only enable us
more fully to appreciate Wordsworth's purpose and the *rationale*
thereof, but also his firm conviction concerning both, which enabled him to remain apparently undisturbed in the midst of sharp
and merciless criticism and the solicitude which it occasioned
among his friends.

In the twelfth book of "The Prelude" Wordsworth tells of the
impairment of his imagination and taste caused by his experience
with the French Revolution, and by his philosophizing on the
nature of Man; also of their restoration. Book XIII continues
the same story. Here, however, he dwells more particularly on
their restoration. In his search for knowledge he had ranged for
a long time "the field of human life, in heart and mind be-
nighted," but as the dawn began to reappear, he

> found
> Once more in Man an object of delight,
> Of pure imagination, and of love.[2]

And as his mental horizon widened, he again began to study,
his knowledge increasing accordingly, and his confidence in feelings

---

[1] Prose Works, I, 50-51.   [2] The Prelude, XIII, 48-50.

that had stood the test of severe trial becoming firmer. His moral vision grew clearer. The promise of his time took on truer proportions. He found less pleasure in hopeful schemes and ambitious projects, and sought rather

> For present good in life's familiar face,
> And built thereon my hopes of good to come.[1]

He turned away from the sources to which he had looked for knowledge concerning Man, to other sources — to modest paths and lonely roads — seeking them enriched with everything he prized, "with human kindness and simple joys." It was in the lowly, simple-hearted folk whom he met here that he found the elements of our constitution in their naturalness. In minds largely untutored by the formal methods of education, but developed by intercourse with Nature and simple life, he found what he deemed to be the universal passions, and heard words expressive of noblest sentiment and truth. All this filled him with hope and peace. His faith in Man returned, and he saw in his fundamental nature much that promised good and fair.

But more than this. So impressed was he with the essential nature of the being in whom he had but a short time before lost faith, and concerning whose destiny he had lost all hope, that it stirred his soul to resolution. He determined to make him the subject of his art. He resolved to sing, and the theme of his song should be.

> No other than the very heart of man,
> As found among the best of those who live.[2]

This resolution was most pronounced in its effect on Wordsworth's poetry. He became the poet of Man as well as the poet of Nature. Indeed, it had its influence upon his most immediate work. This is evident in the "Lyrical Ballads." Many of the poems included in the first volume, and many, also, of the second edition

---

[1] The Prelude, XIII, 62–63.   [2] Ibid., 241–242.

of two volumes, are in harmony with his resolve. In them he deals with human nature in its bare reality and spontaneity; humble folk are the subjects of these simple songs, as is manifest in such poems as "We are Seven," "Simon Lee," "The Complaint of a Forsaken Indian Woman," "The Last of the Flock," "The Idiot Boy," "The Mad Mother," "The Two April Mornings," "The Fountain," and "The Brothers."

There was another reason, closely related to those given above, why Wordsworth chose "humble and rustic life" as the theme of his song. He had by no means yielded the political convictions which had been such an inspiring as well as disturbing factor in his previous life. He was still democratic in his political predilections and beliefs. He had still an antipathy for artificial political class distinctions which brought advantage to some at the expense of others. He deeply sympathized with the poorer classes of society in their toil, suffering, and poverty, much of which was due to social and political wrong, and it was in exaltation, honor, and defense of humanity, as it may be found in such as these, that he was determined to sing; so that all through the " Lyrical Ballads " an intensely human note is struck, and the reasons for it must be taken into consideration in attempting any intelligent criticism.

In these poems there is, of course, a departure from some of the traditions of poetry, and especially a reaction against the conventionalism of the eighteenth century. Such a course could not take place without serious protest. The poems became a veritable storm center; a harsh and unjust criticism followed their publication. Coleridge thought that the preface to the second volume, in which Wordsworth sets forth his aim and theory of poetry, was responsible for much of the later criticism. Wordsworth's contention that poetry differed in no respect from prose save in rime and meter was probably the chief source of offense. Coleridge and others, however, contend that Wordsworth, in the Ballads, wrote better than his theory. On the other hand, Professor Raleigh urges, with considerable plausibility and force, that his shortcomings are largely due to a failure to conform to it. As we are dealing primarily with the content of his poetry, it is not our province to enter upon this debated and debatable field. But much of the criticism relates to the very content itself. Fault is found with his selection of commonplace subjects, ordinary persons, and simple experiences and situations. It was said, and is still said, that he degraded poetry by singing a common song of common persons and things, in common language. Poetry is art and it must not be thus vulgarized. The Muse must not be dragged into the mire. Peasants, vagrants, and humble folk generally, with their petty experiences, do not furnish a sufficiently suggestive and exalted theme for this divine art. Wordsworth sees too much in such people, with their obscure, lowly, and often abject life.

Undoubtedly there is a measure of justice in this. Even the most ardent Wordsworthian hesitates to follow him at times without at least an inward protest. But we ought to try to understand him before uttering hasty criticism. Even a careful reading of his verse, without studying it in relation to the man himself and to the bitter but chastening and sanctifying experience which really gave birth to Wordsworth as the poet of Man, will never enable us to fully understand and appreciate the worth of these ballads. Wordsworth had an intense sympathy and a profound respect for men "as they are men within themselves." With him human nature is a sacred thing. It is neither " common " nor "unclean." He who attempts to explore it treads upon holy ground. Both human affection and human suffering, as involved in the elemental human relations, have something of the divine in them. Now, as we have seen, it is Wordsworth's conviction that the first elements of Man may be best studied in just such people as these who constitute the subjects of these poems. Idealist that he is with reference to Man, Wordsworth is also an intense Realist. He desires to get at the facts regarding human nature. He feels that, by brushing aside all artificiality, conventionalism, and complexity, growing out of society as we find it in the more favored and cultured circles, this may be done; that these feelings coexist in greater simplicity here than elsewhere, and the conduct of rural folk springs from them, and rural occupations render them more comprehensible and durable; that among these people, more than elsewhere, we find these essential emotions incorporated "with the beautiful and permanent forms of nature." Wordsworth had learned this from his association with them. The lonely roads he paced were " open schools " to him, in which he daily read, with keen delight, in words and looks, in sighs and tears, "the passions of mankind." He saw depths of soul revealed in spirits "that appeared to have no depth at all to careless eyes." Hence these became the subject of his poetry. His spiritual eye beheld what the eye of sense cannot see, and he became the interpreter of human nature, apprehending a strength, nobility, glory, and honor in human weakness, suffering, and endurance, and in human love and self-sacrifice. As De Vere says : " He never goes out of his way to find some form of suffering unheard of before; but in his hands ordinary things become extraordinary, because he sees in them, and teaches his readers to see, depths and heights not suspected. The affections he sings are not the mere instincts of temperament brightened by a gleam of fancy; nor have they their root in caprice, self-will, or self-love. They are those nobly-simple affections out of which Nature has built up human society, and which lives in the light of duty." [1]

But it is insisted that in these ballads there is too much subjectivity, or, to put it more baldly, too much egotism. The very theory which underlies them involves a reaction against universally accepted methods of poetry, and exalts the individual will and caprice of the poet.[2] It discards objective sources of inspiration, and depends too much upon meditation and contemplation to

[1] De Vere, Essays Chiefly on Poetry, 112–113.
[2] See, for example, Courthope, The Liberal Men in English Literature, Lecture 3

furnish the afflatus. It *chooses* its materials. There is a volitional reaction on its subject-matter rather than a natural, spontaneous reaction, as though poetry were the product of a mere exercise of will. The result is that, although Wordsworth in practice often is better than Wordsworth in theory, much of his poetry suffers from this arbitrariness — this personal interference with the natural processes and laws of poetic inspiration and composition. We find him substituting personal for universal experience, and, so far as this relates to the content of his poetry, we observe that he sees in common folk much that is uncommon, in ordinary peasants and vagrants much that is extraordinary, in everyday experiences something that is unique and unusual. In other words, in dealing with his subject-matter he sees what other minds fail to see, and affirm cannot be seen. It is merely a subjective or personal contribution to Reality on the part of the Poet.

But here again, may we not be too hasty in our judgment? Reality, even in its most ordinary and familiar forms, is not such a simple thing as it appears on the surface. A more careful contemplation of it usually leads to a change of view. The history of science and philosophy proves this. All knowledge is interpretation of Reality, and minds differ in their capacity to interpret. If this be true in regard to the so-called physical world, it is preëminently true concerning the world of human nature. The poet's genius may perceive what the ordinary mind, unaided, fails to perceive. This does not necessarily make his knowledge less impersonal, objective, or universal. Reality may correspond to the vision, and the poet may simply be the teacher or prophet leading us into further light, as does the genius in science and philosophy, or the prophet in religion. Undoubtedly Wordsworth went to extremes, both in the selection of subjects and in his use of language, and was sometimes betrayed into investing the commonplace with an exaggerated interest and significance. All this must be admitted. But every poet has his lapses and his extremes, and every poet has in a measure the defects of his virtues. Wordsworth is no exception to the rule. Indeed, he conspicuously illustrates it in the "Lyrical Ballads," as well as elsewhere. However, just criticism or evaluation will not magnify these at the expense of the real worth of the poet's work, and in the case of Wordsworth this certainly is not wanting. In regard to human nature there is a careful inquiry into the facts revealed by its essential life. His inquiry is anything but subjective and personal. Hazlitt is wide of the mark in his criticism when he says, " Mr. Wordsworth is the last man to ' look abroad into universality.' " The " Lyrical Ballads," and the theory underlying them, are conspicuous evidence against any such interpretation of Wordsworth's genius. He did look beyond himself, both in imagination and in heart, when writing these simple lays. There is both a natural and an ethical universality to be found in them. He who endeavors to determine that which is elemental is dealing with the universal and the objective, and he who deals with the ideal in interpretation deals with something more than the personal. So if Wordsworth's treatment of human nature, in both its realistic and idealistic aspects, seems at times to be peculiar to himself — if he sees in men what others fail to see — may it not be because, through his genius, he is gifted with a superior vision and insight by which he sees into the life of Man as he sees into the life of things ? This, however, does not necessarily render the vision and interpretation merely subjective, or stamp the poet as an extreme egotist. Subjective, in a sense, they undoubtedly are, but they are also objective and universal in the highest degree, and point to the poet as the real interpreter and prophet of human nature.

Furthermore, the intensely human note found in the " Lyrical Ballads " confutes a somewhat general criticism that Wordsworth's poetry lacks passion. Such a criticism has force only as passion is identified with violent, sensuous, and oftentimes abnormal feeling, such as may be found in a poet, for example, like Byron. In this sense Wordsworth's poetry is not impassioned ; but there is a deeper, truer, nobler, passion than this, and his verse throbs with it — a

passion not to be confounded with tempestuous feeling, mawkish
sentimentalism, or uncontrolled emotion born of personal grief or
misfortune. There is the passion of a profound sympathy and love
for humanity—a passion of fellow-feeling that causes the heart to
beat in sympathy with human sorrow as well as with human joy.
These ballads are saturated with feeling of this sort. Only one thus
possessed could write "The Thorn," "Her Eyes are Wild," "Simon
Lee," "The Complaint of a Forsaken Indian Woman," "The
Last of the Flock," "The Idiot Boy," "The Old Cumberland
Beggar," and, later, "The Two April Mornings," "The Fountain,"
"Ruth," "The Brothers," "Michael," and "The Affliction of Margaret ——." Here the Poet's heart is close to the great heart of humanity, his imagination is warmed by a deep pathos and genuine
passion, and he reveals himself to be a true poet of Man.

Of human nature and human experience, then, as he thus found
it in Racedown and Alfoxden, and read it with a poet's insight, the
"Lyrical Ballads" are but the poetic expression. These simple
lays are the actualization of the noble resolve formed after Man
was revealed to him in lowly life.

> Of these, said I, shall be my song; of these,
> If future years mature me for the task,
> Will I record the praises, making verse
> Deal boldly with substantial things; in truth
> And sanctity of passion, speak of these,
> That justice may be done, obeisance paid
> Where it is due: thus haply shall I teach,
> Inspire; through unadulterated ears
> Pour rapture, tenderness, and hope, — my theme
> No other than the very heart of man,
> As found among the best of those who live —
> Not unexalted by religious faith,
> Nor uninformed by books, good books, though few —
> In Nature's presence: thence may I select
> Sorrow, that is not sorrow, but delight;
> And miserable love, that is not pain
> To hear of, for the glory that redounds
> Therefrom to human kind, and what we are.

Be mine to follow with no timid step
Where knowledge leads me : it shall be my pride
That I have dared to tread this holy ground,
Speaking no dream, but things oracular.[1]

Nihil humani a me alienum puto is preëminently Wordsworth's motto. It runs through the contents of these early volumes like a theme through a symphony. These simple songs, while they record the joys of simple life, are also burdened with the heart's weight of suffering, with its griefs and sorrows, with its mysterious and unintelligible experience, as well as with the sublime strength and virtuous humanity which they reveal in humble folk ; and if poetry be "an image of Man and Nature," then, so far as the "Lyrical Ballads" purport to be the image of Man, it does not appear, after conceding all of the Poet's shortcomings, that he degraded his art in dealing with human nature, but rather must it be said, in the words of a brother poet,

He sang a lofty song of lowly weal and dole.

[1] The Prelude, XIII, 232–253.

CHAPTER VII

THE "LYRICAL BALLADS" (CONTINUED). NATURE AND HER RELATION TO MAN

Wordsworth's contribution to the "Lyrical Ballads" reveals two classes of poems: one in which the Poet is chiefly concerned with Man; the other in which he is primarily interested in Nature and in Nature's relation to Man. The first class has already been considered. Let us now turn to the second. Here may be found poetry which is regarded as peculiarly Wordsworthian — poetry which, with that of a similar character, to be considered later, gives Wordsworth his peculiar historical significance as a poet of Nature. It is in poetry such as this that he manifests his remarkable power to "see into the life of things." In these early poems "the vision and the faculty divine" are already apparent. Indeed, if we may ascribe to Wordsworth a philosophy at all, the fundamentals of it may be found in this second class of poems contained in the "Lyrical Ballads."

Proceeding in chronological order, there are four poems, all breathing the same spirit, belonging to the year 1798. The first of these is entitled "Lines written in Early Spring." In a prefatory note Wordsworth says it was "actually composed while I was sitting by the side of the brook that runs down from the *Comb*, in which stands the village of Alford, through the grounds of Alfoxden. It was a chosen resort of mine. The brook ran down a sloping rock, so as to make a waterfall, considerable for that county; and across the pool below had fallen a tree — an ash if I rightly remember — from which rose perpendicularly, boughs in search of the light intercepted by the deep shade above. The boughs bore leaves of green, that for want of sunshine had faded into almost lily-white;

and from the underside of this natural sylvan bridge depended long and beautiful tresses of ivy, which waved gently in the breeze, that might, poetically speaking, be called the breath of the waterfall. This motion varied of course in proportion to the power of water in the brook." [1] This unique spot was a meeting place of Wordsworth, Coleridge, and their Alfoxden friends. Coleridge himself refers to it in a poem the first line of which reads, "This lime-tree bower, my prison." Wordsworth now puts himself in touch with Nature, just as in earlier years. He seeks her for her own sake, and drinks deep draughts from her wells of inspiration.

This early poem was undoubtedly inspired by his natural surroundings. In the very first verse expression is given to his intuition of the unity of Nature. He hears a thousand notes while sitting in this favorite grove, steeped in a peculiar mood — a mood in which pleasant thoughts give rise to sad thoughts. Yet Nature's voices are not discordant. The thousand notes are blended into a beautiful harmony. His mystical sense not only perceives individual, isolated sounds, but apprehends Nature's notes as a melodious whole. The sad thoughts suggested by pleasant thoughts were the outcome of the Poet's soul harking back to those conditions of Man which had previously thrown him into a state of moral despair. Some, too, were doubtless suggested by contemplating present social and political conditions. This seems probable from the second verse, where, after pointing out the fact that Nature had linked his human soul to her fair works, he confesses much grief "to think what man has made of man." The psychological law of suggestion by contrast is here in operation. Nature's "thousand blended notes," causing pleasant thoughts, occasion grief also, because of the contrast suggested between the natural and the human world.

As the poem progresses we are introduced to Wordsworth's poetic faith, which is at the same time his philosophic faith. He notes the periwinkle trailing its wreaths through primrose tufts, and

[1] Poetical Works, edited by William Knight, I, 268 n.

confesses to a belief that every flower is possessed of conscious
life. It has the power of conscious enjoyment.

> And 't is my faith that every flower
> Enjoys the air it breathes.[1]

But it is not the flowers alone that are thus highly endowed. Birds
also possess this capacity. Every motion of theirs seems to the
Poet to be " a thrill of pleasure." And even the budding twigs, as
they spread their fan " to catch the breezy air," make it impossible
for Wordsworth to think otherwise than that they too have a capacity
for enjoyment. Here are two aspects of his conception of Nature :
First, the so-called vegetable world, usually supposed to be a world of
unconscious life, is not merely a living world, but a *conscious* world,
and therefore a world of mind, for all conscious life is mental life.
In the second place, the conscious life of both the vegetable and
the animal world seems to be a pleasure-consciousness. In these two
realms, *to be* is *to be joyous*. With him, according to the Poet's
own confession, these conceptions attain unto the dignity of a faith,
and a faith which is of the nature of a revelation. This is in keeping with what he says about speaking no dream, but things oracular.
Here the mysticism of the Poet is again manifest. Furthermore,
it ought to be noted that here he does not apprehend Nature as
imbedded in a spirit life, but rather conceives of things themselves
as possessed of spirit. Every flower, for instance, is represented
as enjoying the air it breathes, as though it had a soul of its own.

The next poem is entitled " To my Sister." It is inspired by
" the first mild day of March," when each minute is "sweeter than
before." The robin is singing in the tall larch by the Poet's door.
There is " a blessing in the air " that yields a sense of joy to the
bare trees and mountains, and to the green grass of the field. The
Poet expresses a wish that his sister join him in a day of idleness
in the woods. Not even a book shall divert their attention from
natural objects. Nature is pulsating not only with life, but with the
spirit of love also. Everywhere love abounds. It is an attribute of

[1] Lines written in Early Spring, 11–12.

Man, but is not confined to him alone. It pervades all Nature, and Man and Nature are knit together by this spiritual bond into a spiritual kingdom. On this mild March day the Poet feels it operative, not only among his fellows but also between them and Nature:

> Love, now a universal birth,
> From heart to heart is stealing,
> From earth to man, from man to earth.[1]

Futhermore, Nature is inspiring and illuminating. She exists in close relation to the human mind and heart, and Man may derive more from one moment's communion with her than from " years of toiling reason." She helps Man to moral resolution. She reveals moral laws, and inspires him to conform to them. Her spirit is a spirit of beneficence, in communion with which Man finds and frames the measure or ideal of his soul, and in harmony with which he endeavors to tune it.

> One moment now may give us more
> Than years of toiling reason:
> Our minds shall drink at every pore
> The spirit of the season.
>
> Some silent laws our hearts will make,
> Which they shall long obey:
> We for the year to come may take
> Our temper from to-day.
>
> And from the blessed power that rolls
> About, below, above,
> We 'll frame the measure of our souls:
> They shall be tuned to love.[2]

There is progress here in Wordsworth's conception of Nature beyond the position taken in the previous poem. The all-animating Spirit of Nature is a spirit of *Love*, which, in its relation to the spirit of Man, incites to moral resolution and endeavor, and furnishes the ethical standard or measure for the human soul. There is a moral order in the universe. Things and men are subject to

---

[1] To my Sister, 21–23. [2] Ibid., 25–36.

its universal sway. It "rolls about, below, above." It holds the
stars in their courses. It binds things together in a mighty system.
The law of social interaction is the same as the law of corporeal
things. The law governing Man's relation to things is the same as
that governing the relation of things to things, and the relations of
men to men. It is the law of love, which is the heart of the world,
and Man's heart should beat in harmony with it. Once more
Wordsworth conceives of all Nature as possessed of a unitary life,
which life is that of an all-animating Soul.

"Expostulation and Reply" is written in the same spirit as the
poem just considered. In a prefatory note Wordsworth informs us
that it was "a favorite among the Quakers," doubtless because of
the mysticism involved. The Poet represents his friend as re-
monstrating with him for dreaming his time away, sitting on an
old gray stone by Esthwaite Lake. He is urged to take to his books
instead, and imbibe "the spirit breathed from dead men to their
kind." To this the Poet makes reply, in which he brings out again
his belief in Nature as a source of inspiration and knowledge. The
"mighty sum of things" has a voice which reaches the human
mind and heart. Man must not always be *seeking* truth. There
is a time for quiet meditation, and for communion with the Spirit
of the Universe. The mind must be passive as well as active.
It must be open to the subtle influences and powers with which it
is in relation. Therefore let us occasionally dream away the hours,
and feed our minds "in a wise passiveness." Let us listen to the
voice "of things for ever speaking," and learn the lesson intended
for the receptive soul. It is Wordsworth's familiar story of a spiritualized Nature close to the spirit of Man, speaking a language
which his heart and mind can understand, and bearing a message
of wisdom and truth :

> " The eye — it cannot choose but see ;
> We cannot bid the ear be still ;
> Our bodies feel, where'er they be,
> Against or with our will.

" Nor less I deem that there are Powers
Which of themselves our minds impress;
That we can feed this mind of ours
In a wise passiveness.

" Think you, 'mid all this mighty sum
Of things for ever speaking,
That nothing of itself will come,
But we must still be seeking?

" — Then ask not wherefore, here, alone,
Conversing as I may,
I sit upon this old grey stone,
And dream my time away." [1]

Here, again, we meet with Wordsworth's indefiniteness concerning his real conception of Nature. We have a spiritualized world, but he does not represent all things as pervaded by one Spiritual Presence, but conceives of spiritual Powers which impress our minds, and of "things for ever speaking." There is an inclination here to believe that things themselves possess conscious spirits.

In similar vein is the poem "The Tables Turned." Here Wordsworth brings out still more explicitly Nature's relation as a teacher of Man. The same friend is urged in turn to quit his books and to come forth "into the light of things" and learn of Nature. Books are dull and full of endless strife. Nature, on the other hand, is full of inspiration and harmony. She is a teacher of truth and wisdom. There is not only music but wisdom in the linnet's song, and the throstle is no mean preacher. Indeed, Nature is full of resources. Hers is "a world of ready wealth" to bless the mind and heart of Man:

Spontaneous wisdom breathed by health,
Truth breathed by cheerfulness.[2]

From her we may learn more concerning ourselves, more of things moral, than from the wisdom of the ages:

[1] Expostulation and Reply, 17-32.   [2] The Tables Turned, 19-20.

> One impulse from a vernal wood
> May teach you more of man,
> Of moral evil and of good,
> Than all the sages can.[1]

Both science and art, as teachers, are inferior to her. Their leaves are barren; their methods are fruitless, so far as introducing us to the real meaning of things is concerned. Science is destructive of beauty. She disfigures Nature. Analysis kills the soul of things. "We murder to dissect." The analytical method of approach to Nature is the method of the cold, logical intellect, which fails to yield the richest results. It furnishes an arid waste for the spirit's activity. We need the warm, sympathetic, watchful, receptive heart to get at Nature's secret meanings — to hear things tell the story of their spiritual significance for the soul:

> Sweet is the lore which Nature brings;
> Our meddling intellect
> Mis-shapes the beauteous forms of things: —
> We murder to dissect.

> Enough of Science and of Art;
> Close up those barren leaves;
> Come forth, and bring with you a heart
> That watches and receives.[2]

The attitude toward Science manifest in this poem is similar to that taken later in "A Poet's Epitaph." It does not mean that Wordsworth is really hostile to scientific investigation. What he desires is that men should not lose the soul of Nature in their mental attitude toward her. His poetic intuition of the unity of things is so pronounced that he is opposed to any method of approach to the study of Nature by analysis that loses its way in mere manifoldness and variety of parts. For him Nature is so evidently grounded in a spiritual unity, her beauty and loveliness are so full of inspiration and meaning, that he does not want us to lose the important lessons of wisdom which she imparts. This poem,

---

[1] The Tables Turned, 21–24.   [2] Ibid., 25–32.

contrary to the two immediately preceding, conceives of the spiritual unity of Nature. One Spirit animates things.

Lord Morley, in his excellent Introduction,[1] referring to this poem, says : " It is best to be entirely sceptical as to the existence of system and ordered philosophy in Wordsworth. When he tells us that ' one impulse from a vernal wood may teach you more of man, of moral evil and of good, than all the sages can,' such a proposition cannot be seriously taken as more than a half-playful sally for the benefit of some too bookish friend. No impulse from a vernal wood can teach us anything at all of moral evil and of good. When he says that it is his faith, ' that every flower enjoys the air it breathes,' and that when the budding twigs spread out their fan to catch the air, he is compelled to think ' that there was pleasure there,' he expresses a charming poetic fancy and no more, and it is idle to pretend to see in it the fountain of a system of philosophy." This is certainly a misapprehension of Wordsworth's meaning. There is, of course, not a formally developed system of philosophy to be found in the poetry of Wordsworth, but there are certain fundamental conceptions and beliefs which dominate his thought and faith, and these are embodied in the poems just considered. There cannot be even the shadow of reasonable doubt on this matter when we read these lyrics in connection with what has already been revealed on the subject by the history of the Poet as far as we have traced it, and in view of the evidence yet to be presented. In almost every book of "The Prelude" this faith in a Spirit (sometimes spirits) of Nature sustaining a moral relationship to the spirit of Man is expressed. As we have seen, the Poet represents himself as having been guided from childhood, through youth, up to manhood, by this moral Spirit, receiving direction and wisdom from it. This is especially manifest in the account and interpretation of his Hawkshead experiences, which were considered in the second chapter. He conceives of the Spirit of Nature performing an important moral office in relation to him.

[1] The Complete Poetical Works of William Wordsworth, p. lxv.

Her visitings that came to him with "soft alarm," as well as her "severer interventions," constituted, in his judgment, a ministry to which he owed the calm existence which was his when worthy of himself.[1] He declares that the "Wisdom and Spirit of the Universe" intertwines "the passions that build up our human soul" by the power of high and enduring things. It purifies "the elements of feeling and thought" and sanctifies pain and fear to our highest good.[2] That Nature is a moral teacher, consciously imparting her lessons through fear and desire, through pain and pleasure, is a similar conclusion, to which he comes when he interprets another incident of his Hawkshead life.[3] In Book II of "The Prelude" he acknowledges with "grateful voice" his obligations to Nature for what he has learned of her, especially in things moral. Here, immediately after an interesting account of his unique communion with, and mystical intuition of, Nature, he adds :

> If this be error, and another faith
> Find easier access to the pious mind,
> Yet were I grossly destitute of all
> Those human sentiments that make this earth
> So dear, if I should fail with grateful voice
> To speak of you, ye mountains, and ye lakes
> And sounding cataracts, ye mists and winds
> That dwell among the hills where I was born.
> If in my youth I have been pure in heart,
> If, mingling with the world, I am content
> With my own modest pleasures, and have lived
> With God and Nature communing, removed
> From little enmities and low desires,
> The gift is yours; if in these times of fear
> This melancholy waste of hopes o'erthrown,
> If, 'mid indifference and apathy,
> And wicked exultation when good men
> On every side fall off, we know not how,
> To selfishness, disguised in gentle names
> Of peace and quiet and domestic love,
> Yet mingled not unwillingly with sneers

[1] The Prelude, I, 340–355.   [2] Ibid., 401–414.   [3] Ibid., 464–474.

> On visionary minds; if, in this time
> Of dereliction and dismay, I yet
> Despair not of our nature, but retain
> A more than Roman confidence, a faith
> That fails not, in all sorrow my support,
> The blessing of my life; the gift is yours,
> Ye winds and sounding cataracts! 't is yours,
> Ye mountains! thine, O Nature! Thou hast fed
> My lofty speculations; and in thee,
> For this uneasy heart of ours, I find
> A never-failing principle of joy
> And purest passion.[1]

What more conclusive evidence can be demanded of Wordsworth's faith in Nature's moral ministry than that which is presented here? He acknowledges with gratitude the moral service she has rendered. He says that if in youth he has been *pure in heart;* that if, content to commune with God and Nature, he has been "removed from little enmities and low desires"; that if, in a time when men were deserting high ideals and falling into lives of selfishness, a time of dereliction and dismay, he preserved a sturdy faith in human nature, it was due to the ministry of the winds and sounding cataracts, and to the mountains — to Nature. She had not only fed his mind's lofty speculations, but at the time of his writing he finds in her "a never-failing principle of joy and *purest* passion." What is the significance of such language if it does not mean that Nature is possessed of spirit and that she was a source of *moral* inspiration to Wordsworth, that she was a moral teacher and guide? All of the offices performed by Nature, mentioned in the above quotation, are *moral* offices, and they are exercised for the benefit of his soul. This was Wordsworth's faith, and it is proclaimed over and over again in his poetry.

Again, we have seen how, when a student at Cambridge, he conceived of Nature as endowed with life, and beheld her full of moral meaning. Is this not evident in the words:

---

[1] The Prelude, II, 419–451.

> To every natural form, rock, fruit, or flower,
> Even the loose stones that cover the highway,
> I gave a moral life: I saw them feel,
> Or linked them to some feeling: the great mass
> Lay bedded in a quickening soul, and all
> That I beheld respired with inward meaning.[1]

Again, it will be recalled how, when he was still a student at Cambridge, during a summer vacation, the Spirit of Nature laid hold of him, and bond unknown to him was given that he should be a dedicated soul, else be guilty of sinful disobedience. It was from the Spirit of Nature that he learned at this time the important lesson of his life work, and learned it as a moral obligation.[2] And so it was in London; the Spirit of Nature was upon him there.

> The soul of Beauty and enduring Life
> Vouchsafed her inspiration.[3]

And here in the great metropolis he was gradually, under her direction, led to a love of Man. In his own judgment she was constantly rendering him a *moral* service. And after he had passed through the fires of the French Revolution, and through the mental anguish and spiritual darkness caused by his disappointment, we later find him turning back and reviewing these critical years, and acknowledging his great indebtedness to the sustaining power of Nature. In the course of this acknowledgment he proclaims her a moral teacher. He speaks of the

> breezes and soft airs,
> Whose subtle intercourse with breathing flowers,
> Feelingly watched, might teach Man's haughty race
> How without injury to take, to give
> Without offence.[4]

Furthermore, in contrasting his attitude toward Nature, after his mind had fallen a prey to the spirit of speculation and rational criticism, with his attitude toward her in early youth, in an

[1] The Prelude, III, 122–143.   [3] Ibid., VII, 766–767.
[2] Ibid., IV, 306–338.   [4] Ibid., XII, 10–14.

apostrophe he addresses the Spirit of Nature both as a *rejoicing* spirit and as a teacher of the mind and heart:

> O Soul of Nature! excellent and fair!
> That didst rejoice with me, with whom I, too,
> Rejoiced through early youth, before the winds
> And roaring waters, and in lights and shades
> That marched and countermarched about the hills
> In glorious apparition, Powers on whom
> I daily waited, now all eye and now
> All ear; but never long without the heart
> Employed, and man's unfolding intellect.[1]

And what more positive testimony could we have of Wordsworth's faith in Nature as invested with Spirit, and of that Spirit as an ethical one, teaching Man the serious and weighty lessons of the moral life, than may be found in the following words from the thirteenth book of " The Prelude " ? Speaking of the beginning of the dawn, after his long wandering through the skeptic's night, he says:

> 'T was proved that not in vain
> I had been taught to reverence a Power
> That is the visible quality and shape
> And image of right reason; that matures
> Her processes by steadfast laws; gives birth
> To no impatient or fallacious hopes,
> No heat of passion or excessive zeal,
> No vain conceits; provokes to no quick turns
> Of self-applauding intellect; but trains
> To meekness, and exalts by humble faith;
> Holds up before the mind intoxicate
> With present objects, and the busy dance
> Of things that pass away, a temperate show
> Of objects that endure; and by this course
> Disposes her, when over-fondly set
> On throwing off incumbrances, to seek
> In man, and in the frame of social life,
> Whate'er there is desirable and good
> Of kindred permanence, unchanged in form
> And function, or, through strict vicissitude
> Of life and death, revolving.[2]

[1] The Prelude, XIII, 93–101.   [2] Ibid., XIII, 19–39.

In fact, two conceptions are peculiarly prominent in Wordsworth's earlier poetry. The first is that Nature is suffused with Spirit; and the second is that she is a teacher, and preëminently a *moral* teacher, of Man. This is apparent in what has just been said. It is evident, also, in the four poems interpreted above, and it will be made eminently manifest — evident beyond question — in the chapters following. We shall find either one or both of these conceptions brought out explicitly in more than a score of poems. Nothing is more peculiarly distinctive of Wordsworth as a poet of Nature than this. Indeed, it is the feature of his verse that differentiates him from the large majority of poets in their attitude toward Nature.

As to the second point urged by Lord Morley, namely, that Wordsworth's declaration concerning Nature's life as joyous must be interpreted merely as a " charming fancy," it may be said that inasmuch as the Poet regards Nature as possessed of Spirit, and as one of the constitutional capacities of Spirit is its capacity for pleasure, why is not a literal interpretation of Wordsworth's declaration really the correct one ? If as Spirit she *can* rejoice, then this "first mild day of March," with the trailing periwinkle in blossom, with the birds singing, and with the twigs budding with a new life, is evidence to the Poet that she *does* rejoice. This is not an isolated declaration of his faith in Nature's joyousness. We find the same belief expressed in other poems. In the beautiful poem " I wandered lonely as a cloud," the sparkling waves outdo the dancing daffodils in glee. In the poem beginning " Three years she grew in sun and shower," Lucy, a child fashioned by Nature, is to manifest Nature's own joyous life.

> She shall be sportive as the fawn
> That wild with glee across the lawn
> Or up the mountain springs.[1]

Again, in the poem entitled " To the Daisy " (1802) he addressed this little flower as " cheerful Flower," and as alert and *gay*. And

[1] Three years she grew in sun and shower, 13–15.

this is not merely figurative language. The entire poem speaks of the ministry of Nature to him through this common flower. Nature is possessed of a life of her own, and this life is a joyous life. She ministers to the Poet through this flower of the field, which evidently reflects the cheerful spirit of Nature, banishing melancholy and bringing delight to his own soul. Again, in "The Prelude," in his address to Nature, quoted above, he proceeds:

> O Soul of Nature! excellent and fair!
> That didst rejoice with me, with whom I, too,
> Rejoiced.

So that, when he declares that it is his

> faith that every flower
> Enjoys the air it breathes,

he simply utters what is the necessary implication of his conception of Nature as possessed of Spirit, or of things as having a spiritual life.

"The Old Cumberland Beggar" brings out some of Wordsworth's characteristic teaching in respect to both Nature and Man. It was composed at Racedown and Alfoxden in 1798 and published in 1800, and was inspired by the war of the political economists "upon mendicity in all its forms, and by implication, if not directly, on alms-giving also." [1] It shows us how close the Poet was to both Man and Nature, and also how near they are to each other in his judgment. Wordsworth's optimism is also brought out in this poem in a more pronounced manner than heretofore. The essential universality of goodness is affirmed. A spirit of Good is associated with all things. It cannot be divorced even from the meanest and most degraded, the vilest and most brutish, of Nature's forms, much less from Man, even in his lowest estate:

> 'T is Nature's law
> That none, the meanest of created things,
> Of forms created the most vile and brute,
> The dullest or most noxious, should exist

[1] Poetical Works, edited by William Knight, I, 299 n.

> Divorced from good — a spirit and pulse of good,
> A life and soul, to every mode of being
> Inseparably linked. Then be assured
> That least of all can aught — that ever owned
> The heaven-regarding eye and front sublime
> Which man is born to — sink, howe'er depressed,
> So low as to be scorned without a sin.[1]

The old beggar, who has been reduced to the lowest terms of existence, and is apparently one of the most helpless of men, must not be regarded as utterly useless. Indeed, he performs a helpful ministry to society, by keeping alive the record of past deeds of charity, and by calling forth a spirit of beneficence. His extremity is an opportunity for kindness on the part of others. Thus he becomes a moral force. Therefore he should be allowed to roam at will, receiving alms which are "not robbed of their Christian grace and spirit." Do not imprison him, but let him continue to live "in the eye of Nature," and "in the eye of Nature let him die." Wordsworth has great respect for a being who owns "the heaven-regarding eye and front sublime," and, as in the earlier poems of the "Lyrical Ballads," he shows his regard for the nature of Man as Man.

"Peter Bell: A Tale," was composed in the summer of 1798, but was not published until 1819. The poem was composed "under a belief that the Imagination not only does not require for its exercise the intervention of supernatural agency, but that, though such agency be excluded, the faculty may be called forth as imperiously and for kindred results of pleasure, by incidents, within the compass of poetic probability, in the humblest departments of daily life."[2] In it will be found a conception of Man's relation to Nature different from that which has been presented heretofore.

Part First opens with a description of the life and character of Peter Bell. He was a crude man, being feared much more than respected. Though he roved far and wide, travel failed to improve either his heart or his mind, and though he lived much with Nature,

[1] The Old Cumberland Beggar, 73–83.
[2] Poetical Works, edited by William Knight, II, 2 n.

she seemed never to have awakened in him a worthy response. He was indifferent to, if not, indeed, ignorant of, her charms. That she had any lesson to teach, that in her beauteous forms there was any spiritual meaning, never seemed to have dawned on his soul. She had not found the way to the heart of this lawless and insensate man.

Nevertheless, Nature and Peter Bell were not total strangers. It is evident that they had frequently been together, and that he had been affected by her influence, but to his detriment. Her sterner influences had left their impress upon body and soul, and he reflected many of her wild and savage moods.

> " A savage wildness round him hung
> As of a dweller out of doors;
> In his whole figure and his mien
> A savage character was seen
> Of mountains and of dreary moors.
>
> " To all the unshaped half-human thoughts
> Which solitary Nature feeds
> 'Mid summer storms or winter's ice,
> Had Peter joined whatever vice
> The cruel city breeds.
>
> " His face was keen as is the wind
> That cuts along the hawthorn-fence;
> Of courage you saw little there,
> But, in its stead, a medley air
> Of cunning and of impudence.
>
> " He had a dark and sidelong walk,
> And long and slouching was his gait;
> Beneath his looks so bare and bold,
> You might perceive, his spirit cold
> Was playing with some inward bait." [1]

Although much of the above description refers to the influence of Nature on Peter's physical being, still there is the thought that Nature's wildness and savagery found an echo in his soul, and that

[1] Peter Bell, 291–310.

this spiritual state was reflected in his bodily life. Occasionally her influence on character is for evil rather than for good. The presentation of this thought is not limited to this poem alone ; Wordsworth refers to it again in " Ruth," where a passionate young man finds certain conditions of Nature really more harmful than helpful to character :

> The wind, the tempest roaring high,
> The tumult of a tropic sky,
> Might well be dangerous food
> For him, a Youth to whom was given
> So much of earth — so much of heaven,
> And such impetuous blood.[1]

So that this can hardly be regarded as a mere passing thought in the Poet's mind, but rather as his conviction concerning Nature's baneful influence on Man under certain conditions.

After thus describing Peter Bell, Wordsworth proceeds to tell his tale. Traveling alone one beautiful November night, Peter meets an ass gazing into a stream. Finding no one near, he decides to steal the beast, and leaping upon his back endeavors to ride away ; but the animal refuses to move, and Peter soon discovers the reason why. A peculiar object in the water arrests his gaze, which, on investigation, reveals itself to be the body of a dead man, the owner of the ass. After removing the corpse from the water, Peter mounts the beast and journeys toward the home of its late master. His mind is full of fear and compunction. As he rides along, Nature seems to wear a peculiar aspect. Sounds take on a strange character and vague meaning. When he reaches his destination, the pathetic scenes which he is called upon to witness in the family of the dead man touch his heart — a heart already more or less softened by uncanny experience and by mingled feelings of fear and remorse. The " Spirits of the Mind," too, may have exercised their offices on Peter Bell. His fear was also aggravated by vague apprehensions of an avenging Nature. The result

[1] Ruth. 121–126.

is, that this reckless and depraved man forsakes a life of folly and wrongdoing, and becomes "a good and honest man."

In this simple poem the Poet goes back to his boyhood experiences at Hawkshead, described in "The Prelude." The same conception of Nature's relation to the moral nature of Man is brought out. Just as the boy, after stealing a woodcock snared by another, heard "low breathings" among the solitary hills coming after him, so Peter, struggling with his conscience in the presence of Nature, as he journeys over a lonely plain, feels himself pursued by a withered leaf, and is in sore mental and moral distress.

> When Peter spied the moving thing,
> It only doubled his distress;
> "Where there is not a bush or tree,
> The very leaves they follow me —
> So huge hath been my wickedness!"[1]

And, as in the case of Wordsworth, when he had plundered the raven's nest, Nature seemed to assume a peculiar and unearthly aspect—"the loud dry wind" blowing through his ear with "strange utterance," and the sky seeming "not a sky of earth," and the clouds moving with a peculiar motion — so Peter hears something he does not like in the echo of the rocks in response to the ass's "long and clamorous bray"; and when he brays again, more ruefully than before, the sound falls on Peter's ear with strange, transforming power — so strange, indeed, that Nature assumes a different appearance:

> What is there now in Peter's heart!
> Or whence the might of this strange sound?
> The moon uneasy looked and dimmer,
> The broad blue heavens appear to glimmer,
> And the rocks staggered all around.[2]

Furthermore, as in the Hawkshead days, after Wordsworth had seized by stealth a boat on Esthwaite Lake,

---

[1] Peter Bell, 706-710.   [2] Ibid., 481-485.

> a huge peak, black and huge,
> As if with voluntary power instinct
> Upreared its head,[1]

and, "growing in stature," seemed to stride after him "with measured motion like a living thing," so with Peter, rocks are transformed into fantastic objects, which seem to assume a kind of spiritual life, and to stare ominously at the frightened man.[2]

There is, undoubtedly, a subjective note in all this. Wordsworth brings before us here the belief presented in the first book of "The Prelude." There he interprets the strange experience of his boyhood as Nature's ministry. She was at work with his soul, "purifying the elements of feeling and of thought," and sanctifying his nature through discipline of pain and fear. In Peter Bell repentance is wrought through the power of Nature, conscience, and possibly the "Spirits of the Mind."[3] In some respects Nature's power is even more manifest than in the Poet's case. With Wordsworth she was dealing with an impressionable, callow, and morally sensitive youth. But in the case of Peter Bell she was laboring with a hardened sinner, to whose heart, for many years, it was impossible for her to find the way. But she conquered him at last, and he became submissive to her will.

Two important lessons are contained in this poem : first, that Nature exerts a powerful moral influence on Man ; and second, that in some instances, in cases where the soul is not in harmony

---

[1] The Prelude, I, 378–380.   [2] Peter Bell, 681–690.

[3] In Part Third of the poem, Wordsworth speaks of "potent Spirits" "that play with soul and sense" — Spirits that "trouble friends of goodness, for most gracious ends." He invokes these Spirits to try "what may be done with Peter Bell!" Wordsworth was such a believer in "spirits" of Nature of different kinds — souls of things, souls of "lonely places," the soul of the universe, etc.—that it is difficult to determine whether here he is expressing a belief in "Spirits of the Mind," or merely indulging in "poetic license." Lines 736–785 indicate a real belief in the existence of these "potent Spirits." But the main fact is that Nature and conscience coöperating are chiefly responsible for bringing Peter Bell to a consciousness of his wickedness, and to repentance. If, in this interpretation, too great a part in Peter's repentance and reform is ascribed to Nature, it may be said that, at least, it is in harmony with Wordsworth's general teaching.

with moral law, her influence may prove harmful. These two conceptions amount to convictions with Wordsworth, and the first is undoubtedly fundamental in his thinking.

Thus Man, Nature, and Nature's relation to Man were the sources of Wordsworth's poetical inspiration during these Alfoxden days. Whatever may be said of the poems written at this time which deal primarily with Man, we cannot fail to see in them a nobility of soul in the Poet's sympathy for men as he finds them in the humbler walks of life, in the tribute that he pays to their humanity, in the defense of their essential rights, and in the determination to exalt their virtues. No serious-minded student can help being impressed by the exalted conception of human nature which these poems contain. Stripping Man of all artificiality, and reducing his nature to its naked, fundamental elements, the Poet declares it to be "good." Optimism is the faith presented in the "Lyrical Ballads" — not a blind, naïve confidence in Man's constitution, but a faith originally strong, gradually undermined by the weakness and excesses of men, and by a barren critical analysis of the human spirit, and reëstablished by actual contact with men in the natural manifestations of their essential life. Whatever, then, may be our judgments concerning these simple poems as works of art, we can sympathize with Hazlitt's confession after hearing Coleridge read them : " In ' The Thorn,' ' The Mad Mother,' and ' The Complaint of a Poor Indian Woman,' I felt that deeper passion and pathos, which have since been acknowledged as the characteristics of the author ; and, the sense of a new style, and a new spirit in poetry came over me. It had to me something of the effect that arises from the turning up of the fresh soil, or the first welcome breath of spring." [1]

And so, too, with respect to the poems of Nature written at Alfoxden ; they breathe a most wholesome atmosphere and reveal a mind in closest touch with the natural world. Compared with the conventional treatment of Nature common in much of

[1] Hazlitt, *The Liberal*, II, 371.

preceding English poetry, they come like a fresh breeze from vernal field and wood. They disclose not merely the body, but the soul of Nature. They teach us that she and Man are members of a spiritual kingdom in which her function is to minister to his mental and moral need in wisdom and love. They reveal such an insight into the life of things, such an intuition into the very heart of Reality, that we can appreciate the observation of Coleridge to Hazlitt, made before these ballads had appeared in print, that "his philosophical poetry," by which undoubtedly he referred chiefly to his poems of Nature, "had a grand and comprehensive spirit in it, so that his soul seemed to inhabit the Universe like a palace, and to discover truth by intuition rather than by deduction." [1] Intuition undoubtedly it was, for there is no reasoning in these ballads. There is an immediate perception of the inner nature of corporeal Being. But how rich and profound the intuition, giving us an apprehension of things as instinct with life, possessed of a spirit of joy, wisdom, and love, and performing a holy ministry in their relation to the spirit of Man!

[1] Coleridge, *The Liberal*, II, 371.

CHAPTER VIII

THE "LYRICAL BALLADS" (CONCLUDED). "LINES COMPOSED A FEW MILES ABOVE TINTERN ABBEY"

Notwithstanding the beauty of their natural surroundings, and the delightful society it was their privilege to enjoy, the Wordsworths did not abide long in Alfoxden. This, however, was not due to disinclination, but to the fact that the house in which they were living was not available for another year. Coleridge was considerably perturbed over Wordsworth's departure. In a letter to Cottle, the publisher, he manifests not only this but also his recognition of Wordsworth as a poet of Nature. He writes: "Whether we shall be able to procure him a house and furniture near Stowey we know not, and yet we must; for the hills, and the woods, and the streams, and the sea, and the shores would break forth into reproaches against us if we did not strain every nerve to keep their Poet among them. Without joking, and in serious sadness, Poole and I cannot endure to think of losing him." [1] Evidently the house was not procured, for, after arranging with Coleridge to make a visit to Germany, the Wordsworths left Alfoxden, June 26, 1798, and, after spending a week with Coleridge at Stowey, and a week with Cottle at Bristol, where Wordsworth completed arrangements for the publication of a volume of poems, they left for a brief journey to the Wye. The journey is of importance because of its associations with Wordsworth's immortal poem "Lines composed a few miles above Tintern Abbey." Concerning the circumstances under which the poem was written, he says: "No poem of mine was composed under circumstances more pleasant for me to remember than this. I began it upon leaving Tintern, after

[1] Knight, Life of William Wordsworth, I, 155.

crossing the Wye, and concluded it just as I was entering Bristol in the evening, after a ramble of four or five days, with my sister. Not a line of it was altered, and not any part of it written down till I reached Bristol. It was published almost immediately after in the little volume of which so much has been said in these Notes, the 'Lyrical Ballads,' as first published at Bristol by Cottle." [1] The poem deserves special consideration, for in it we shall find the Wordsworthian creed concerning Nature and Man, and their relations, quite complete, and set to beautiful and " impassioned music." As Mr. Myers says : " The 'Lines written above Tintern Abbey' have become, as it were, the *locus classicus*, or consecrated formulary of the Wordsworthian faith. They say in brief what it is the work of the poet's biographer to say in detail." [2] We may search Wordsworth's entire body of verse without finding a better expression of the fundamentals of his faith.

Five years before, after crossing Sarum Plain, to visit his old college friend Robert Jones, Wordsworth had made a journey to the Wye. The memory of the "beauteous forms" of this lovely country had evidently lingered with him, and he now tells us something of their ministry to his soul during this long interim. These beautiful objects have not been unremembered or unfelt by him, even when he was far removed from them and engrossed with the perplexities of a somewhat unsettled life. Rather have they been with him " in lonely rooms " and in the midst of the wearying din of town and city. He has felt their influence in the form of pleasing and deep-seated sensations, bringing peace and tranquillity to his soul; also in those quiet, subtle, unremembered pleasures which prompt many of the kindly acts that make up so much of a good man's life. But more than this : their influence was responsible for a mystical and consoling mood, in which the Poet was almost completely released from the life of body and sense, and was permitted to rise unfettered into the higher life of the spirit, catching a vision of the inner nature of things —

[1] Poetical Works, edited by Knight, II, 51 n.   [2] Myers, Wordsworth, 33.

> that blessed mood,
> In which the burthen of the mystery,
> In which the heavy and the weary weight
> Of all this unintelligible world,
> Is lightened : — that serene and blessed mood,
> In which the affections gently lead us on, —
> Until, the breath of this corporeal frame
> And even the motion of our human blood
> Almost suspended, we are laid asleep
> In body, and become a living soul :
> While with an eye made quiet by the power
> Of harmony, and the deep power of joy,
> We see into the life of things.[1]

This mystic mood, to which Wordsworth was subject, and through which much of what he teaches was revealed, is here super-induced, not by *direct contact* with Nature, as was the case in his boyhood and youth, but by *remembered* Nature — by *recalling* the "beauteous forms" with which he had previously come in contact. Thus Nature, not only immediately, through the eye of sense, but *mediately*, through the power of memory, was able, by a remembered harmony, to lay him asleep in body, and permit him to "become a living soul," with a power to "see into the life of things."

But if what has been said concerning Nature's power to inspire such a mystic vision be merely a foundationless belief, still there is no doubt in the poet's mind concerning her power to console and heal the stricken spirit. Certainly it was so in his case. These lovely forms, as they came to him through memory, proved a refuge in the hour of disappointment and sorrow, in those days of darkness and sore distress occasioned by his experience with the course of political events during the French Revolution, when, in the midnight of his soul, he was unable to see even a ray of hope in his darkness and despair. To these remembered scenes he had turned for help, and Nature came to his relief. This is his confession :

[1] Lines composed a few miles above Tintern Abbey, 37–48.

                                              If this
       Be but a vain belief, yet, oh! how oft —
       In darkness and amid the many shapes
       Of joyless daylight; when the fretful stir
       Unprofitable, and the fever of the world,
       Have hung upon the beatings of my heart —
       How oft, in spirit, have I turned to thee,
       O sylvan Wye! thou wanderer thro' the woods,
       How often has my spirit turned to thee![1]

Once more we see how thoroughly a child of Nature Wordsworth was. He sought comfort from her in his darkest days, even when, indeed, he was deserting her and viewing her with the eye of a critic rather than with the eye and spirit of a lover and poet. Through long-continued habit he turned to her for succor. It becomes more and more evident that this intimate relation which he sustained to Nature, or rather which, as he believed, she sustained to him, must be regarded as one of the most powerful forces in his spiritual life and development as a Poet.

But the poem grows in interest, showing, as it does, his state of mind as he stands again in the actual presence of these former scenes, and Past, Present, and Future seem to engage his consciousness. In the midst of these attractive surroundings he has not only a " sense of present pleasure " but an agreeable consciousness that the present moment has promise for the future. At least so he dares to hope, although, undoubtedly, he has changed in some respects since his former visit. And it is well to note the character of the change. *Then* he roamed through Nature's wilds impelled by a regard amounting almost to blind passion. Her forms were an appetite, a love. No other interest than that furnished by the eye was necessary to compel his devotion. Her beauty and sublimity, appealing to his senses, were sufficient to compel subjection to her sovereignty. She was all in all to him. That time is no more ; a change has been wrought. Yet he does not mourn the change ; a gain compensates the loss. *Now* Nature appeals to him

---

[1] Lines composed a few miles above Tintern Abbey, 49–57.

in a different way. He is no longer steeped in mere personal or
subjective feeling. She awakens feelings and thoughts that lead
beyond themselves — that own "a remoter charm." As he beholds her he often hears

> The still, sad music of humanity,
> Nor harsh nor grating, though of ample power
> To chasten and subdue.[1]

Nature now leads him to Man with his spiritual burden, chastening
and subduing his soul. She not only charms him with her beauty
and loveliness, but calls attention to the human world in which he
lives, with its weight of sad and sorrowful experience. But more
than this : she has also powerfully affected his intellectual and
emotional life. He has gained such an insight into her real life
that he has felt "a presence" disturbing him "with the joy of
elevated thoughts." He has had a sense of an all-pervading Spirit
in Nature, in such close relations to his soul as to awaken a sublimer consciousness of its immanence and activity, both in Nature
and in Man, than he had ever before experienced. In it both
things and men live and move and have their being. It is because
of this sublime and profound insight that he regards Nature with
such deep affection. This is why he finds in her an anchor for
his noblest thoughts, a "nurse," a "guide," a "guardian" of his
heart, and the very soul of his moral being.

> And I have felt
> A presence that disturbs me with the joy
> Of elevated thoughts; a sense sublime
> Of something far more deeply interfused,
> Whose dwelling is the light of setting suns,
> And the round ocean and the living air,
> And the blue sky, and in the mind of man:
> A motion and a spirit, that impels
> All thinking things, all objects of all thought,
> And rolls through all things. Therefore am I still
> A lover of the meadows and the woods,

[1] Lines composed a few miles above Tintern Abbey, 91-93.

And mountains; and of all that we behold
From this green earth; of all the mighty world
Of eye, and ear, — both what they half create,
And what perceive; well pleased to recognise
In nature and the language of the sense
The anchor of my purest thoughts, the nurse,
The guide, the guardian of my heart, and soul
Of all my moral being.[1]

Here is insight — insight of the true poet and mystical philosopher — and as a result we have the most complete expression of his conception of the nature of Reality yet given by Wordsworth. Heretofore he has, indeed, told of a Spirit pervading all Nature, and of Nature as ministering to Man's soul, but never before has he approached so near to identifying this omnipresent Spirit with the activity of things and minds. Indeed, with reference to Man, he has at no previous time brought this Universal Spirit into such close relationship with him as to conceive of the human mind as its dwelling place, and of the Spirit itself as the impelling power of human thought.

It is this immanence of a Spirit in Nature and Man, and the conception of it as the active, animating Power in both, so superbly described in the beautiful lines of this beautiful poem, that has led many of the readers of Wordsworth to regard him as a Pantheist. A Power so deeply interfused with Nature and Man, which has as its dwelling not only the light of setting suns, the vast ocean, the universal air, and infinite sky, but also the self-conscious and self-determining mind of Man; which is the impelling power of all thinking things, and of the objects of all thought; that rolls through all things — such a Power, it is said, is "the All" of the Pantheist. Language like this seems to identify Nature and Man with the Ground of all Reality. Indeed, his own kinsman-biographer feels it necessary to offer at least a quasi-apology for the Poet's apparent lack of orthodoxy manifest in this poem. He says: "If also, as is not improbable, he [the reflective reader] should be of

---

[1] Lines composed a few miles above Tintern Abbey, 93-111.

the opinion that a 'worshiper of nature' is in danger of divinizing the creation and of dishonouring the Creator, and that, therefore, some portions of this poem might be perverted to serve the purposes of a popular and pantheistic philosophy, he will remember that the author of the 'Lines on Tintern Abbey,' composed also the 'Evening Voluntaries,' and that he who professes himself an ardent votary of nature, has explained the sense in which he wishes these words to be understood, by saying, that

> By grace divine,
> Not otherwise, O Nature, we are thine." [1]

But this apology, or explanation, is unnecessary, because there is no Pantheism here. Thorough-going Pantheism does not speak of a Universal Spirit, or of a God, or of an Absolute, as *dwelling in* Nature, but *identifies* Nature with the Absolute. All forms are modes of its energizing or functioning. Neither does Pantheism speak of the Universal Spirit as *dwelling in* the mind of Man. It *identifies* the human mind with the Universal Being. It too is a mode of the Absolute's activity. Both things and minds are merely the Absolute individualized, and they sustain the same relation to it that billows sustain to the sea, to use the figure of Spinoza, the prince of modern Pantheists. The sea does not exist apart from the billows, nor do the billows exist apart from the sea. They are, *ultimately* considered, one and the same. So with the Absolute in its relation to things and minds. The latter do not exist apart from the former. They have no essential being, no separate individuality, no being-for-self, according to Pantheism. They exist only as modes of the one Ultimate Being.

Furthermore, Pantheism really cancels the personality of both God and Man. All being is governed by an inner law of necessity, and therefore there is no such thing as self-determining being. But the power of self-determination is the very core of personality ; hence Pantheism precludes the possibility of personality in either

[1] Memoirs, I, 120.

God or Man. The *necessary* implication of all this is that there can be no moral life in God or Man, for how can there be morality without self-consciousness and self-determination ? In other words, with Pantheism there is no real selfhood.

Now Wordsworth's conception of a Spirit present in all things, and in the mind of man — a Spirit which is the impelling power of both — is very far removed from such a philosophy. He brings out, in the lines quoted above, the existence of three distinct natures — a Universal Presence, a world of corporeal things, and a world of finite spirits. He does not identify the Universal Spirit with "the light of setting suns," nor with "the round ocean," nor with "the living air," nor with "the blue sky," nor with "the mind of man." He merely affirms that these are its "*dwelling*," and that Spirit is their *impelling power*. Only the *immanence* of the Absolute or Universal Spirit in the finite is declared. Pantheism is not involved in such a statement. The Poet is merely giving expression to his faith in the immanence of Spirit in the world — a faith which is in thorough accord with Theism.

Neither does this notable poem warrant the inference that Wordsworth is an Idealist. He is sometimes represented as such in his ontology — in his doctrine of the ultimate nature of things. It is said that he affirms all Reality to be mental in its essential nature. However, this is neither the explicit teaching of this poem, nor a necessary implication of it. The Poet does not say that corporeal things are minds, nor does he identify them with an Infinite Mind. What he does say is that Mind or Spirit is present *in* things. Whether so-called material being, as material, has any reality at all is not revealed in this poem. There were times in his childhood, as we shall see later in the "Ode. Intimations of Immortality," when in his trance-experiences the physical world seemed canceled and he apprehended merely a spiritual world. But there is no evidence that the extreme mental attitudes represented in these abnormal or supernormal moods ever attained to the dignity of a permanent faith with him. In the poem under consideration, Wordsworth's teaching concerning corporeal Reality is that there is a world of things, but that this world is not dead or inert, but alive with Spirit. He does not determine the *ultimate* metaphysical relation of things to this Spirit more than to say that it is their impelling Power. But if he does not deal definitely and ultimately with the relations of so-called matter to Spirit, it is because here he is primarily the poet and not the systematic philosopher. He is not reasoning about Reality, but recording a vision of it. Indeed, in the poetry of Nature considered thus far, he is really not a philosopher at all. He is a poet — a poet with mystical insight. He has a vision born of mystical feeling, in which he apprehends a Spirit, or a Presence, which is neither things nor finite minds, but dwells in them. This Presence is

> A motion and a spirit, that impels
> All thinking things, all objects of all thought,
> And rolls through all things.[1]

He is giving utterance to a refined Theistic view of God, things, and finite minds, rather than to either a Pantheistic or an Idealistic view. And if his intuition of the relations of this Spirit to things and minds does not completely satisfy, it is hardly, in the final analysis, less satisfactory than the conclusions of Philosophy. At least it does not involve the difficulties inherent in Pantheism — the cancellation of the reality of the finite, and of personality in both God and Man. And yet it preserves to us the satisfying truth of the Divine immanence in the world, which constitutes the main strength of Pantheism. And how immeasurably superior is the Poet's teaching to that crude, unphilosophic, unpoetic, Deistic doctrine of God's relation to the world which obtained in the age preceding, which despiritualized Nature and robbed the world of God's presence, conceiving of him as afar off — a Creator who, having made his world, withdrew from it, and from his transcendent throne looks down upon a huge machine, running like a wound-up clock, and, as Carlyle remarks, "sees it go!"

[1] Lines composed a few miles above Tintern Abbey, 100-102.

This poem embodies Wordsworth's prevailing conception of Nature. There is no conception here of individual things possessing souls. It is the Universal Soul that is present in things. The Spiritual unity of Nature is preserved. This is very apparent in the words:

> Whose dwelling is the light of setting suns,
> And the round ocean and the living air,
> And the blue sky, and in the mind of man:
> A motion and a spirit, that impels
> All thinking things, all objects of all thought,
> And rolls through all things.[1]

Pursuing the analysis of the poem still further, we find that Wordsworth continues to speak of Nature and of her relations to Man. Turning in thought to his sister, to pay her a kindly tribute, he again gives expression to his regard for Nature. She is the faithful friend of Man, and ministers to his need. Her loyalty can never be impeached. She has never been found guilty of treason to the heart that loves her. She so ministers to the mind through her beauty, through the knowledge she imparts, and the thoughts she inspires, through her solaces and joys, that all the evil men can do, and all the dullness and " dreary intercourse of daily life," can neither overcome us, nor disturb our faith in a beneficent order of things.

> And this prayer I make,
> Knowing that Nature never did betray
> The heart that loved her; 't is her privilege,
> Through all the years of this our life, to lead
> From joy to joy: for she can so inform
> The mind that is within us, so impress
> With quietness and beauty, and so feed
> With lofty thoughts, that neither evil tongues,
> Rash judgments, nor the sneers of selfish men,
> Nor greetings where no kindness is, nor all
> The dreary intercourse of daily life,
> Shall e'er prevail against us, or disturb
> Our cheerful faith, that all which we behold
> Is full of blessings.[2]

[1] Lines composed a few miles above Tintern Abbey, 97–102.   [2] Ibid., 121–134.

There are in these lines, either by implication or by explicit statement, essentially all of the dominant Wordsworthian conceptions concerning Nature and her relation to Man contained in the poems already considered, but in a more pronounced form. Here is a creed full of moral and spiritual elevation, and Wordsworth seems to believe it with his whole mind and heart. He smites the hard rock in the wilderness of human life, and from it flows a veritable stream of living water, full of healing for human souls. Nowhere in literature can be found a more refined Spiritualism, and a more indomitable Optimism, than is here expressed.

Wordsworth closes this immortal poem with a confession that he had long worshiped at Nature's shrine, and that he came to the banks of the Wye "unwearied in that service," nay, even with a warmer affection for his divine Mistress — a "far deeper zeal of holier love." So that the "beauteous forms" which greet his eye and minister to his spirit, as he stands near these waters that roll "from their mountain-springs with a soft inland murmur," are more dear to him than heretofore.

Of the poems which constitute the first edition of the "Lyrical Ballads," this one, so peculiarly characteristic of Wordsworth's poetic genius and faith, was doubtless the last composed. It was written in July, 1798, and is a fitting close to a period of gradual mental and spiritual restoration, in which his former faith in, and love for, both Man and Nature were not only restored but also strengthened and enriched. He has recovered completely from his "moral disease," and has emerged from the trying ordeal, a better self, chastened and subdued, and "with a stronger faith his own." It is a fitting close, also, to a period in which his faith gradually took form — in which it became articulate, and crystallized into a kind of "substance of doctrine," a creed affirming the essential goodness of Man, and the spiritual nature of things; that resolves the Universe into a spiritual kingdom, wherein Love is law, and "all which we behold is full of blessing"; a creed that bridges the chasm between Nature and Man, bringing them together into closest relations, in which the function of the former is to minister to the intellectual, æsthetic, and moral needs of the latter, feeding his soul with truth, beauty, and goodness, fortifying him against all evil, and enabling him to bear the "burthen of the mystery" — "the heavy and the weary weight of all this unintelligible world."

In conclusion it may be said that, whatever be the final verdict in regard to the literary merit of the "Lyrical Ballads,"[1] no one can successfully deny that they represent a noble ethical aim, a lofty conception of the poet's function, a decided growth in mental and spiritual power, a profound love for, and deep insight into, the heart both of Nature and of Man, and a sublime poetical and, in a sense, philosophical faith, that breathes inspiration, hope, and love in such large measure, and with such deep earnestness, that it cannot fail to prove a moral and spiritual tonic to every thoughtful soul who drinks in the simple melody of these songs, and reflects seriously upon their wholesome content.

[1] Cf. especially Francis Jeffrey, Poems, in Two Volumes.

CHAPTER IX

GERMANY AND RETURN. POETRY OF NATURE

On September 16, 1798, Wordsworth, Dorothy, and Coleridge left England for Germany. Coleridge left the Wordsworths at Hamburg, going to Ratzeburg, and thence to Göttingen. The Wordsworths went to Goslar, where they remained until February 10. The Poet was not idle here, and these winter months witness the production of a goodly number of poems, all of which bear the usual marks concerning Nature. His principal conceptions and beliefs are constantly in evidence.

Following a chronological order, we first meet with the poem "There was a Boy," which is an "extract," as Wordsworth called it later, from "The Prelude." It was composed in 1798 and published in 1800 as a separate poem. Later, however, it took its place in the autobiographical work. In his Preface to the edition of 1815 Wordsworth refers to it in a manner which evinces at once its personal character, and also throws light on the development of his imagination under the influence of Nature. "In the series of Poems placed under the head of Imagination," he says, "I have begun with one of the earliest processes of Nature in the development of this faculty. Guided by one of my own primary consciousnesses, I have represented a commutation and transfer of internal feelings, coöperating with external accidents to plant, for immortality, conjoined impressions of sound and sight in the celestial soil of the Imagination."[1] And then, referring to this poem, which tells of a boy of his acquaintance who, with the palms of his hands pressed together, used "to blow mimic hootings to the silent owls," he adds: "The Boy, there introduced, is

[1] Prose Works, edited by Knight, II, 215-216.

listening, with something of a feverish and restless anxiety, for the recurrence of the riotous sounds which he had previously excited; and, at the moment when the intenseness of his mind is beginning to remit, he is surprised into a perception of the solemn and tranquillising images which the Poem describes." [1] This poem reveals a peculiarity of Wordsworth's genius of which we shall speak more at length when considering the "Ode. Intimations of Immortality." It is his conception of Nature as passing beyond the gates of sense, engaging the imagination, warmed by a strong mystical feeling, and resulting finally in poetic insight. This peculiarity is manifest in the words:

> And, when there came a pause
> Of silence such as baffled his best skill:
> Then sometimes, in that silence, while he hung
> Listening, a gentle shock of mild surprise
> Has carried far into his heart the voice
> Of mountain-torrents; or the visible scene
> Would enter unawares into his mind,
> With all its solemn imagery, its rocks,
> Its woods, and that uncertain heaven received
> Into the bosom of the steady lake.[2]

As Professor Edward Caird says: "By such electric strokes, even more than by the direct expression of his poetic creed, though that also is not wanting, Wordsworth makes us feel that it is one spirit that speaks in man and nature, and that, therefore, the poet's vision is no mere playing with metaphors, but a real discovery of 'a presence far more deeply interfused.' The poet, with trembling and watchful sensibility, seems to stand between the worlds, and catches the faintest sounds of recognition that are carried from one to the other." [3]

Another interesting Nature poem bears the cumbersome title "Influence of Natural Objects in calling forth and strengthening the Imagination in Boyhood and early Youth." It was composed in

---

[1] Prose Works, edited by Knight, II, 215–216.   [2] There was a Boy, 16–25.
[3] Caird, Essays on Literature and Philosophy, I, 177

1799, but not published until 1809. Later it appeared as part of "The Prelude." It is, of course, as the title indicates, a poem that deals with Nature's influence on the soul in the earlier years of life. According to the conception here presented, Nature is pervaded by a universal Presence. This Presence is the "Wisdom and Spirit of the universe"; it is the "Soul" and "Eternity of thought." It gives to "forms and images a breath and everlasting motion." The Poet represents it as having come into relations with him in the very dawn of childhood, as having intertwined for him the passions which constitute the soul. It fashioned his spirit not by objects of man's crude construction, but rather by bringing him into contact with Nature's lofty and enduring works, which proved to be a means of purification and a sanctifying force. Such was the fellowship sustained by him thus early with Nature, and which she vouchsafed in generous measure. The poem has already been quoted in connection with Wordsworth's interpretation of his experience when, by act of stealth, he seized a boat on Esthwaite Lake and, under the influence of a guilty conscience, Nature seemed to take on the form of a moral avenger. It contains not only Wordsworth's conception of Nature as animated by an eternal Spirit of Wisdom, but also as a builder, fashioner, and purifier of Man in his earliest years.

"The Simplon Pass" was composed probably in 1799, but not published until 1845. Later it, too, was included in "The Prelude." It records a description of Switzerland scenery as Wordsworth beheld it when, in 1790, in company with his friend Jones, he crossed the Alps by way of this well-known Pass. In the poem it is apparent how much Nature was to the Poet even at this time. But it has also another feature of interest. It is not so markedly Wordsworthian as the conception emphasized heretofore. It seems to conceive of Nature as symbolical of Spirit rather than as possessed of life and mind. Her forms are conceived of as types and symbols of spiritual life. She works as if possessed of Spirit. This is evident from the last half of the poem as it appears in its early form:

The rocks that muttered close upon our ears,
Black drizzling crags that spake by the wayside
As if a voice were in them, the sick sight
And giddy prospect of the raving stream,
The unfettered clouds and region of the heavens,
Tumult and peace, the darkness and the light —
Were all like workings of one mind, the features
Of the same face, blossoms upon one tree,
Characters of the great Apocalypse,
The types and symbols of Eternity,
Of first, and last, and midst, and without end.[1]

However, this symbolical conception of Nature does not often occur in Wordsworth. He is too much a poet of insight or intuition to rest in symbolism. With him, as a rule, Nature does not behave *like* Spirit, but Nature *is* corporeal Reality animated by Spirit.

"Nutting" is a poem more distinctively characteristic of its author than the one just considered. It, also, was written in Germany in 1799, and was originally intended to be part of "The Prelude," but was finally excluded. It strikes a subjective note, disclosing his own peculiar feelings as a boy. In the Preface he says, "These verses arose out of the remembrance of feelings I had often when a boy, and particularly in the extensive woods that still stretch from the side of Esthwaite Lake towards Graythwaite."[2] The poem itself describes a nutting excursion taken in company with his sister, and the feelings of remorse experienced by him on looking upon his ruthless ravage of Nature in pursuit of his object, which he regards as a desecration. The riches of the woods are acquired, but only by mercilessly mutilating a hazel tree, and despoiling its immediate surroundings. The boy does not long exult in his newly acquired wealth without a mingled feeling of sorrow and remorse because of his wantonness, and soon becomes conscious of "a spirit in the woods":

---

[1] The Simplon Pass, 10–20.
[2] Poetical Works, edited by Knight, 70 n.

> Then up I rose,
> And dragged to earth both branch and bough, with crash
> And merciless ravage: and the shady nook
> Of hazels, and the green and mossy bower,
> Deformed and sullied, patiently gave up
> Their quiet being: and unless I now
> Confound my present feelings with the past,
> Ere from the mutilated bower I turned
> Exulting, rich beyond the wealth of kings,
> I felt a sense of pain when I beheld
> The silent trees, and saw the intruding sky,—
> Then, dearest Maiden, move along these shades
> In gentleness of heart; with gentle hand
> Touch — for there is a spirit in the woods.[1]

There is a reminder here of other boyhood experiences during the Hawkshead days previously referred to. It is worthy of note that this feeling concerning Nature's moral relation to Man not only took possession of Wordsworth when a boy, but even now he is not quite sure whether he is confounding present with past feelings. This is in line with interpretations of former experiences which he narrates in " The Prelude," one of which, as we have just seen, was written about this time; so that this conception of Nature must not be regarded as merely a state of mind belonging to him as a boy, but rather as representing what by this time had attained to the dignity and power of a definite conviction, or faith. Here again is evinced that strong ethical sense with which Wordsworth seems to have been endowed, and through which Nature so often appealed to him. It makes him feel guilty of gross violence. He has ruthlessly despoiled her face, and now struggles with compunctions of conscience, and has a weird consciousness of " a spirit in the woods."

But there is still another point to be noticed here. Attention has been called to the fact that Wordsworth's conception of Nature as possessed of spirit is not always the same. He sometimes conceives of all corporeal things as animated by one consciousness;

[1] Nutting, 43–56.

at other times he represents things as having souls. But there is
still another conception to which he occasionally gives expression.
Not only things but *places* are invested with spirit life, not merely
in a poetic but in a real sense. The conception of "a spirit in the
woods" is an illustration. But this does not stand alone. There
are other examples to be found in his poetry, as, for instance, in
"The Prelude," where he conceives of the "Presences of Nature
in the sky and on the earth," of the "Souls of lonely places," etc.,
as performing a moral ministry similar to that implied in "Nutting."
What other interpretation can be put upon this apostrophe?

> Ye Presences of Nature in the sky
> And on the earth! Ye Visions of the hills!
> And Souls of lonely places! can I think
> A vulgar hope was yours when ye employed
> Such ministry, when ye through many a year
> Haunting me thus among my boyish sports,
> On caves and trees, upon the woods and hills,
> Impressed upon all forms the characters
> Of danger or desire; and thus did make
> The surface of the universal earth
> With triumph and delight, with hope and fear,
> Work like a sea? [1]

The fact is that Wordsworth's soul would every now and then hark
back to primitive man, and frame conceptions of Nature-spirits
very like those which obtained in early times.

A well-known poem, written in 1799, and published in 1800,
bears the title "A Poet's Epitaph." Wordsworth here presents
his views of what really constitutes a poet and differentiates him
from other men. The statesman, lawyer, theologian, soldier, physician, scientist, and moralist are warned away from the poet's
grave, because they are not in touch with his mood or in sympathy with his mental attitude; but the humble poet is welcomed,
for the simple reason that he is a poet, and is possessed, therefore,
of his love for, and insight into, Nature. His attitude toward her

[1] The Prelude, I, 464-474.

is far removed from that of the scientist or philosopher, who "would peep and botanize upon his mother's grave." The poet is no such "fingering slave" as this. He is possessed of no such "ever-dwindling soul." Rather does he live on terms of fellowship with Nature, receiving her inspirations and profound impulses.

> He murmurs near the running brooks
> A music sweeter than their own.
>
> .   .   .   .
>
> The outward shows of sky and earth,
> Of hill and valley, he has viewed;
> And impulses of deeper birth
> Have come to him in solitude.
>
> In common things that round us lie
> Some random truths he can impart, —
> The harvest of a quiet eye
> That broods and sleeps on his own heart.[1]

He views her externals, but has also insight into her inner life. The poet reaches the heart of things not by the cold processes of the logical intellect — by analysis and dissection, and conclusions therefrom — but by sympathy, love, meditation, mystical brooding, and intuition. It is thus that insight is gained. He is Nature's friend and confidant, to whom she reveals her deeper life and mind, and to whom she speaks her spiritual message. Wordsworth is undoubtedly giving expression here to his own experience, describing his own mental processes as a poet, for, as we have seen and shall continue to see, it is thus that he deals with Nature and that Nature deals with him. Seldom does he reason about her in his poetry; he meditates, broods, and thus receives the vision.

Another poem, very beautiful indeed, and very interesting, too, from the standpoint of our special study, is the well-known poem "Three years she grew in sun and shower," composed in the Hartz Forest. He describes a girl as Nature would fashion her were she to be her own — a girl in whom her different moods

---

[1] A Poet's Epitaph, 39-52.

and the beauty and grace of her fairest forms would be reflected.
The poem expresses implicit faith in Nature's consummate art.

> " Myself will to my darling be
> Both law and impulse : and with me
> The Girl, in rock and plain,
> In earth and heaven, in glade and bower,
> Shall feel an overseeing power
> To kindle or restrain.
>
> " She shall be sportive as the fawn
> That wild with glee across the lawn
> Or up the mountain springs ;
> And hers shall be the breathing balm,
> And hers the silence and the calm
> Of mute insensate things.
>
> " The floating clouds their state shall lend
> To her ; for her the willow bend ;
> Nor shall she fail to see
> Even in the motions of the Storm
> Grace that shall mould the Maiden's form
> By silent sympathy.
>
> " The stars of midnight shall be dear
> To her ; and she shall lean her ear
> In many a secret place
> Where rivulets dance their wayward round,
> And beauty born of murmuring sound
> Shall pass into her face.
>
> " And vital feelings of delight
> Shall rear her form to stately height,
> Her virgin bosom swell ;
> Such thoughts to Lucy I will give
> While she and I together live
> Here in this happy dell." [1]

This is delightful, and it is really expressive of Wordsworth's faith
in Nature's moulding or fashioning power. He is not giving vent
merely to a charming fancy. We have seen it manifest over and

[1] Three years she grew in sun and shower, 7–36.

over again that the Poet regards it as one of Nature's functions to mould both the body and the soul of Man, and here Wordsworth shows, in exquisite verse, just how skillfully she can perform her office, and by what methods it is accomplished. Where, in all literature, can be found such a beautiful conception and presentation of Nature's relation to Man? In many respects it is unique — far removed from the conceptions of Nature to be found in previous English poetry; nor is it wide of the truth as viewed from the standpoint of biological science in its emphasis of the influence of physical environment on our bodily and mental life.

There are, however, several poems of this period which present Nature in another relation to Man. The Matthew poems, and the beautiful and pathetic poem entitled " Ruth," are of this character. According to the former, Nature is sometimes, through memory and the subtle laws of association, the source of sadness and sorrow. In "The Two April Mornings," Matthew, the aged village schoolmaster, is traveling merrily along with his young friend to spend a day among the hills. But soon the old man realizes that Nature wears an aspect similar to that worn by her on a like day long ago — a day on which he pursued his sport until suddenly he came upon his daughter's grave and, on turning from it, met a fair maiden, the very sight of whom made him painfully conscious of his own loss. This beautiful April morn, so like that of thirty years ago, vividly recalls his previous experience and fills his heart with sadness. Thus Nature occasionally begets sorrow.

The same truth is brought out in " The Fountain." Here the streamlet with its murmuring sound recalls to Matthew happy days of yore, never to be lived over again. It makes him conscious of the flight of time and of the decay of old age, of children dead and of no one remaining to love him as he desires. Though the day be delightful and the surroundings such as would ordinarily bring joy to the heart and inspire the usually tuneful Matthew, the streamlet's music, through the subtle working of the laws of suggestion which operate in memory, fills him with a pensive melancholy.

Nature once more awakens feelings of sadness. This conception of her relation to Man is not merely a passing thought with Wordsworth. We shall meet with it again in the poetry of the Grasmere period, in an even more pronounced form. However, it occupies a comparatively subordinate position in his apprehension of Nature's functioning in her relation to the human soul.

In " Ruth " Wordsworth expresses a belief similar to that already referred to in " Peter Bell " — a belief that, under some circumstances, Nature's influence may prove morally harmful. But he refers also to her healing power. This beautiful poem, which was a great favorite with Coleridge, was composed in Germany in 1799, and published in 1800. According to its author, it was suggested by an account given him by a wanderer. It is a pathetic love story. A red-blooded, high-spirited, soldierly youth from the Western world wooes and weds a British maid. For a time she is blissfully happy, but a young man of such " impetuous blood " is sometimes incited to evil by Nature herself. Her beautiful forms furnish food for voluptuous thought. To persons of a certain constitution or temperament danger lurks in the very heart of Nature. And so it was with this " youth from Georgia's shore." The roaring tempest and the tumultuous tropical sky would awaken the impetuosity of his own nature. Any irregularity of sights and sounds that would " impart a kindred impulse " to his mind

> seemed allied
> To his own powers, and justified
> The workings of his heart.[1]

Even the beauty of Nature's fair forms contributed to sensuous thought. The languorous breezes communicated their own state to him, and the stars themselves exerted a malign influence. However, such persons are not altogether at a moral disadvantage with reference to Nature. The passions which usually animate them are often sources of good, and productive of wholesome sentiment,

[1] Ruth, 130–133.

because of their relation to natural beauty. They predispose toward
morality because of their sensitiveness to Nature's salutary influence, and the Poet thinks this may have been the case with the
youth.

> Yet, in his worse pursuits I ween
> That sometimes there did intervene
> Pure hopes of high intent :
> For passions linked to forms so fair
> And stately needs must have their share
> Of noble sentiment.[1]

However, according to the Poet's story, notwithstanding this constitutional predisposition toward Nature's helpful influence, set over
against a temperamental susceptibility to her harmful power, the
youth became " the slave of low desires "— a man without self-control, going from bad to worse, and ultimately deserting his young
bride, who, with a broken heart, and with reason destroyed, is soon
committed to the madhouse. But even here Wordsworth seems
desirous of making out a good case in favor of Nature ; for he
says that, at times, even in the midst of hours of sadness, there
came other hours in which her sweet ministry brought something
of healing to Ruth's wretched spirit.

> Yet sometimes milder hours she knew,
> Nor wanted sun, nor rain, nor dew,
> Nor pastimes of the May ;
> — They all were with her in her cell ;
> And a clear brook with cheerful knell
> Did o'er the pebbles play.[2]

It is evident from the poems considered above that this brief
period spent in the little city near the Harz Forest was a fruitful
one. Wordsworth's genius was awake, and a number of very beautiful and important poems were the result of his creative work. It
is manifest, too, that the subject which most engrossed him was
Nature, and especially Nature in her relation to Man. Little, if
indeed anything, new is presented on this favorite theme save

[1] Ruth, 139–144.   [2] Ibid., 199–204.

the conception that certain places are possessed of spirits, and the presentation of the truth that Nature, under certain conditions, exerts a depressing influence on the human soul. In the main there is simply a repetition of certain fundamental conceptions and beliefs which have ruled his mind ever since the dawn of his mental and spiritual restoration.

But there is evidence of still further activity of mind during this winter at Goslar, the results of which are far-reaching in their character. As Professor Knight says: "Absence from his own country in that cold season, and amongst the unsympathetic burghers of Goslar, had a curious effect on Wordsworth. It not only drove him back on his former life, and stirred him up to memorialise the scenes and incidents of his native land, but it led him to think of writing his own life in verse; and during that winter he blocked out the large design of 'The Recluse' (as he narrates at length in his preface to 'The Excursion'), and kept it before him as the months passed on." [1] The nature of the design of this elaborate work will be considered later. As we have already seen, poems which afterwards became incorporated as parts of "The Prelude" were written in Germany, and the first lines of this autobiographical poem were composed on his journey from "the melancholy walls of Goslar" to Göttingen, to visit his friend Coleridge, a journey which took place on February 10, 1799. After remaining with Coleridge about three weeks, the Wordsworths returned to their native land.

Wordsworth and his sister left Germany, according to Dorothy's letter to Mrs. Poole, because they found it more expensive to live there than they had expected, if they were to enjoy " any tolerable advantages." They went to Sockburne to visit old friends, the Hutchinsons. The nine months spent here record very little of interest. In September Wordsworth made a tour to the Lake District with Coleridge and his brother, John Wordsworth, apparently to indulge his love for Nature. This tour is noteworthy

[1] Knight, The Life of William Wordsworth, I, 182–183.

because it was largely responsible for his decision to locate at Grasmere. For some time he and his sister had been at a loss to know where to settle. This was of course a hindrance to steady work, so that the months spent at Sockburne were comparatively unproductive. On this autumn excursion Coleridge, as stated by Wordsworth in a letter to his sister, "was much struck with Grasmere and its neighborhood," and apparently Wordsworth himself was impressed by its beauty— so much so, indeed, that he wrote to his sister saying that he contemplated building a house by the lake, and thought his brother John would provide the money for buying the ground. This soon resulted in a decision to make Grasmere their home.

Although there is very little information concerning his life at Sockburne, there are indications that Wordsworth was not altogether idle during these months. From one of Coleridge's letters we can infer that he was at times busy with his metrical autobiography. Coleridge was ambitious to have him push forward this important work. In a letter dated October 12, 1799, he writes to Wordsworth: "I long to see what you have been doing. O let it be the tail-piece of 'The Recluse'! for of nothing but 'The Recluse' can I hear patiently. That it is to be addressed to me makes me more desirous that it should not be a poem of itself. To be addressed, as a beloved man, by a thinker, at the close of such a poem as 'The Recluse,' a poem *non unius populi*, is the only event, I believe, capable of inciting in me an hour's vanity — vanity, nay, it is too good a feeling to be so called; it would indeed be a self-elevation produced *ab extra*." [1] It is quite probable that he worked on the poem in a more or less desultory fashion during his stay at Sockburne.

Having decided to move to Grasmere, after securing Dove Cottage, Wordsworth and his sister Dorothy set out on foot for their future home. His letter to Coleridge describing their journey is a fine piece of prose — a letter that only an ardent lover of Nature could write. It furnishes an unusual illustration of his

[1] Memoirs, I, 159.

remarkable powers of minute observation and description. In minuteness and delicacy of detail it might almost be taken for an extract from his sister's Journal.

It is evident from this letter that these two journeyed to their new home apparently as though they were on an excursion to gratify an almost insatiate thirst for natural beauty. Apparently there was no hurry to reach their destination. They turned aside in quest of other sights than those which greeted them on the road. Now and then they stopped to look back on scenes already enjoyed. At all times, and on all sides, they were engaged with beauty, eager to drink in the loveliness of all natural forms, and in this letter the Poet records his observations with great minuteness. His attitude toward Nature on this journey is very interesting. He is not dealing with her so much in the large and more heroic aspects of her being as in the more minute and delicate manifestations, although it is evident, in his reference to the journey in "The Recluse," that his interest in the former was not wanting. He observes and describes after the manner of a landscape artist. The softer and more delicate relations arrest and hold his gaze in an unusual manner. Furthermore, he views Nature more as a descriptive poet than as a poet of insight. It is the eye of sense that holds sovereign sway, rather than the vision and the gleam. He is more interested in the body of Nature than in her soul, in her forms and accidents than in her essential life. Perceptive consciousness predominates over imagination and spiritual intuition. This is not infrequently the case in his poetry also, as is manifest here and there in "The Prelude" and "The Excursion," as well as in a number of minor poems; so that we have in Wordsworth both the descriptive poet and the poet of spiritual penetration. He sees Nature clothed with beauty as with a garment, and also invested with an inner beauty of soul. He reaps the harvest of the eager, luxurious eye of sense, and also of the quiet and brooding eye of spirit. He beholds Nature in her corporeal particularity and manifoldness, as well as in her essential ideality and unity.

These two attitudes, so often met with in Wordsworth's poetry, are not necessarily opposed in his case. Seldom did he rest completely in the report of eye and ear, and compose a poem constituting merely a minute metrical reproduction of what he had seen and heard. Rather did he take the contribution of sense and work it over with his imagination. In such instances the idealization at times scarcely represented anything beyond a mere artistic selection and re-arrangement of sense materials. Such poetry did not reveal "the gleam," "the vision," the interpretation — the seeing into the life of things. At other times, however, imagination would brood over the matter thus presented, and, awakened by mystical feeling, the vision would dawn in the form of a revelation of Nature's mind and heart. The careful observation manifest in his descriptive poetry was in a sense really a pre-condition of his poetry of insight. His exquisite organic sensibility, his fixedness of gaze and hearing, his close observation, seemed to superinduce, either directly, or indirectly through memory, a mystical, idealizing mood, sometimes very light, and attended only with faint gleams of insight, but at other times deeper in its character, with fuller and more significant vision.

CHAPTER X

GRASMERE. POEMS OF NATURE

In "The Recluse"[1] Wordsworth reveals the motive that impelled him to locate at Grasmere. He went there on Nature's invitation. The natural environment was so attractive, appealing so powerfully to his æsthetic sense, and promising such aid to his poetic mind, that, added to the possibilities of a simple life, it constituted a motive sufficiently persuasive to lead him to a decision, which, he says, was sanctioned by Reason also. Late in December he and Dorothy reached the beautiful vale, and soon were settled in a humble cot. Here Wordsworth entered upon what may be regarded as the most productive period of his life — a period in which his poetic genius reached the very height of its development and power, and gave to the world a body of verse that entitles him to high rank among English poets.

If, as we have seen, he was greatly dependent upon Nature for inspiration and subject-matter in much of his previous poetic activity, this was preëminently the case in the lovely Grasmere Vale. And if, as was the case in his earlier poetry, Nature ministered to him with a loving and bountiful hand, so here, to a still greater degree, the very riches of her generous heart seem to have been poured out for his inspiration and delight, and the establishment of his mind and heart in wisdom and love. Here his fellowship with Nature, the mistress of his soul, was supreme, and in their sacred communion he heard her gracious heart throb, and listened to the deeper pulsations of her spirit.

Many are the descriptions of the Lake District, but none as satisfactory as Wordsworth's "Guide." This, however, contains very little material relating to Grasmere, and even that does not pertain to

---

[1] The real title is the " Home at Grasmere."

natural scenery. But the poems of this period abound in descriptions of local surroundings, and "The Recluse" especially shows us, in a general way, the loveliness of their environment. Wordsworth seems to be enchanted by the beauty of the vale, and, with the ever-faithful Dorothy by his side, he thinks that no being "since the birth of man had ever more abundant cause to give thanks." His "boon is absolute," and to him "surpassing grace has been vouchsafed." Thus, filled with appreciation, gratitude, and delight, he breaks forth in verse which reveals the lovely forms with which they are surrounded.

> Embrace me then ye Hills, and close me in,
> Now in the clear and open day I feel
> Your guardianship; I take it to my heart;
> 'T is like the solemn shelter of the night.
> But I would call thee beautiful, for mild
> And soft, and gay, and beautiful thou art,
> Dear Valley, having in thy face a smile
> Though peaceful, full of gladness. Thou art pleased,
> Pleased with thy crags, and woody steeps, thy Lake,
> Its one green Island and its winding shores;
> The multitude of little rocky hills,
> Thy Church and cottages of mountain stone
> Clustered like stars some few, but single most,
> And lurking dimly in their shy retreats,
> Or glancing at each other cheerful looks,
> Like separated stars with clouds between.
> What want we? have we not perpetual streams,
> Warm woods, and sunny hills, and fresh green fields,
> And mountains not less green, and flocks, and herds,
> And thickets full of songsters, and the voice
> Of lordly birds, an unexpected sound
> Heard now and then from morn till latest eve,
> Admonishing the man who walks below
> Of solitude, and silence in the sky?[1]

There is something really unique in the way all this appeals to the Poet, calling forth a response similar to that which his soul yielded in the early days of Cockermouth and Hawkshead, for he adds:

[1] The Recluse, 110-133; Knight, The Life of William Wordsworth, I, 235-236.

Nowhere (or is it fancy) *can* be found
The one sensation that is here; 't is here,
Here as it found its way into my heart
In childhood, here as it abides by day,
By night, here only; or in chosen minds
That take it with them hence, where'er they go.
'T is but I cannot name it, 't is the sense
Of majesty, and beauty, and repose,
A blended holiness of earth and sky,
Something that makes this individual Spot,
This small abiding-place of many men,
A termination, and a last retreat,
A centre come from wheresoe'er you will,
A whole without dependence or defect,
Made for itself; and happy in itself,
Perfect contentment, unity entire.[1]

Dorothy Wordsworth's Grasmere Journal is full of minute descriptions of local scenery, and records numerous excursions through the immediate and neighboring surroundings, all of which indicate the resources that Nature possessed for the Poet's soul to feed on, and how he availed himself of her generous bounty. Wordsworth's peculiar susceptibility to Nature is especially marked here in Grasmere, and results in a large body of poetry having Nature as its fountain-head of inspiration.

But, as heretofore, Nature was not to be the only source of his poetic incentive and delight. Man did not lose his hold upon the Poet's imagination and love. In him, too, he expects to find a subject for reflection, and for tuneful verse. He comes to this favored place with no false conceptions of Man, as though the majesty of his surroundings here had bred in him a like frame of mind. Nature at her best is not all-sufficient in the work of moral development. The Poet expects to find Man in this beautiful vale, as elsewhere, a mixture of good and evil. Nevertheless, he finds him existing here under far better conditions than in the city, and this itself is to be regarded as "a mighty gain." In this

[1] The Recluse, 136-151; Knight, The Life of William Wordsworth, I, 236.

quiet place the laborer is happy. Here, too, he is a freeman. No extremes of poverty are known, and want is not too great to be relieved. Here, too,

> may the heart
> Breathe in the air of fellow-suffering
> Dreadless, as in a kind of fresher breeze
> Of her own native element, the hand
> Be ready and unwearied without plea
> From tasks too frequent, or beyond its power
> For languor, or indifference, or despair.
> And as these lofty barriers break the force
> Of winds, this deep Vale, — as it doth in part,
> Conceal us from the storm, — so here abides
> A power and a protection for the mind,
> Dispensed indeed to other solitudes,
> Favoured by noble privilege like this,
> Where kindred independence of estate
> Is prevalent, where he who tills the field,
> He, happy man! is master of the field,
> And treads the mountain which his fathers trod.[1]

To find Man thus existing added to Wordsworth's peace of mind, and ministered to the poetic within him. The really *human* aspect of his surroundings appealed to an imagination and heart always responsive to Man, and thus early, as we find in "The Recluse," they are warming to the human side of his environment. He sees a grove of firs on the mountain side, and learns from a widowed dame in the cot below that it was planted by herself and her husband. A simple incident like this in the life of lowly folk stirs his imagination and feeling, and he asks:

> "Is there not
> An art, a music, and a strain of words
> That shall be like the acknowledged voice of life,
> Shall speak of what is done among the fields,
> Done truly there, or felt, of solid good
> And real evil, yet be sweet withal,
> More grateful, more harmonious than the breath,
> The idle breath of softest pipe attuned

[1] The Recluse, 367–383; Knight, The Life of William Wordsworth, I, 243.

To pastoral fancies? Is there such a stream,
Pure and unsullied, flowing from the heart
With motions of true dignity and grace?
Or must we seek that stream where Man is not?
Methinks I could repeat in tuneful verse,
Delicious as the gentlest breeze that sounds
Through that aerial fir-grove, could preserve
Some portion of its human history
As gathered from the Matron's lips, and tell
Of tears that have been shed at sight of it,
And moving dialogues between this pair,
Who in their prime of wedlock, with joint hands
Did plant the grove, now flourishing, while they
No longer flourish, he entirely gone,
She withering in her loneliness. Be this
A task above my skill; the silent mind
Has her own treasures, and I think of these,
Love what I see, and honour humankind." [1]

The human side of his genius, which was rooted in the intense humanity of his nature, was ever seeking the human in his environment, and usually found it, and the Poet was inspired by it to simple and heartfelt song.

Thus, with Nature in this peaceful vale ministering to the eye and ear of sense, as well as speaking a language to the inner spirit; with human conditions conducive to the comfort, freedom, and self-respect of Man; with the faithful and affectionate sister by his side, sharing his household joys, and joining in his frequent wanderings about the lake, through wood and field, over hills and mountains; with the company of Captain John, the " never-resting Pilgrim of the sea"; and the anticipated fellowship of the Hutchinsons, the sisters of his heart; and, finally, with Coleridge, the brother of his soul, an expected visitor, Wordsworth found himself in circumstances which not only filled him with joy and gratitude, but also acted as a powerful incentive to his genius.

It might be well, for the sake of convenience and clearness, to study Wordsworth's mental attitude, first in his smaller and less

[1] The Recluse, 401-426; Knight, The Life of William Wordsworth, I, 244.

important poems, from the date of his settlement in Dove Cottage to the time of his removal from Grasmere Vale, and then in the larger and, in some respects, more important compositions belonging to this period. Many of the minor poems are concerned with Nature and Man. Concerning Nature there is a tuneful reiteration and elaboration of his faith, and a still further disclosure of the mental process involved in his mystical apprehension of the world of things. Two poetical fragments of this period call for only brief consideration. The first begins "On Nature's invitation do I come." It is a part of " The Recluse." The exact date of its composition is uncertain, but it was probably written early in 1800, Wordsworth having moved to Dove Cottage during the last of December, 1799. It states the reason for his coming to Grasmere. He was lured to Grasmere Vale chiefly by the beauty and loveliness of the country. He came on Nature's invitation, and Reason sanctioned the choice. It was not simply the *man* but the *poet* that made the decision.

The second fragment begins, "Bleak season was it, turbulent and wild." This also is part of " The Recluse," and, like the previous fragment, was not published until 1851. It refers to the Poet's journey on foot, with his sister Dorothy, from Sockburne to Grasmere. In the case of any other poet we might interpret the casual reference to strength drawn from Nature, and the apparent questionings of the naked trees and icy brooks, to mere poetic license in the form of anthropomorphism or personification of Nature, but not so in this particular instance. All of this is in such complete harmony with Wordsworth's conception of Nature in her relation to Man, that it is not forcing the interpretation to say that the poem is expressive of his conviction.

A poem intimately related to this memorable journey to Grasmere is " Hart-leap Well," because the story and many of the images were gathered at this time, Wordsworth and his sister having visited the well. The poem was composed in 1800, and published the same year. It was a favorite with Charles Lamb.

The tale that it relates was told to Wordsworth by an aged peasant. It is a story of a remarkable hunt, in which a knight and his party pursued a hart which led them a wonderful chase. Finally, with men and dogs exhausted, Sir Walter alone overtook the stag lying dead at a spring. On further examination he found the animal had taken three surprising leaps from the brow of a hill. Sir Walter, in admiration of the " gallant stag," had a pleasure-house built there and a basin framed for the spring below, naming it Hart-leap Well. He also erected a monument of three pillars on the brow of the hill from which the hart leaped. Wordsworth makes the story an occasion for piping " a simple song for thinking hearts," and Part II of the poem gives us the simple lay, the story of which is as follows :

As he was passing from Hawes to Richmond he came to this spot, which seemed the very picture of desolation and decay. Inquiring of a shepherd concerning the place, he learned that it was once " a jolly place," but now it is accursed because of the cruel chase. The Poet finds himself not far removed from the shepherd's way of thinking, and proceeds to state his own belief. In it he calls attention to the fact that the hart fell observed by Nature, and " his death was mourned by sympathy divine." The Spirit that pervades Nature exercises a providence over the animal creation. The waste and gloom are peculiar in character. " This is no common waste, no common gloom," says the Poet, and he affirms that they constitute one of Nature's ways of teaching an important lesson. They are a reproof to men who seek their pleasure in the suffering of other creatures. In due time, however, she will repair the place, and clothe it again with living beauty.

This poem contains not only the usual Wordsworthian conception of a Spirit in Nature, but the Poet, more nearly than heretofore, identifies this Spirit with God, or the divine Spirit. It mourns with a " sympathy divine "; it exercises a providential care over the animal world. This Being, whose presence is in the clouds and air, and in the leaves of the groves, is a personal Being, who

loves *his* (not *her*) unoffending creatures. Up to this time Wordsworth has been slow to use the words " he " and " divine " in
speaking of this Presence in Nature. In his previous references to
the Spirit of Nature he has used the pronouns " she " and " her."
Here he personifies Nature in the language used in speaking of its
attributes, and apparently regards it as the Being whom Faith calls
God. Speaking of its functions, it is interesting to note also that,
whereas heretofore he has pointed out Nature's relations to so-
called inanimate objects, and to the organic world as represented
in plants, trees, birds, and men — making no specific reference to
the brute world — *now* he calls attention to another article of his
Nature-creed, namely, that the universal Spirit of Nature " main-
tains a deep and reverential care " for the animal creation, and
manifests disapproval when Man seeks his pleasure at the expense
of suffering on the part of its unoffending members.

A group of poems published under the general head of " Poems
on the Naming of Places " also belongs to this period. In an
" advertisement " Wordsworth explains his object in naming
certain places, and writing poems in consequence. He says : " By
Persons resident in the country and attached to rural objects, many
places will be found unnamed, or of unknown names, where little
Incidents will have occurred, or feelings been experienced, which
will have given to such places a private and peculiar interest. From
a wish to give some sort of record to such Incidents or renew the
gratification of such Feelings, Names have been given to Places by
the Author and some of his Friends, and the following Poems
written in consequence." [1]

Included in this group are the poems " It was an April morning : fresh and clear," " To Joanna," " There is an Eminence,
— of these our hills," " A narrow Girdle of rough stones and
crags," and " To M. H." — all of them written and published in
1800. In these poems we have Wordsworth's nearness to Nature
again indicated, and also his peculiar mental attitude toward her.

[1] Poetical Works, edited by William Knight, II, 153.

There is often a ravishing rapture in all that he beholds, the impressions of eye and ear pushing beyond the boundaries of sense, to sink deep into the Poet's heart, and to be transfigured by the imagination. It is not mere sensuous enjoyment and description, but idealization, profoundly affected by mystical feeling. There are at times decided indications of the vision and the gleam. This is evident in at least the first poem of the group, entitled " It was an April morning : fresh and clear," suggested to the Poet on the banks of a wild and beautiful brook. " I roamed," he says, " up the brook

> in the confusion of my heart,
> Alive to all things and forgetting all.
> At length I to a sudden turning came
> In this continuous glen, where down a rock
> The Stream, so ardent in its course before,
> Sent forth such sallies of glad sound, that all
> Which I till then had heard appeared the voice
> Of common pleasure : beast and bird, the lamb,
> The shepherd's dog, the linnet and the thrush,
> Vied with this waterfall, and made a song
> Which, while I listened, seemed like the wild growth
> Or like some natural produce of the air,
> That could not cease to be." [1]

This power to fixate the sense of sight or sound, or both, on the external stimulus until the object sank into the imagination, to be worked over into a new product, resulted, as we have already seen, in a kind of apprehension of Nature which is peculiar to Wordsworth's genius. The vision then becomes the joint product of sense-perception and imagination, which, often suffused by mystical feeling, seemed to constitute that poetic insight which characterizes so much of his verse. In the above poem there is a tendency to abstract the various sounds from their objects, and fuse them into one song, which seemed " like some natural produce of the air." Here is the unifying tendency of the mystical poet — the intuition of the one in many, the synthetic apprehension of the manifold

[1] It was an April morning : fresh and clear, 18–30.

of sound as one song, as though it were an harmonious creation of the natural world.

This peculiarity of Wordsworth's poetic genius is also illustrated in the second poem of the group, "To Joanna." Here the Poet shows the same concentration of sense, and the gradual transfiguring of its material by the imagination. On a summer morning's walk, accompanied by Joanna, they came into the presence of a tall rock on Rotha's banks. As he carefully scanned the rock he was delighted to find its various colors, suddenly unified by the synthetic force of their beauty, imaged in his heart. Joanna, noting his steady gaze, and beholding the ravishment in his eyes, laughed aloud, and her laugh echoed and reëchoed through the mountains. Wordsworth's idealizing faculty was evidently at work with sounds, and, as a result, as Charles Lamb says, the mountains and all the scenery seemed absolutely alive. Whatever may have been the reality, his description indicates that his "ear was touched with dreams and visionary impulses."

In the short poem "There is an Eminence,— of these our hills," there is still another example, or illustration, of Wordsworth's conception of the healing or restoring power of Nature. The eminence that "rises above the road by the side of Grasmere Lake towards Keswick," he says,

"often seems to send
Its own deep quiet to restore our hearts." [1]

The same may be said of the poem "A narrow Girdle of rough stones and crags." This is a poem of moral import, but it reveals also how Wordsworth's daily life seemed to be in close touch with Nature. To commune with her was apparently his daily bread.

The poem "To M. H."— to Mary Hutchinson, his future wife — is a description of a nook which was named for her. The powerful impression that Nature, even in her less imposing forms, makes upon the Poet is manifest here also. "If," he says, in speaking of this sequestered spot,

[1] There is an Eminence, — of these our hills, 7–8.

> " a man should plant his cottage near,
> Should sleep beneath the shelter of its trees,
> And blend its waters with his daily meal,
> He would so love it, that in his death-hour
> Its image would survive among his thoughts." [1]

It is important that the student of Wordsworth should note such lines as these, if he would understand that deep, abiding, and at times almost all-possessing power of Nature in his soul. A man thus attached to Nature, if he could sing the Poet's song at all, must needs make her its subject.

In the next poem to be considered, Wordsworth again calls attention to the fact that the beauty and joyousness of Nature may at times be even *directly* the source of pain and grief. There is a mood in which her beautiful forms seem unbearable. They seem to accentuate the sadness and melancholy of the soul. A true psychology of this mood may be found in the law of suggestion by contrast. It is the mood expressed in Burns's famous ballad " **Ye** Banks and Braes." The Scottish bard is made almost insufferably sad by Nature's beauty, because it reminds him of departed joys.

> Ye banks and braes o' bonnie Doon,
> How can ye bloom sae fresh and fair?
> How can ye chant, ye little birds,
> And I sae weary fu' o' care?
> Thou'lt break my heart, thou warbling bird,
> That wantons thro' the flowering thorn:
> Thou minds me o' departed joys,
> Departed never to return. [2]

Wordsworth closely approached this mood in " 'T is said, that some have died for love," but, if we be not mistaken, there is a slight difference in the way in which Nature intensifies the man's sorrow. It is not so much because she recalls former happiness, as that by her beauty and freshness she furnishes a contrast to his own melancholy condition of mind. The man in his lamentation over his dead

---

[1] To M. H., 18–22.   [2] Burns, Ye Banks and Braes, 1–8.

Love finds Nature anything but a comforter. She aggravates his sorrow, and he breaks forth :

> " Oh, move, thou Cottage, from behind that oak !
> Or let the aged tree uprooted lie,
> That in some other way yon smoke
> May mount into the sky !
> The clouds pass on ; they from the heavens depart :
> I look — the sky is empty space ;
> I know not what I trace ;
> But when I cease to look, my hand is on my heart.
>
> " O ! what a weight is in these shades ! Ye leaves,
> That murmur once so dear, when will it cease ?
> Your sound my heart of rest bereaves,
> It robs my heart of peace.
> Thou Thrush, that singest loud — and loud and free,
> Into yon row of willows flit,
> Upon that alder sit ;
> Or sing another song, or choose another tree.
>
> " Roll back, sweet Rill ! back to thy mountain-bounds,
> And there for ever be thy waters chained !
> For thou dost haunt the air with sounds
> That cannot be sustained ;
> If still beneath that pine-tree's ragged bough
> Headlong yon waterfall must come,
> Oh let it then be dumb !
> Be anything, sweet Rill, but that which thou art now.
>
> " Thou Eglantine, so bright with sunny showers,
> Proud as a rainbow spanning half the vale,
> Thou one fair shrub, oh ! shed thy flowers,
> And stir not in the gale.
> For thus to see thee nodding in the air,
> To see thy arch thus stretch and bend,
> Thus rise and thus descend, —
> Disturbs me till the sight is more than I can bear.[1]

Although these words must be read "in character," still we have been prepared for them in the poem " The Two April Mornings." If

---

[1] 'T is said, that some have died for love, 13-44.

it cannot be said, with Professor Knight, that Wordsworth appreciated this mood "as fully as the opposite, or complementary one, which finds expression in the great 'Ode. Intimations of Immortality,'"[1] it can at least be said that he was alive to the fact that there are moods in which Nature may prove to be something other than a source of joy—in which, indeed, she can become a real source of pain and sorrow, disturbing and oppressing the soul. This is not an uncommon mood with poets. We have found it in Burns. Tennyson, too, was subject to it. With him

> Tears from the depth of some divine despair
> Rise in the heart, and gather to the eyes,
> In looking on the happy Autumn-fields,
> And thinking of the days that are no more.[2]

It is also manifest in his pathetic little poem "Break, break, break," where the sight of the sea seems to superinduce the mood:

> Break, break, break,
>   On thy cold gray stones, O Sea!
> And I would that my tongue could utter
>   The thoughts that arise in me.
>
> O well for the fisherman's boy,
>   That he shouts with his sister at play!
> O well for the sailor lad,
>   That he sings in his boat on the bay!
>
> And the stately ships go on
>   To their haven under the hill;
> But O for the touch of a vanish'd hand,
>   And the sound of a voice that is still!
>
> Break, break, break,
>   At the foot of thy crags, O Sea!
> But the tender grace of a day that is dead
>   Will never come back to me.

It may be found also in Browning, as, for example, in his lyric entitled "May and Death":

[1] Poetical Works, II, 181 n.   [2] The Princess.

I wish that when you died last May,
    Charles, there had died along with you
Three parts of Spring's delightful things;
    Ay, and, for me, the fourth part too.

Coleridge once said concerning the words,

"and that uncertain heaven received
Into the bosom of the steady lake,"

to be found in the poem "There was a Boy," that he should have
recognized them anywhere, and adds, "Had I met these lines
running wild in the deserts of Arabia, I should have instantly
screamed out 'Wordsworth!'"[1] The same thing might be said of
the poem "To the Cuckoo." It is preëminently a characteristic
poem. The idealizing, visionary character of the Poet's genius is
revealed in it. The tendency to unsubstantialize the corporeal, to
abstract the quality from the object, and universalize it is very
marked. Here sound is abstracted from the bird, and is conceived
of merely as a "wandering voice." The cuckoo loses its identity
— its substantial reality — and its song becomes the thing
considered. But it becomes an incorporeal, "visionary thing,"
"a voice," "a mystery." The particularity of sense is lost in
the universality or abstract generality of the mystical imagination.
The real subject is canceled, and the attribute is made the subject.
And this mystical idealization does not stop here, but the trance
becomes still deeper, until the corporeal world of sense recedes
under the spell of the cuckoo's voice, and the solid earth itself becomes an unsubstantial place. The peculiar vision and gleam that
were with him in his boyhood are still with him, and his ethereal
conception of Nature is without doubt largely attributable to the
mystical dream. If this poem be carefully read, it will be noticed
that, first, the sense of sound is arrested by the cuckoo's voice.
Immediately the process of abstraction seems to begin, and the
substantial object of sense gradually fades away, the cuckoo's
note alone becoming the reality. But it is no longer a definitely

[1] Knight, The Life of William Wordsworth, I, 184.

localized affair. There is a mysterious, invisible everywhereness about it. It seems to pass from hill to hill. It is "at once far off, and near." It seems to be merely a widely diffused voice. Under its spell consciousness becomes more and more dreamy and visionary, until the solid earth of normal sense perception is transformed into "an unsubstantial fairy place" — a subjective world, apparently of the mind's own creation, but superinduced by actual sense impressions in the form of the cuckoo's notes. By some strange psychologic alchemy an ideal world is created, which supplants the world commonly recognized as real.

In the poem "To the Daisy," written in 1802 and published in 1807, Wordsworth continues to speak of Nature's ministry to himself. In various ways her kindly offices are performed through this common but beautiful flower of the fields, which is "by many a claim" the Poet's darling. This little flower banishes melancholy. To it he owes

> Some apprehension;
> Some steady love; some brief delight;
> Some memory that had taken flight;
> Some chime of fancy wrong or right;
> Or stray invention.[1]

But it ministers to his moral nature also, teaching him sympathy, humility, and wisdom. In words like the following we see again how far from correct is Lord Morley's interpretation of Wordsworth when he affirms that in poetry like this, where he represents Nature as teaching moral lessons, he is merely giving utterance to a charming fancy:

> If stately passions in me burn,
> And one chance look to Thee should turn,
> I drink out of an humbler urn
>   A lowlier pleasure;
> The homely sympathy that heeds
> The common life our nature breeds;
> A wisdom fitted to the needs
>   Of hearts at leisure.[2]

[1] To the Daisy, 44–48.   [2] Ibid., 49–56.

At morn this little flower brings gladness to his soul, its cheer-fulness and rest breeding in him a corresponding temper, and oft, at evening, it has eased the burden of his heart.

> Fresh-smitten by the morning ray,
> When thou art up, alert and gay,
> Then, cheerful Flower! my spirits play
>   With kindred gladness:
> And when, at dusk, by dews opprest
> Thou sink'st, the image of thy rest
> Hath often eased my pensive breast
>   Of careful sadness.[1]

Indeed, there is a further obligation that he owed to this flower of the summer fields.

> An instinct call it, a blind sense;
> A happy, genial influence,
> Coming one knows not how, nor whence,
>   Nor whither going.[2]

This is no exaggeration of Nature's influence upon Wordsworth. One who studies his history will be impressed by this sensitiveness and susceptibility of the Poet to the smaller and less pretentious forms of Nature. That which in another poet might seem to be affectation or poetic exaggeration is in Wordsworth but the natural expression of a daily experience. A daisy speaks in divers ways to his soul. It breathes words of love and solace, of cheer and wisdom, to a heart peculiarly receptive and in close sympathy with any message it may utter. He understands Nature's speech, whether it be uttered by the flower of the field, or by the mighty suns and systems that roll in space. All forms of Nature have a message for him. Often it is merely personal in character, but often, too, it is so important, in the Poet's judgment, as to take on the form of a message to others, and, because of his poetic insight and gift of song, he feels himself a chosen instrument to proclaim it to the world. The proclamation of his belief becomes "oracular."

[1] To the Daisy, 57–64.   [2] Ibid., 69–72.

A number of short poems—the majority of which, to use
a phrase of Wordsworth, are "breathings of simple nature"—
were written at Grasmere between the years 1801 and 1805
—the year memorable for the completion of "The Prelude."
Among them are "The Sparrow's Nest," "To a Butterfly," "The
sun has long been set," "My heart leaps up when I behold," "The
Redbreast chasing the Butterfly," "To the Small Celandine,"
"To the Same Flower," the well-known sonnet—"It is a beauteous Evening, calm and free," two more poems to the daisy,
"The Green Linnet," "Yew-Trees," "At the Grave of Burns,"
"Thoughts suggested the Day following, on the Banks of Nith,
near the Poet's Residence," "To a Highland Girl," "The Solitary
Reaper," "Yarrow Unvisited," "I wandered lonely as a cloud,"
"The Kitten and Falling Leaves," "The Small Celandine," and
"To a Sky-Lark." In some of these poems there is little more
than descriptive poetry. The deeper emotional nature does not
predominate. When this is the case, the description is both beautiful and accurate. As Professor Raleigh says: "His descriptions
never stray far from the object before him, and sometimes are the
work of the most delicate observation. The poem on 'The Green
Linnet' was praised by Coleridge for its accurate loveliness:—

> Amid yon tuft of hazel trees,
> That twinkle to the gusty breeze,
> Behold him perched in ecstasies,
>   Yet seeming still to hover;
> There! where the flutter of his wings
> Upon his back and body flings
> Shadows and sunny glimmerings,
>   That cover him all over.[1]

Beauties like this are most frequent in his least ambitious poems,
where his mind plays at ease and has time for observation. When
his heart is deeply stirred the description is almost drowned in
the emotion."[2]

[1] The Green Linnet, 25-32.   [2] Raleigh, Wordsworth, 151.

But among these "breathings of simple nature" there are some that bear also marks of the Poet's deeper insight, and in others we have at least hints at his general Nature-faith. In "The Solitary Reaper," for example, is seen the tendency, noted elsewhere, to abstract attributes from their objects, or functions from their agents, and, delocalizing them, to conceive of them as realities, and to render them practically ubiquitous. Sounds first heard by the ear of sense penetrate deep into the Poet's heart and, by a strange, mystical, psychical process, are transformed from particular and local impressions of sense into sounds without "a local habitation and a name," as was noted in the case of Joanna's laugh, and the cuckoo's twofold shout. In "The Solitary Reaper" it is the maiden's song, as she reaps and binds the grain, that fills the vale to overflowing.

> Alone she cuts and binds the grain,
> And sings a melancholy strain;
> O listen! for the Vale profound
> Is overflowing with the sound.[1]

Only a mystical poet could apprehend such a sound as filling the entire vale, as though the very atmosphere were vibrant with it.

In the two poems referring to Burns may be found some of Wordsworth's fundamental teaching concerning Nature. They were written in 1803, while he was making a tour in Scotland with Dorothy and Coleridge. He very naturally visited the grave of Burns, and it was natural, too, that he should be inspired to sing of the dead poet, with whom, though so unlike, he had, nevertheless, much in common. Neighbors they were, and loving friends they might have been. Both were children of Nature, both loved Nature, and both sang of Nature. In the second poem Wordsworth recognizes that Burns was schooled by Nature — that the soul of the poet was fashioned by her art — and he asks by what rules she trains a mind like this in a manner far transcending the art of the schools.

[1] The Solitary Reaper, 5-8.

> Proud thoughts that Image overawes,
> Before it humbly let us pause,
> And ask of Nature from what cause
>   And by what rules
> She trained her Burns to win applause
>   That shames the Schools.[1]

In the poem " I wandered lonely as a cloud," composed in
1804, is seen how Wordsworth apprehends Nature as joyous, and
also how her joy is soon reflected in him. Just as his heart leaps
up when he beholds a rainbow in the sky, so, when he sees ten
thousand dancing daffodils more gleeful than the sparkling waves
dancing beside them, they awaken in him an irresistible joy. " A
poet," he says, " could not but be gay, in such a jocund company."
But there is here, also, another example of his mystical idealization—the usual intense observation, then the mental representation
or memory image, followed by pensive brooding, and transfiguration.

> I gazed — and gazed — but little thought
> What wealth the show to me had brought:
>
> For oft when on my couch I lie
> In vacant or in pensive mood,
> They flash upon that inward eye
> Which is the bliss of solitude;
> And then my heart with pleasure fills,
> And dances with the daffodils.[2]

In a Fenwick note, the third and fourth lines of the preceding
stanza are attributed to Mrs. Wordsworth. However, the poet has
appropriated them in such a manner as to make them thoroughly
his own. They express his own sentiment, and illustrate his poetical method of dealing with Nature.

A striking example of Nature's influence on Wordsworth is given
in " Elegiac Verses," a poem written in memory of his brother,
Captain John Wordsworth, whose ship was wrecked February 6,
1805, the Captain going down with the craft. Wordsworth, who

---

[1] Thoughts suggested the Day following, on the Banks of Nith, etc., 37–42.
[2] I wandered lonely as a cloud, 17–24.

was deeply attached to his brother, was greatly shocked and sad-
dened by the disaster. In a previous poem, "Elegiac Stanzas,"
his state of mind is apparent. He says,

> " A power is gone, which nothing can restore;
> A deep distress hath humanised my Soul," [1]

and adds,

> " The feeling of my loss will ne'er be old." [2]

In similar vein he tells of his profound loss in a letter to a friend,
which also reveals how dear the brothers were to each other.
" For myself, I feel that there is something cut out of my life
which cannot be restored. I never thought of him but with hope
and delight. We looked forward to the time, not distant, as we
thought, when he would settle near us — when the task of his life
would be over, and he would have nothing to do but reap his
reward. By that time I hoped also that the chief part of my labours
would be executed, and that I should be able to show him that he
had not placed a false confidence in me. I never wrote a line without a thought of giving him pleasure; my writings, printed and
manuscript, were his delight, and one of the chief solaces of his
long voyages." [3] But what helps him bear such a profound grief?
In this great misfortune he finds relief through the ministrations
of a little flower; its beauty and grace seem to contribute to his
comfort and peace:

> That was indeed a parting! oh,
> Glad am I, glad that it is past;
> For there were some on whom it cast
> Unutterable woe.
> But they as well as I have gains; —
> From many a humble source, to pains
> Like these, there comes a mild release;
> Even here I feel it, even this Plant
> Is in its beauty ministrant
> To comfort and to peace. [4]

---

[1] Elegiac Stanzas, 35–36.   [3] Myers, William Wordsworth, 70.
[2] Ibid., 39.   [4] Elegiac Verses, 41–50.

It was really remarkable how Wordsworth apparently linked all things with Nature. As one reads the poem "The Kitten and Falling Leaves," telling of Wordsworth and his infant Dora watching a kitten as it leaped up to catch the falling leaves, one is really amazed at the manner in which the Poet associates apparently insignificant things with Nature's power. Wordsworth was conscious of this fact, and there was evidently conviction and method in his art, for we find in a note in Henry Crabb Robinson's "Diary, Reminiscences, and Correspondence," bearing the date of September 10, 1816, that Wordsworth "quoted from 'The Kitten and Falling Leaves' to show he had connected even the kitten with the great, awful, and mysterious powers of Nature." The poem speaks for itself on this point:

> Yet, whate'er enjoyments dwell
> In the impenetrable cell
> Of the silent heart which Nature
> Furnishes to every creature ;
> Whatsoe'er we feel and know
> Too sedate for outward show,
> Such a light of gladness breaks,
> Pretty Kitten ! from thy freaks,—
> Spreads with such a living grace
> O'er my little Dora's face.[1]

The poems thus far considered in this chapter represent the greater part of Wordsworth's work between 1800 and 1805 — unusually fertile years — with the possible exception of the work done on "The Prelude." There is, however, an interesting piece of prose belonging to the year 1805, in the form of a letter relating to landscape gardening, that ought to be introduced here, as it illustrates in a unique way some of Wordsworth's fundamental conceptions of, and attitudes toward, Nature, and reveals in another way the functioning of his æsthetic nature. Sir George Beaumont, a landscape painter, had his country-seat at Coleorton and was at this time rebuilding Coleorton Hall, and laying out the grounds.

[1] The Kitten and Falling Leaves, 95-104.

This work was the occasion of an exchange of opinions in the correspondence between Wordsworth and Sir George "on the principles of beauty in Houses, Parks, and Gardens." [1] In a letter written by the Poet from Grasmere, October 17, 1805, he gives, at considerable length, his views on landscape architecture. They show that his beliefs concerning Nature constituted for him not merely a poetic but also a practical creed, and reveal how thoroughly he was possessed of the idea of Nature as animated by spirit.

The principles which Wordsworth lays down for observance in the art of gardening are, first, that we must not build a mansion regardless of its natural surroundings. Nature should be consulted when we must thus interfere with her preserves, and only that should be done which good taste can sanction. The Poet is not in sympathy with the system in vogue in his time, and favors getting back to the simplicity of Nature, preserving much of her wild beauty. Nothing should be attempted which she cannot appropriate or adopt. "Let Nature be all in all, taking care that everything done by man shall be in the way of being adopted by her." We should accept her leadership, take hints from her, and try to complete her plans. In laying out grounds we ought to appeal to, and try to move the affections of, men and women of good sense — those who have the deepest perception of Nature's beauty. Nature tries to reach such, and she ought to be assisted in this respect. "All just and solid pleasure in natural objects rests upon two pillars, God and Man. Laying out grounds, as it is called, may be considered as a liberal art, in some sort like poetry and painting: and its object, like that of all the liberal arts, is, or ought to be, to move the affections under the control of good sense; that is, those of the best and wisest: but, speaking with more precision, it is to assist Nature in moving the affections, and, surely, as I have said, the affections of those who have the deepest perception of the beauty of Nature; who have the most valuable feelings, that is, the most permanent, the most independent, the most ennobling,

[1] Memoirs, I, 344.

connected with Nature and human life. No liberal art aims merely at the gratification of an individual or a class; the painter or poet is degraded in proportion as he does so; the true servants of the Arts pay homage to the human kind as impersonated in unwarped and enlightened minds. If this be so when we are merely putting together words or colours, how much more ought the feeling to prevail when we are in the midst of the realities of things; of the beauty and harmony, of the joy and happiness of loving creatures; of men and children, of birds and beasts, of hills and streams, and trees and flowers; with the changes of night and day, evening and morning, summer and winter; and all their unwearied actions and energies, as benign in the spirit that animates them as they are beautiful and grand in that form and clothing which is given to them for the delight of our senses." [1]

Close to Nature as this letter shows the Poet to be, and jealous for her beauty and leadership, it also indicates how close he is to Man, and how much he is interested in his welfare. According to Wordsworth the establishment of great country-seats ought not to be accomplished at the expense of banishing men from the neighborhood. "What then shall we say of many great mansions with their unqualified expulsion of human creatures from their neighbourhood, happy or not; houses, which do what is fabled of the upas tree, — breathe out death and desolation! I know you will feel with me here, both as a man and a lover and professor of the arts. I was glad to hear from Lady Beaumont that you did not think of removing your village. Of course much here will depend upon circumstances, above all, with what kind of inhabitants, from the nature of the employments in that district, the village is likely to be stocked. But, for my part, strip my neighbourhood of human beings, and I should think it one of the greatest privations I could undergo. You have all the poverty of solitude, nothing of its elevation. In a word, if I were disposed to write a sermon (and this is something like one) upon the subject of taste

[1] Memoirs, I, 350–351.

in natural beauty, I should take for my text the little pathway in Lowther woods, and all which I had to say would begin and end in the human heart, as under the direction of the Divine Nature, conferring value on the objects of the senses, and pointing out what is valuable in them." [1]

The year 1806 was a productive year. This is indicated by a number of poems, especially sonnets, which also are "simple breathings of Nature," and in which Wordsworth shows himself to be still in close fellowship with her. The group of Nature-poems of this year includes another cuckoo poem, "Yes, it was the mountain Echo." Here the cuckoo's "two-fold shout" still has a charm for the Poet. In connection with it a suggestion is brought out, born of his mystical consciousness, to which the cuckoo's song so often appealed. Does not mortal life also hear two voices? One is of the earth and is heard by sense, but the other is heard by the inward ear and speaks of immortality. We have answers, or echoes, from " beyond the grave," and to these we should harken, for they are of God. Wordsworth brings this suggestion before us in the last three verses of the poem, after contrasting the echo of the cuckoo's song with the song itself, the latter being "like her ordinary cry, . . . but oh, how different!"

> Hears not also mortal Life?
> Hear not we, unthinking Creatures!
> Slaves of folly, love, or strife —
> Voices of two different natures?
>
> Have not *we* too? — yes, we have
> Answers, and we know not whence;
> Echoes from beyond the grave,
> Recognised intelligence!
>
> Such rebounds our inward ear
> Catches sometimes from afar —
> Listen, ponder, hold them dear;
> For of God, — of God they are. [2]

[1] Memoirs, I, 351 – 352.   [2] Yes, it was the mountain Echo, 9–20.

Other poems showing the Poet's intimacy with Nature are the sonnets "Admonition," "Beloved Vale! I said, when I shall con," "With how sad steps, O Moon, thou climb'st the sky," and the well-known sonnet "The world is too much with us; late and soon." In the famous sonnet last mentioned he enters a protest against our preoccupation with social and business cares, and our indifference to the resources which Nature offers to the human spirit. It also indicates how much Wordsworth valued her as a refuge for his own soul.

> The world is too much with us; late and soon,
> Getting and spending, we lay waste our powers:
> Little we see in Nature that is ours;
> We have given our hearts away, a sordid boon!
> This Sea that bares her bosom to the moon;
> The winds that will be howling at all hours,
> And are up-gathered now like sleeping flowers;
> For this, for everything, we are out of tune;
> It moves us not. — Great God! I'd rather be
> A Pagan suckled in a creed outworn;
> So might I, standing on this pleasant lea,
> Have glimpses that would make me less forlorn;
> Have sight of Proteus rising from the sea;
> Or hear old Triton blow his wreathèd horn.

Two more Nature-sonnets of this year are entitled "Brook! whose society the Poet seeks," and "There is a little unpretending Rill." In the former the very familiar conception of Nature as pervaded by a Spirit life is again brought out. Were our Poet to typify the brook, he would not, like Grecian artists, give her human fleshly form. She should be no naiad. Something nobler than this should constitute the type, or symbol, of the sparkling stream whose society the poet and the painter seek.

> It seems the Eternal Soul is clothed in thee
> With purer robes than those of flesh and blood,
> And hath bestowed on thee a safer good;
> Unwearied joy, and life without its cares.[1]

It must be evident to every one who reads these Nature-poems, written during the first years spent in Grasmere, that we have in Wordsworth a soul enjoying closest companionship with a revered and much-loved Mistress, who ministers unto him out of the abundance of her riches. Daily he sits at her board and partakes of a bountiful repast. Sometimes the food merely satisfies his appetite of sense; the eye and ear are ever alert to feed upon the beauty of the vale. But often she ministers to a more refined taste, and his soul feeds on the deeper spiritual beauty of the natural world, as seen in this most favored spot. At times he seems to see and hear all that field and wood, mountain and lake, afford, and indulges in the delights of a ravished sense; again, he sits down in "a wise passiveness" of soul and receives, through his spiritual eye and ear, the lessons which his great Teacher imparts. The heavens and the earth speak to him, and he understands their language, and interprets it to others in the beauty and melody of song. Verily, as poet, during these delightful years, he is the high priest of Nature, and as he stands before her altar, he reverently proclaims her message of solace and healing, of joy and love, of truth and wisdom, to a needy world.

CHAPTER XI

GRASMERE (CONTINUED). "THE BROTHERS." "MICHAEL."
"RESOLUTION AND INDEPENDENCE." "THE AFFLICTION
OF MARGARET——." POLITICAL SONNETS

Preoccupied with Nature as Wordsworth undoubtedly was during
the five years since entering Grasmere Vale, nevertheless Man also
received earnest and affectionate consideration. He was a subject
too dear to be neglected, and, as we have seen in "The Recluse,"
just after the Poet had settled in Dove Cottage, he saw men here
under conditions far more hopeful than those of the city, and therefore looked upon them with expectancy, believing that in them also
he should find a source of fellowship, and a subject for his simple
song. An examination of the poetry of these years shows that his
expectations were realized, for there are a number of poems which
manifest the human side of the Poet's nature as open and sensitive to the human side of his environment.

These poems may be divided into two classes — those dealing
with men in their essential nature as men, and those dealing with
men as living under certain social conditions, and organized under
political government. The first class bear the real Wordsworthian
marks. He proves to be "a faithful painter of rural manners"
and a true delineator of those passions that constitute our fundamental life. Paternal love, for example, is the theme of his song
in "The Childless Father," where poor old Timothy, across whose
threshold a coffin bearing his lost child had recently passed, arouses.
himself from his grief and responds to the call of the chase, going
forth to the fray "with a tear on his cheek." Again, "The
Brothers" is a simple, pathetic tale of fraternal love. Between two
orphans there exists a love which is a benediction to behold. The
older brother leaves home to follow the sea, in order that he may

be of more service to the younger. After many years he returns. He does not venture to inquire for his brother, but visits the country churchyard. He knows the spot where his parents are buried. He finds another grave and is left in mingled doubt, apprehension, and hope. The village priest appears, and the stranger asks the history of some of the graves. This leads the priest to tell the story of the orphans, and it is not long before the stranger learns of his brother's death. At the close of the tale the vicar invites him to partake of his hospitality, but his heart is too full. He goes to a neighboring town and writes to the priest revealing his identity. This simple story, having its basis in fact, illustrates the nature of Wordsworth's genius. He seizes upon a few facts involving the basal affections, as manifest in these simple people, which furnish a foundation for poetic idealization. Many of his poems are idealized biography of rustic folk, in which the Poet shows a profound reverence for Man as Man. As he came in contact with these rural people he found them possessed of strong attachments and deep feeling. He observed the domestic affections to be especially intense. It was his aim in this simple, pathetic poem, as well as in others, to give an illustration of them as he knew they existed among the people in the North of England.

A pastoral poem of similar import, and written about the same time, is entitled " Michael." It also has a basis in fact, and here we find Wordsworth again drawing a picture of domestic affection as he found it existing among people in certain parts of the North. He introduces an interesting bit of mental history before entering upon his story. It illustrates once more how he was led to Man by the hand of Nature. He says :

> " It was the first
> Of those domestic tales that spake to me
> Of Shepherds, dwellers in the valleys, men
> Whom I already loved ; — not verily
> For their own sakes, but for the fields and hills
> Where was their occupation and abode.
> And hence this Tale, while I was yet a Boy

> Careless of books, yet having felt the power
> Of Nature, by the gentle agency
> Of natural objects, led me on to feel
> For passions that were not my own, and think
> (At random and imperfectly indeed)
> On man, the heart of man, and human life." [1]

The subject of the tale is an aged shepherd who lived in Grasmere Vale. His only child, a son, had been his hope and joy from infancy. When the boy had reached the age of eighteen, owing to pecuniary misfortune, it was deemed wise to send him to a kinsman in the city, in the hope that he might be able to retrieve his parents' loss. Before the boy left home, his father took him to a dell in the mountains, where they had carried stone to build a sheepfold. Here the father told his son the story of his love for him from birth, and gave him wholesome counsel. He asked him to lay the corner stone of the sheepfold, which would serve as a memorial of this sacred hour. But, alas! the young man failed to profit by it, and soon dishonored his father's love. Soon after reaching the city he gave himself up to evil ways, which resulted in moral disaster. Finally, he was driven "to seek a hiding-place beyond the seas." The father, broken-hearted, but sustained by the power of his love, survived seven years after learning of his son's downfall. He continued building the sheepfold, but sank into his grave before completing the work, and the place, which, to him and his ancestors, had been for generations the object of affection and toil, soon became the property of strangers.

This simple tale is another portrayal of human love — the deep, constant, abiding love of a man in humble station for his offspring. "Michael" and "The Brothers" were both written for a purpose. An earnest, ethical aim lies back of them, which, when understood, reveals Wordsworth's deep regard and concern for human nature. This is brought out in a letter from the Poet to Charles James Fox, written in 1802. He was much pleased with

[1] Michael, 21–33.

Fox's "sensibility of heart" as manifested in his "public character."
He decided to send him a copy of the second edition of the
"Lyrical Ballads," simply because these poems were contained in
it. In doing so, he says :

"It appears to me that the most calamitous effect which has
followed the measures, which have lately been pursued in this
country, is a rapid decay of the domestic affections among the
lower orders of society. This effect the present Rulers of this
country are not conscious of, or they disregard it. For many years
past, the tendency of society amongst almost all the nations of
Europe has been to produce it. But recently, by the spreading of
manufactures through every part of the country, by the heavy taxes
upon postage, by work-houses, Houses of Industry, and the inven-
tion of Soup Shops, &c., &c.,— superadded to the increasing dis-
proportion between the price of labour and that of the necessaries
of life,— the bonds of domestic feeling, as far as the influence of
these things has extended, have been weakened, and, in innumer-
able instances, entirely destroyed. The evil would be the less to
be regretted, if these institutions were regarded as palliatives to a
disease ; but the vanity and pride of their promoters is so subtly
interwoven with them that they are deemed great discoveries and
blessings to humanity. In the meantime, parents are separated from
their children, and children from their parents ; the wife no longer
prepares with her own hands a meal for her husband, the produce
of his labour ; there is little doing in his house about which his
affections can be interested, and but little left in it which he can love.
I have two neighbours, a man and his wife, both upwards of eighty
years of age — they live alone ; the husband has been confined to
his bed many months, and has never had, nor till within these few
weeks has ever needed, anybody to attend to him but his wife.
She has recently been seized with a lameness, which has often
prevented her from being able to carry his food to his bed, the
neighbours fetch water for her from the well, and do other kind
offices for them both ; but her infirmities increase. She told my

servant two days ago that she was afraid they must both be boarded out amongst some other Poor of the parish; (they have long been supported by the parish), but she said it was hard, after having kept house together so many years, to come to this, and she was sure 'that it would burst her heart.' I mention this fact to show how deeply the spirit of independence is, even yet, rooted in some parts of the country. These people could not express themselves in this way without an almost sublime conviction of the blessings of independent domestic life. If it is true, as I believe, that this spirit is rapidly disappearing, no greater curse can befal a land.

"I earnestly entreat your pardon for having detained you so long. In the two poems, "The Brothers" and "Michael," I have attempted to draw a picture of the domestic affections, as I know they exist amongst a class of men who are now almost confined to the North of England. They are small, independent proprietors of land, here called Statesmen, men of respectable education, who daily labour in their own little properties. The domestic affections will always be strong among men who live in districts not crowded with population, if these men are placed above poverty. But if they are proprietors of small estates which have descended to them from their ancestors, the power which these affections will acquire among such men is inconceivable by those who have only had an opportunity of observing hired labourers, farmers, and the manufacturing poor. Their little tract of land serves as a kind of permanent rallying point for their domestic feelings, as a table upon which they are written, which makes them objects of memory in a thousand instances, when they would otherwise be forgotten. It is a fountain fitted to the nature of social man, from which supplies of affection, as pure as his heart was intended for, are daily drawn. This class of men is rapidly disappearing.

"You, sir, have a consciousness, upon which every good man will congratulate you, that the whole of your public conduct has, in one way or other, been directed to the preservation of this class of men and those who hold similar situations. You have felt that the most sacred of all property is the property of the poor. The two poems which I have mentioned were written with a view to show that men who do not wear fine clothes can feel deeply. '*Pectus enim est quod disertos facit, et vis mentis. Ideoque imperitis quoque si modo sint aliquo affectu concitati, verba non desunt.*'

"The poems are faithful copies from nature, and I hope, whatever effect they may have upon you, you will at least be able to perceive that they may excite profitable sympathies in many kind and good hearts, and may in some small degree enlarge our feelings of reverence for our species, and our knowledge of human nature, by showing that our best qualities are possessed by some whom we are too apt to consider, not with reference to the points in which they resemble us, but to those in which they manifestly differ from us. I thought, at a time when these feelings are sapped in so many ways, that the two poems might co-operate, however feebly, with the illustrious efforts which you have made to stem this and other evils, with which the country is labouring; and it is on this account alone that I have taken the liberty of thus addressing you." [1]

This letter reveals a heart beating in sympathy for the humbler classes of society, and a conviction that the best elements of our nature may be found there. Furthermore, it shows how much of Wordsworth's poetry was grounded in an earnest purpose to utilize his powers for their betterment, and therefore for the betterment of his country. No great English poet, with the possible exceptions of Spenser, Milton, and Tennyson, had such a profound consciousness of the ethical import of his art, and consecrated his gifts to such lofty ends. He bears the burden of these simple people on his heart, and exalts the virtuous humanity in them. Of such as these would he record praises, and of such would he speak that justice might be done, and obeisance paid where it is due. It must be insisted upon, in any final judgment on Wordsworth's poetry, that the reason for the simple and homely theme, the seeking

[1] Knight, The Life of William Wordsworth, I, 218-221.

"for present good in life's familiar face," is the feeling on the part of Wordsworth that here, among men in lowly station, pursuing simple tasks, and exemplifying the basic virtues, we find humanity at its best. Here the poet had heard

> From mouths of men obscure and lowly, truths
> Replete with honour; sounds in unison
> With loftiest promises of good and fair.[1]

He reads human nature as illustrated in such characters as Michael, and Leonard in "The Brothers," and feels that of such is not only the kingdom of heaven, but of such must be the kingdom of earth if society is to realize its highest good. Here, in these two poems, we find him exalting the domestic affections, and he hopes, as indicated in the letter to Fox, to excite "profitable sympathies" in good hearts and to "enlarge our feelings of reverence for our species." Coleridge, who is certainly no mean critic, so felt the beauty, sacredness, and force of this ethical purpose of Wordsworth that, after reading the second volume of the "Lyrical Ballads," he wrote to Godwin : "I should judge of a man's heart and intellect, precisely according to the degree and intensity of the admiration with which he read these poems. Perhaps instead of heart, I should have said taste, but when I think of 'The Brothers,' of 'Ruth,' and of 'Michael,' I recur to the expression, and am enforced to say *heart*. If I die, and the booksellers will give you anything for my life, be sure to say ; 'Wordsworth descended on him like the Γνῶθι σεαυτόν from heaven, by showing to him what true poetry was, he made him know that he himself was no Poet.'"[2]

Of course these three poems are far in advance of many of the poems of the first edition of the "Lyrical Ballads," which evoked much severe criticism and ridicule. But even in this second edition occasional triviality is manifest, and here also we can see the human

[1] The Prelude, XIII, 183–185.
[2] Paul, William Godwin : His Friends and Contemporaries, II, 79. Cf. Knight, The Life of William Wordsworth, I, 224.

motive back of it all. This, of course, does not necessarily justify such poetry, but it explains how one who could write the " Lines composed a few miles above Tintern Abbey," " Three years she grew in sun and shower," " Hart-leap Well," " Ode to Duty," and " Ode. Intimations of Immortality " was led to write verse that met with unsparing criticism and contempt.

These objectionable qualities are manifest in the poem " Alice Fell; or, Poverty." It is a homely story of a little girl weeping because her old weather-beaten cloak was torn by a wheel while she was riding behind a post chaise. The poem, written in 1802 and published in 1807, was ridiculed by his critics. Wordsworth, in a subsequent publication, adds a note explaining the circumstances under which it was written, and the thoroughly human motive back of it. He says: " Written to gratify Mr. Graham of Glasgow, brother of the author of ' The Sabbath.' He was a zealous co-adjutor of Mr. Clarkson, and a man of ardent humanity. The incident had happened to himself, and he urged me to put it into verse for humanity's sake. The humbleness, meanness if you like, of the subject, together with the homely mode of treating it, brought upon me a world of ridicule by the small critics, so that in policy I excluded it from many editions of my poems, till it was restored at the request of some of my friends, in particular my son-in-law, Edward Quillinan."[1] That others appreciated Wordsworth's verse of this character is evident from Charles Lamb's letter to him, written in 1815, after the revision of the poem. Referring to Wordsworth's critics he said, " I am glad that you have not sacrificed a verse to those scoundrels."[2]

" Resolution and Independence," or the story of an old leech-gatherer, is one of Wordsworth's masterpieces. Of course, a critic of the old school could hardly expect to find poetic inspiration in such a humble and obscure person. His vocation places him but a little higher in the social scale than the vagrants in whom our Poet could discern something worthy of consideration, and from

[1] Poetical Works, edited by William Knight, II, 272-273 n.   [2] Ibid., 276 n.

whom he felt he could learn important lessons. But Wordsworth regards him with favor, and does not seem to think it disrespectful or degrading to the Muse to sing of this old man's pursuing a very humble calling. The old man proves to be an object lesson to the Poet, and he proceeds to embody it in noble verse. The poem is based largely on fact, and the story runs as follows :

On a beautiful morning after a storm, when "all things that love the sun are out of doors," as Wordsworth journeys over the moor, sharing in the joyousness of Nature, he soon finds himself in a different mood, oppressed with "fears and fancies" concerning his future. As a matter of fact he is thinking that thus far he had pursued the poet's calling with comparatively little success, pecuniary or otherwise. His material resources are limited, and on this bright morning he is looking forward to an uncertain future. He reflects on the fact that the poet's life, although having a glad beginning, frequently ends in "despondency and madness." As he walks along, striving with these "untoward thoughts," he comes across an old man standing motionless beside a pool. He is bent almost double with extreme age. Soon the old man takes his staff and stirs the pool, gazing fixedly on the muddy water. Wordsworth approaches him with a stranger's greeting, and receives a gentle and courteous acknowledgment. Then, in response to a question, the old man explains the nature of his occupation. He is a leech-gatherer. Being old and poor, he must engage in this "employment hazardous and wearisome," enduring frequent hardships to gain a livelihood. The heroism of this man, struggling with the infirmities of age and poverty, come to Wordsworth as a kind of heavenly admonishment. However, his former fears return. The uncertain fate of poets still disturbs him. What does the future hold in store for him, with "mighty Poets in their misery dead"? And so, "perplexed and longing to be comforted," he renews his question, asking the aged man how he lives, and what is the real nature of his vocation. To this he replies, explaining how he travels hither and thither gathering leeches, as well as the method by which he secures them. But, he adds, once they were plentiful; now, however, they are hard to find; yet he perseveres, finding them wherever he can. Then the old man turns to converse cheerfully on other subjects. His unyielding, unconquerable spirit, laboring under most discouraging difficulties, handicapped by age, comes as a rebuke to Wordsworth for yielding to fears concerning his own future lot, and inspires him with courage and resolution.

In this poem, and a number of others to be analyzed in this chapter, Wordsworth illustrates what he confesses in "The Prelude":

> When I began to enquire,
> To watch and question those I met, and speak
> Without reserve to them, the lonely roads
> Were open schools in which I daily read
> With most delight the passions of mankind,
> Whether by words, looks, sighs, or tears, revealed;
> There saw into the depth of human souls,
> Souls that appear to have no depth at all
> To careless eyes.[1]

In the leech-gatherer he finds a man of indomitable will, carrying on his work bravely, though bowed with age, though obliged to walk far and wide, to meet hazardous situations, and to behold ever-dwindling returns for his labor. In Michael, the peasant, as we have seen, he finds a strength of love that makes things endurable, "which else would overset the brain, or break the heart." In Leonard, the orphan boy, he finds an example of self-sacrificing, brotherly love that leads him to give up all and brave all in behalf of another. In poor Margaret, as we shall soon see, he finds a fidelity of heart that makes a mother's love consume her very life in mourning for her lost son. And so we meet in his poetry with numerous examples which illustrate the fact that Wordsworth is teaching the lessons he learned from lowly folk, and is carrying out the resolution referred to in "The Prelude":

[1] The Prelude, XIII, 160–168.

Of these, said I, shall be my song; of these,
If future years mature me for the task,
Will I record the praises, making verse
Deal boldly with substantial things; in truth
And sanctity of passion, speak of these,
That justice may be done, obeisance paid
Where it is due: thus haply shall I teach,
Inspire; through unadulterated ears
Pour rapture, tenderness, and hope, — my theme
No other than the very heart of man,
As found among the best of those who live.[1]

What loftier subject for poetry could he have than these elemental passions and basic virtues, the exercise of which give life worth, and without which society could not exist?

To these subjects Wordsworth could and did give genuine poetic treatment. He had sufficient imagination to accomplish the task. As Professor Raleigh says concerning this poem "Resolution and Independence," referring to its dramatic action: "The management of it shows Wordsworth at his greatest. He had not loved and studied Nature in vain. The man is compared to certain natural appearances which have something of mystery and dignity about them — to a huge boulder, deposited, none knows how, on a hill-top — to a slow-moving cloud, seen from afar, untroubled by the tumult of the winds — to a sea-beast that has crawled out of its native element to taste the strange warmth of the sun. Before he delivers his message the Leech-gatherer is felt to be 'a man from some far region sent.' And when he has delivered his message, the old pauper on the lonely moor has won a place beside the great heroic figures of history, or epic, or drama." [2]

"The Affliction of Margaret ——," composed in 1804 and published in 1807, is another of these intensely human portraits. It is a story of a widow mourning for her lost son. Like other poems, it was founded on fact, which is used as a basis for idealization. It was taken, says Wordsworth, "from the case of a poor widow who lived in the

[1] The Prelude, XIII, 232–242.   [2] Raleigh, Wordsworth, 183.

town of Penrith. Her sorrow was well known to Mrs. Wordsworth, to my sister, and, I believe, to the whole town. She kept a shop, and when she saw a stranger passing by, she was in the habit of going out into the street to enquire of him after her son." [1] In the poem Margaret bewails her loss, not knowing whether her son is living or dead, and utters a plaintive plea for his return. Wordsworth portrays with unusual skill, and in beautiful verse, her mental distress. The afflicted woman is almost overcome by her ignorance concerning the young man's whereabouts. It breeds all sorts of misgivings and fears. Her imagination tortures her with horrible pictures of the possible fate that may have befallen him:

> Perhaps some dungeon hears thee groan,
> Maimed, mangled by inhuman men;
> Or thou upon a desert thrown
> Inheritest the lion's den;
> Or hast been summoned to the deep,
> Thou, thou and all thy mates, to keep
> An incommunicable sleep. [2]

Receiving no earthly tidings, she looks for tidings from another world. If he be dead, possibly his ghost may appear; but she finds no truth in the belief that man may have intercourse with the dead. She gains no sight of him for whom she waits day and night, "with love and longings infinite." Her mental condition gives rise to manifold apprehensions:

> My apprehensions come in crowds;
> I dread the rustling of the grass;
> The very shadows of the clouds
> Have power to shake me as they pass;
> I question things and do not find
> One that will answer to my mind;
> And all the world appears unkind. [3]

And then comes the climax of her sorrow. It is hinted at, indeed, in the last line of the verse just quoted. She begins to experience

---

[1] Poetical Works, edited by William Knight, III, 7 n.
[2] The Affliction of Margaret ——, 50–56.   [3] Ibid., 64–70.

that spiritual isolation which is the curse of profound grief. She is
brought to realize in her extremity that each heart knows its *own*
bitterness; that it cannot be shared with or by another :

> Beyond participation lie
> My troubles, and beyond relief:
> If any chance to heave a sigh,
> They pity me, and not my grief.
> Then come to me, my Son, or send
> Some tidings that my woes may end;
> I have no other earthly friend![1]

Here is a poet who knows the human heart. He has sounded
its depths. He is acquainted with grief, which, more than anything else, reveals the abysmal deeps of the spirit. He knows
the passions of the soul, not in their superficial tumult, but in
their profound undercurrents. It is poems like this, and like
" Ruth, " " Michael," " The Brothers," and the sad tale of the
ruined cottage, as told in " The Excursion," that demonstrate how
truly Wordsworth is the poet of Man. He seems to have a remarkable insight into human nature. He knows a father's heart,
as, for example, in " Michael," " The Two April Mornings," and
" The Fountain." He knows a mother's heart, as is seen in " The
Affliction of Margaret——." He knows a brother's heart, as is
manifest in " The Brothers." He knows a lover's heart, as is indicated in " Ruth." He knows the heart of Man — its fundamental
fears and loves, its joys and sorrows, its virtues and vices, as is
illustrated in the large body of verse concerning Man already
considered, and as will be further manifest in the churchyard
biographies related in " The Excursion." Had Wordsworth dealt
with the human heart in all of his poetry as he has dealt with it
in these poems, no critic worthy of consideration could have found
reasonable fault with him. But, to quote Professor Raleigh again,
referring to " The Affliction of Margaret——," " Poetry like this
is not to be produced voluminously in a single lifetime."[2] In his
best poetry of Man the true Wordsworth is seen, and, as seen from

[1] The Affliction of Margaret ——, 71–77.   [2] Raleigh, Wordsworth, 36.

this point of view, he towers high above his brother-poets. He is a keen mental observer, a spiritual psychologist, with profound sympathies that aid his insight, and lead him to deal with human sorrow in such a manner as to bring calm and healing to the souls of men. In reading these compositions one can understand what he meant when he said to Lady Beaumont, " To be incapable of a feeling of poetry, in my sense of the word, is to be without love of human nature and reverence for God."

In view of this remarkable poem, and others of similar import already considered, it is difficult to understand the oft-repeated objection, that Wordsworth's poetry lacks passion. Here is pathos, and passion of the noblest character, intense and profound, but restrained. It does not storm the human breast, and becloud the mind. It is passion subject to rational control that is to be found here, as in most of Wordsworth's poetry of Man. " It was part of his faith, a main article of his moral creed, that ' the Gods approve the depth and not the tumult of the soul ' ; and that ' passion itself is highest reason in a soul sublime.' " [1]

We see in such pictures that this period, dating from his coming to Grasmere Vale down to 1808, was one in which the intensely human side of Wordsworth was wide awake, and had much to do in superinducing a poetic mood in which his feelings, imagination, and reflection centered in Man. He still sings, not of the high and mighty, but, as of old, of lowly folk, the humblest of mankind, and the result is the production of some of his best verse. However, during these years he dealt not only with human nature as illustrated in particular individuals or characters, but also with Man's social and political condition. He writes poems which evince a deep interest in the social and political events and conditions of his time. In them a genuine humanity and patriotism are manifest. He betrays not only a love for his own people and country, but also a true cosmopolitan spirit. A number of these poems seem to have been inspired by a visit to Calais in 1802, when political

[1] Hudson, Studies in Wordsworth, 116

conditions were in sharp contrast with the promise and hope of a previous visit. To his mind they evidently did not augur well. He also seems anxious about the effect of conditions there on his own country because of the close proximity of France to England. He fears the power of Napoleon, and is anxious about the threatened liberties of the people. Not only political but social conditions disturb him, especially as they exist in England. The increase of wealth has been attended by an increase in the complexity of life, and by a commercializing and materializing tendency. This mental state gives rise to two well-known sonnets, which are among his best. In one, "O Friend! I know not which way I must look," the "vanity and parade" of his country is lamented, and a feeling expressed that the march of wealth is productive of mischief. The greater sonnet of the two, the famous sonnet on Milton, shows him in despair over the state of things at home :

> Milton! thou shouldst be living at this hour:
> England hath need of thee: she is a fen
> Of stagnant waters: altar, sword, and pen,
> Fireside, the heroic wealth of hall and bower,
> Have forfeited their ancient English dower
> Of inward happiness. We are selfish men;
> Oh! raise us up, return to us again;
> And give us manners, virtue, freedom, power.[1]

But such words are sometimes supplanted by others which breathe a stronger faith and hope, especially with reference to politics, as in the sonnet, "It is not to be thought of that the Flood," wherein he says that it is impossible to think of British freedom perishing in "bogs and sands," and in the sonnet, "When I have borne in memory what has tamed," in which he expresses shame for his "unfilial fears," and shows his appreciation of England as "a bulwark for the cause of men."

Anxious moods, however, seem to predominate, as they often will with a patriotic observer of events, and especially with the patriotic poet whose sensitive soul is full of a strong love of freedom. As a

---

[1] Milton! thou shouldst be living at this hour, 1–8.

consequence, there are still other sonnets dedicated to liberty, or, as he puts it later, to " National Independence." Napoleon's sway and ambitious projects seem to be a disturbing influence with him. Most of these sonnets are born of his observations and reflections concerning the movements of the French " Tyrant." The sonnets " One might believe that natural miseries," " There is a bondage worse, far worse, to bear," "These times strike monied worldlings with dismay," " England! the time is come when thou shouldst wean," and " When looking on the present face of things" reveal his state of mind so far as events of the time are concerned. " To the Men of Kent," " In the Pass of Killicranky," " Lines on the Expected Invasion," and "Anticipation" are poems written really in anticipation of a possible, if not indeed a probable, invasion of England by Napoleon. The French conqueror had amassed a large army for this purpose, and the English people were on fire with patriotic zeal to defend their land and liberties. It was natural that such a liberty-loving poet as Wordsworth should celebrate in advance, by anticipation, the inevitable result of such an attempt on the part of the French ruler.

We have another evidence of Wordsworth's humanity in "Lines" composed in September, 1806, in expectation of the death of Charles James Fox, Minister for Foreign Affairs. Professor Knight, in a note appended to the poem, says : " Wordsworth's sadness on this occasion, his recognition of Fox as great and good, and as 'a Power' that was 'passing from the earth,' may have been due partly to personal and political sympathy, but also probably to Fox's appreciation of the better side of the French Revolution, and to his welcoming the pacific proposals of Talleyrand, perhaps also to his efforts for the abolition of slavery." [1] In this year matters reached a crisis with England. Napoleon had conquered the Germans. Another power had been laid low, and on November 21 of this year he issued a decree for the blockade of England. Wordsworth, as a consequence, writes another sonnet " dedicated

[1] Poetical Works, edited by William Knight, IV, 48–49 n.

to Liberty," entitled "November, 1806," in which he recognizes the fact that England's safety now depends upon herself, and again anticipates rejoicing over victory,

> if they who rule the land
> Be men who hold its many blessings dear,
> Wise, upright, valiant; not a servile band,
> Who are to judge of danger which they fear,
> And honour which they do not understand.[1]

If many of the "Poems dedicated to National Independence and Liberty" are to be fully understood, they must be read in the light of the spirit of the times — the social and political movements of the age; otherwise we shall miss their true import. Furthermore, they must be read with a consciousness that we are dealing with a poet whose heart is close to Man — who views events with a liberty-loving eye and soul, with a heart that throbs not only with a profound love for his own country, and its free institutions, but with a universal love, a love for Man as Man. Poet of Nature that he is — as much so, if indeed not more so, during his residence in Grasmere Vale than at any other time in his whole career — he is also the poet of Man, with a deep and abiding interest in those conditions which make for social and political welfare. In his soul sounds "the still sad music of humanity," and his poet's heart and mind are enlisted in the service of humanity's sacred cause.

[1] November, 1806, 10-14.

CHAPTER XII

GRASMERE (CONTINUED). "THE PRELUDE." "ODE TO DUTY." "CHARACTER OF THE HAPPY WARRIOR"

If we could place no further work to Wordsworth's credit, during his residence in Grasmere Vale, than the poems already considered, they would bear testimony to the fertility of his genius, and are of sufficient number and quality to give him a recognized place in English poetry. But, as a matter of fact, they do not represent the greater part of his work during this period, nor his most important contributions to literature. A large part of his time and effort was spent on more ambitious productions, some of which, at least, constitute a fair measure of his claim to immortality. The productions referred to include the autobiographical poem "The Prelude"; the famous "Ode to Duty"; the well-known poem "Character of the Happy Warrior"; and the great "Ode. Intimations of Immortality from Recollections of Early Childhood." These poems throw a bright light on the development of Wordsworth, both as a poet of Nature and as a poet of Man. They are important, too, not only from the standpoint of his personal psychology, but also as giving an insight into the content of his philosophic faith. Therefore they call for careful examination, and a strict regard for chronology requires that we begin with "The Prelude."

As far back at least as the Racedown days Wordsworth had in mind the composition, sooner or later, of a work that should really be his *magnum opus* — a work of large scope, more or less philosophical in character, and having for its subject, "Nature, Man, and Society." In a letter written to James Losh, in 1798, he says: "I have written 706 lines of a poem which I hope to make of considerable utility. Its title will be, The Recluse, or Views of Nature, Man, and Society." [1] According to the Bishop of Lincoln, Coleridge wrote to Wordsworth in the summer of 1799, urging him to steady work on "The Recluse." He says, "I am anxiously eager to have you steadily employed on 'The Recluse.'" [2] Again, as was stated in a previous chapter, Coleridge writes to him at Sockburne, October 12, 1799, saying: "I long to see what you have been doing. O let it be the tail-piece of 'The Recluse,' for of nothing but 'The Recluse' can I hear patiently. That it is to be addressed to me makes me more desirous that it should not be a poem of itself. To be addressed, as a beloved man, by a thinker, at the close of such a poem as 'The Recluse,' a poem *non unius populi*, is the only event, I believe, capable of inciting in me an hour's vanity — vanity, nay, it is too good a feeling to be so called; it would indeed be a self-elevation produced *ab extra*." [3] In still another letter, dated December, 1799, he writes from London, saying, "I grieve that 'The Recluse' sleeps." [4] Again, at the close of the fragment "The Recluse," which records the journey of Wordsworth and Dorothy to Grasmere Vale, and their settlement there, we find these words:

> Yet in this peaceful Vale we will not spend
> Unheard of days, though loving, peaceful thoughts.
> A voice shall speak, and what will be the theme? [5]

The theme is indicated in a manuscript note, published in 1814:

> On Man, on Nature, and on Human Life
> Musing in Solitude. [6]

Wordsworth himself, in his preface to "The Excursion," published in 1814, explains the relation of "The Prelude" to this elaborate poem. His explanation throws much light on the entire scheme. In it he says: "Several years ago, when the Author retired to his native mountains, with the hope of being enabled to construct a

---

[1] Knight, The Life of William Wordsworth, I, 148.   [2] Ibid., 195.
[3] Ibid., 201.   [4] Ibid., 202.   [5] Ibid., 254.   [6] Ibid., 254 n.

literary Work that might live, it was a reasonable thing that he should take a review of his own mind, and examine how far Nature and Education had qualified him for such employment. As subsidiary to this preparation, he undertook to record, in verse, the origin and progress of his own powers, as far as he was acquainted with them. That Work, addressed to a dear Friend, most distinguished for his knowledge and genius, and to whom the Author's Intellect is deeply indebted, has been long finished; and the result of the investigation which gave rise to it was a determination to compose a philosophical poem, containing views of Man, Nature, and Society; and to be entitled, 'The Recluse'; as having for its principal subject the sensations and opinions of a poet living in retirement. — The preparatory poem is biographical, and conducts the history of the Author's mind to the point when he was emboldened to hope that his faculties were sufficiently matured for entering upon the arduous labour which he had proposed to himself; and the two Works have the same kind of relation to each other, if he may so express himself, as the ante-chapel has to the body of a Gothic church. Continuing this allusion, he may be permitted to add, that his minor Pieces, which have been long before the Public, when they shall be properly arranged, will be found by the attentive Reader to have such connection with the main work as may give them claim to be likened to the little cells, oratories, and sepulchral recesses, ordinarily included in those edifices." [1]

It is manifest here that the elaborate work "The Recluse" was to consist of three parts, and the autobiographical poem was to constitute the introduction. But "The Recluse," as originally planned, was never finished. "The Excursion," however, which represents the second part, was completed. The First Part of the First Book of "The Recluse" was left in manuscript, and the Third Part was merely planned. "The materials of which it would have been formed, have, however, been incorporated, for the most

[1] The Poetical Works of William Wordsworth, edited by Thomas Hutchinson, 754

part, in the Author's other publications, written subsequently to 'The Excursion.'"[1]

We have already observed that Wordsworth was at work on "The Prelude" in Germany in 1799. This work was continued at intervals during his residence in Town-end, Grasmere Vale, until the poem was completed, in 1805. Eleven of the fourteen books were composed before 1805; the remaining three were completed before June of the same year.[2]

The poem was addressed to Coleridge, who felt greatly pleased and complimented because of the honor thus conferred upon him. After hearing a recitation of the poem, he saw his friend "in the choir of ever-enduring men." The deep impression made upon him is evident in the last verse of his own poem "To William Wordsworth; Composed on the Night after his Recitation of a Poem on the Growth of an Individual Mind":

> And when — O Friend! my comforter and guide!
> Strong in thyself, and powerful to give strength! —
> Thy long-sustained Song finally closed,
> And thy deep voice had ceased — yet thou thyself
> Wert still before my eyes, and round us both
> That happy vision of beloved faces —
> Scarce conscious, and yet conscious of its close
> I sate, my being blended in one thought
> (Thought was it? or aspiration? or resolve?)
> Absorbed, yet hanging still upon the sound —
> And when I rose I found myself in prayer.[3]

The nature of "The Prelude" is indicated in its sub-title, which reads — "Or, Growth of a Poet's Mind; an Autobiographical Poem." In it Wordsworth traces the development of his own mind as a poet. It is invaluable, therefore, in throwing light on his evolution both as a poet of Nature and as a poet of Man. We have already considered it at length in making it in a measure the

---

[1] Poetical Works, edited by William Knight, III, 122 n.

[2] Cf. The Poetical Works of William Wordsworth, edited by Thomas Hutchinson, p. xxviii.

[3] Poetical Works, edited by William Knight, III, 131 n.

foundation of our study of Wordsworth's mental and spiritual development up to the point in his history where he more or less formally enters upon his career as a poet, and we have noted the forces at work with his spirit, as he himself describes them, and also his conceptions of Nature and Man, and their relations as therein contained. The elaborate poem, therefore, does not call for further analysis or consideration here, more than to say that there is the same lack of definiteness in regard to Wordsworth's real conception of Nature that we find elsewhere. All the different modes of his apprehending her are brought out. It is the Presences of Nature that are addressed in Book I of "The Prelude," [1] when he is speaking of the unique experiences of his boyhood. On the other hand, it is of Nature and her overflowing soul that he speaks in Book II,[2] when reviewing the development of his mind during the Hawkshead days. Again, it is to natural objects that, in Book III, he attributes *moral life* when he is a student at Cambridge:

> To every natural form, rock, fruit, or flower,
> Even the loose stones that cover the high-way,
> I gave a moral life.[3]

But on the other hand, he adds,

> the great mass
> Lay bedded in a quickening soul.[4]

In Books VII [5] and VIII [6] it is the Spirit of Nature conceived of as one Spirit that is with him in London and that grants him there the poet's vision of Man. It is of things pervaded by a Spirit of which he speaks in the opening lines of Book XII. It is the "Soul of Nature" that is addressed in the same book when he refers to her relations to him as a boy, and also in the comparison of his weakness with her strength in later years.[7] It is of Nature conceived as a unitary being, and as the inspirer of emotions and moods, that he speaks in the opening lines of Book XIII. In

---

[1] The Prelude, I, 464 f.   [2] Ibid., II, 397 f.   [3] Ibid., III, 127–129.
[4] Ibid., III, 130–131. [5] Ibid., VII, 765 f. [6] Ibid., VIII, 679 f. [7] Ibid., XII, 93 f.

other words, throughout " The Prelude " Nature is spoken of as
things and places animated either by an all-pervading Spirit or by
spirits of their own. His dominant conception, however, is that
Nature is something like Man in his constitution as body-mind or
body-soul. Nature is body possessed of Soul. There is a Spiritual
Presence in things — a conscious spiritual Life, which animates
all objects. It pulsates in the clod ; it breathes in the rock ; it mur-
murs in the brook ; it throbs in the sea ; it moves in the cloud ;
it inhabits the stars ; it rolls in all things, and is the Soul of all ;
it is the " Wisdom and Spirit of the universe," the " eternity of
thought," that gives " to forms and images a breath and everlasting motion," and it is in touch with the spirit of Man as a
teacher, consoler, and guide.

From " The Prelude " we turn to the " Ode to Duty " (composed
in 1805), a poem, of course, of ethical import. Here may be found
Wordsworth's conception of the nature of Man in his highest
endowment. It is of interest also because of the Poet's view of
the ultimate source of Duty, and of his belief in the physical world
as governed by moral law. It is evident from the beginning of
the poem that he considers this ultimate source to be objective.
It lies outside of the human soul. In the magisterial conception
with which the poem opens he figuratively calls Duty the " Stern
Daughter of the Voice of God," just as certain ethical writers are
accustomed to represent conscience as the Voice of the Deity. Its
function, according to Wordsworth, is to guide Man, to check the
erring, to reprove, to guard, and to calm us in " the weary strife of
frail humanity."

But Duty also seems to be a Power in Nature, a Power " that
preserves the stars from wrong "— that strengthens the very heavens
themselves.

> Stern Lawgiver ! yet thou dost wear
> The Godhead's most benignant grace ;
> Nor know we anything so fair
> As is the smile upon thy face :
> Flowers laugh before thee on their beds

> And fragrance in thy footing treads;
> Thou dost preserve the stars from wrong;
> And the most ancient heavens, through
> Thee, are fresh and strong.[1]

Of course this might be regarded merely as a highly poetic and figurative way of conceiving Duty; just as, by the saying that the stars in their courses fight for a man who is in the right, we represent the order of the physical universe as a moral order. All of this carries with it, at least impliedly, a belief in the universe as grounded in righteousness. But in Wordsworth's "Ode to Duty" more than this seems to be meant. It must be remembered that we have repeatedly found the Poet conceiving of the Spirit of Nature from the moral point of view. Its ministry to Man is largely a *moral* ministry. It builds up and fashions his soul largely through *moral* warnings, appeals, suggestions, and inspirations. We have seen, too, how Wordsworth regards Nature as a teacher imparting lessons of sublime ethical import; also, how we "frame the measure of our souls" from the "blessed power that rolls about, below, above." Again, it has been noted how the Spirit of Nature is a Spirit of Love, which binds the world of things and the world of men into one spiritual kingdom; and, further, how it exercises a kind of providence over the animal world, visiting its displeasure upon Man for his inhumanity to the brute creation. We have observed, also, how this Spirit, so moral in its offices, is the Spirit

> Whose dwelling is the light of setting suns,
> And the round ocean and the living air,
> And the blue sky, and in the mind of man:
> A motion and a spirit, that impels
> All thinking things, all objects of all thought,
> And rolls through all things,[2]

and that the Poet, who had often been the object of its gracious ministry, says:

[1] Ode to Duty, 41–48.
[2] Lines composed a few miles above Tintern Abbey, 97–102.

Therefore am I . . . well pleased to recognise
In nature and the language of the sense
The anchor of my purest thoughts, the nurse,
The guide, the guardian of my heart, and soul
Of all my moral being.[1]

It appears, therefore, that Wordsworth, in this majestic ode, has really something more in mind than what ordinarily might be regarded as a highly poetic representation of the moral law in its relation to his own spirit, or, more generally speaking, to the spirit of Man, as well as in its relation to the so-called physical world. He seems, in short, to identify Duty with the voice of the omnipresent Spirit which, in this poem, he calls God. However, it is not meant by this interpretation that the Poet conceives God merely as the moral order of the universe, as is the case with Fichte and others. What he really means is, that all law, whether governing souls or things, is, in the final analysis, *moral* law. The Power that upholds the human world, as well as the Power that holds the stars in their courses, is a Power that makes for righteousness. It is the " nurse," " guide," and " anchor " of our purest thoughts —the very soul of our moral being, and it is also the Power that "preserves the stars from wrong," through which "the most ancient heavens are fresh and strong." It is, according to our Poet, a personal Power, whose " voice " is Nature's law, as well as the measure of Man's moral spirit.

The poem " Character of the Happy Warrior," dated 1806, was probably written in the latter part of 1805. It needs recognition here only because of the light that it throws on the human side of Wordsworth's genius, and on the genuine patriotism of the man, as well as presenting, in a large measure, his ethical view of the life of a true warrior, and his exalted ideal of what a servant of the nation should be. It therefore deals with Man. The poem is a description of an ideal soldier and was suggested by the death of Lord Nelson. He informs us in a prefatory note, however, that Nelson's

---

[1] Lines composed a few miles above Tintern Abbey, 107–111.

" public life was stained with one great crime, so that though many passages of these lines were suggested by what was generally known as excellent in his conduct, I have not been able to connect his name with the poem as I could wish, or even to think of him with satisfaction in reference to the idea of what a warrior ought to be." [1] He further states that he found in his sailor brother, Captain John Wordsworth, many of the qualities portrayed in the poem. Wordsworth very seldom takes one who is conspicuous in the public eye, or exalted in position, as the object or hero of his poems. Lord Nelson constitutes one of the few exceptions to the rule, and even here the noble poem could not be completely devoted to him. The Poet, true to his habit of mind, falls back upon a modest and more or less obscure character as the exemplar of many of the noblest qualities which the poem portrays. Even here he seems to find the best elements of our humanity illustrated in one of humble nature and station. The poem is a "manual of greatness," as Mr. Myers suggests, and an analysis will reveal what qualities are included in it:

Who is the happy warrior, according to Wordsworth ? He is the man of generosity, whose high endeavors guide him ; who is diligent to learn ; who makes his moral being his prime care ; who turns suffering to gain ; who is compassionate and placable, pure and tender, and makes Reason his law ; who rises to high position by open means, and will stand there honorably or retire ; who understands his trust, and stands faithful to it ; whose powers shed a gracious influence about him ; who meets tremendous issues with the joyousness of a lover ; who abides by the law in the midst of conflict, and proves equal to the need of any call. Who is the happy warrior ? He who, though fitted for great and turbulent things, is predisposed to quiet and peace ; who, whether in high or low station, conspicuous or obscure in life, plays the game under favorable or unfavorable circumstances, " where what he most doth value must be won " ; who surmounts fear of danger, nor is betrayed by tender happiness. The happy warrior is the optimist, who confidently

---

[1] Poetical Works, edited by William Knight, IV, 7 n.

looks ahead, ever pressing forward from good to better, making daily progress; who, whether he be destined to earthly applause, or to sink into his grave unknown, finds comfort in himself and in his cause, and in the hour of death confidently awaits the applause of Heaven.

The "Character of the Happy Warrior" should be read in connection with Wordsworth's "Poems dedicated to National Independence and Liberty," in which he often points out what the character of a nation's public servants should be. All of these poems breathe an earnest patriotism, and many of them illustrate the Poet's deep devotion to the best interests of the State, and therefore to Man, as well as his lofty conception of the ideals which ought to control those who govern. Man existing under Government seems to be an engaging theme with Wordsworth, and the political conditions of his time impel him to song. Occasionally we have poems of denunciation, as in the sonnets on Napoleon, and the traitorous Elector of Saxony. Again, there are songs of praise, as in the case of the poems on Charles James Fox, the leader of Parliament, and Lord Nelson, the hero of Trafalgar. Sometimes his song is one of lament over prevailing conditions, and there are notes of anxious fear because of the trend of events; and again, there are songs of hope, with a trumpet call to the brave to stand fast for liberty, and courageously do the duty of the hour. Sometimes he beholds the persistent triumph of wrong, and his faith in God almost gives way, as is evident in the sonnet "October, 1803"; again, faith looks through the clouds and darkness and gains a vision of the ultimate victory of right. Our Poet, despite the beauty of Grasmere Vale, which so persistently enchants him, is not, during these stirring years, merely the poet of Nature, but also the poet of Man, in close touch with him in the humble walks of life, and keeping his eye fixed upon the great social and political issues of the time, solicitous for his well-being — an ardent patriot, guarding with zealous interests the liberties of his own country, and continuing, as of old, "a patriot of the world."

CHAPTER XIII

GRASMERE (CONCLUDED). "ODE. INTIMATIONS OF IMMORTALITY"

From the preceding chapters relating to Wordsworth's life in the delightful Vale of Grasmere it is evident that with him it was a period of great mental activity. It witnessed the composition of a large number of poems, many of which may be regarded as among the finest products of his imagination. Most of them have already been considered. However, one remains which, in the judgment of some critics, more than any other poem of the numerous creations of his genius, entitles him to a seat among the Immortals. This is the celebrated "Ode. Intimations of Immortality from Recollections of Early Childhood," composed 1803–1806. It is, in some respects, one of his most important works, whether viewed from the standpoint of mere art, or from that of poetic insight. Professor Knight says : "Mr. Aubrey De Vere has urged me to take it out of its chronological place, and let it conclude the whole series of Wordsworth's poems, as the greatest, and that to which all others lead up. Mr. De Vere's wish is based on conversations which he had with the poet himself." [1] We have in the ode a description of the trance to which he was subject, with its revelation, and, in a measure, the history of the growth and development of his own mind up to a certain period in his life — in all of which he appears to think his own experience to be representative of that of men in general. The personal psychology and philosophy of mind presented, with their epistemological and ontological implications, are exceedingly interesting. Special attention must be given to these features of the poem, because of their bearing on the Poet's conception of corporeal things, and of the ultimate

[1] Poetical Works, edited by William Knight, VIII, 199 n.

nature of Reality. There is presented, also, Wordsworth's apparent belief in the soul's preëxistence, as well as significant intimations of its immortality. This great ode is a poem which, in the final analysis, deals with Nature and Man.

In an interesting note to Miss Fenwick the Poet says: "This was composed during my residence at Town-end, Grasmere. Two years at least passed between the writing of the four first stanzas and the remaining part. To the attentive and competent reader the whole sufficiently explains itself; but there may be no harm in adverting here to particular feelings or *experiences* of my own mind on which the structure of the poem partly rests. Nothing was more difficult for me in childhood than to admit the notion of death as a state applicable to my own being. I have said elsewhere—

> A simple child,
> That lightly draws its breath,
> And feels its life in every limb,
> What should it know of death!—

But it was not so much from feelings of animal vivacity that my difficulty came as from a sense of the indomitableness of the Spirit within me. I used to brood over the stories of Enoch and Elijah, and almost to persuade myself that, whatever might become of others, I should be translated, in something of the same way, to heaven. With a feeling congenial to this, I was often unable to think of external things as having external existence, and I communed with all that I saw as something not apart from, but inherent in, my own immaterial nature. Many times while going to school have I grasped at a wall or tree to recall myself from this abyss of idealism to the reality. At that time I was afraid of such processes. In later periods of life I have deplored, as we have all reason to do, a subjugation of an opposite character, and have rejoiced over the remembrances, as is expressed in the lines—

> Obstinate questionings
> Of sense and outward things,
> Fallings from us, vanishings, etc.

To that dream-like vividness and splendour which invest objects of sight in childhood, every one, I believe, if he would look back, could bear testimony, and I need not dwell upon it here; but having in the poem regarded it as presumptive evidence of a prior state of existence, I think it right to protest against a conclusion, which has given pain to some good and pious persons, that I meant to inculcate such a belief. It is far too shadowy a notion to be recommended to faith, as more than an element in our instincts of immortality. But let us bear in mind that, though the idea is not advanced in revelation, there is nothing there to contradict it, and the fall of man presents an analogy in its favour. Accordingly, a pre-existent state has entered into the popular creeds of many nations; and, among all people acquainted with classic literature, is known as an ingredient in Platonic philosophy. Archimedes said that he could move the world if he had a point whereon to rest his machine. Who has not felt the same aspirations as regards the world of his own mind? Having to wield some of its elements when I was impelled to write this poem on the ' Immortality of the Soul,' I took hold of the notion of pre-existence as having sufficient foundation in humanity for authorizing me to make for my purpose the best use of it I could as a poet." [1]

Wordsworth, although he says that he did not mean to *inculcate* the doctrine of preëxistence as an article of faith, seems strongly to incline to it as a personal conviction. It appears elsewhere in his poetry, and constitutes the very basis of the ode on immortality. It receives a quasi-indorsement in his conception of childhood, as brought out in " The Prelude," in which he says :

> Our childhood sits,
> Our simple childhood, sits upon a throne
> That hath more power than all the elements.
> I guess not what this tells of Being past,
> Nor what it augurs of the life to come. [2]

[1] Poetical Works, edited by William Knight, VIII, 189–190 n.
[2] The Prelude, V, 507–511.

In " The Excursion " he virtually affirms the doctrine. He asks :

> Ah ! why in age
> Do we revert so fondly to the walks
> Of childhood — but that there the Soul discerns
> The dear memorial footsteps unimpaired
> Of her own native vigour ; thence can hear
> Reverberations ; and a choral song,
> Commingling with the incense that ascends,
> Undaunted, toward the imperishable heavens,
> From her own lonely altar ? [1]

This must be borne in mind in interpreting the poem, which hinges so much on this conception and apparent belief.

The ode opens with a description of the Poet's childhood. There was a time, he says, referring to this early period, when the whole physical universe seemed clothed in celestial light, wearing the aspect of a vision or dream. But that time is no more. The dream has vanished. However beautiful the earth, and however fair all things may be, the Poet knows " there hath passed away a glory from the earth."

Then came a time of grief, due probably to a death in his family. However, he was called away from it, and is now sane, cheerful, and strong. He rejoices in the universal gladness of Nature. Nevertheless, there is still a consciousness of something gone. A tree, or field, or flower reminds him that the visionary gleam has vanished ; that the glory and the dream have passed away.

The Poet then begins to philosophize on this unique experience, which, apparently, in his opinion, is common to all. What does it signify ? Does it not imply that the ordinary conception of birth is erroneous ? It is neither creation nor derivation, but incarnation. The soul exists prior to its connection with the body. It comes to earth from another realm, although not in entire forgetfulness of its previous existence. It brings some of its wealth with it — some of its radiant glory and vision. God is the real home of the soul,

---

[1] The Excursion, IX, 36–44.

and from him as "trailing clouds of glory do we come." The body is its prison house, and not only is much of its original vision clouded by incarnation, but its radiance grows dimmer and dimmer as the earthly life advances. Human infancy is nearest to the Divine Glory. "Heaven lies about us in our infancy." The boy is farther away from it; yet the light is with him, and he beholds its Source. The youth is still farther removed; nevertheless, he is still the Priest of Nature, attended "by the vision splendid." Finally the man perceives its radiance "fade into the light of common day." This is an epitome of life. Undoubtedly, the Poet is here recording his own personal experience; and an experience which he believes to be common to the race. We have, also, his own philosophy of mind — or, if not a philosophy, at least the expression of an apparent conviction, based upon the unique psychical experiences described. How beautiful his words, and how definite his description, of the progress of the soul from the preëxistent state through its earthly career!

> Our birth is but a sleep and a forgetting:
> The Soul that rises with us, our life's Star,
>   Hath had elsewhere its setting,
>   And cometh from afar:
>   Not in entire forgetfulness,
>   And not in utter nakedness,
> But trailing clouds of glory do we come
>   From God, who is our home:
> Heaven lies about us in our infancy!
> Shades of the prison-house begin to close
>   Upon the growing Boy,
> But He beholds the light, and whence it flows,
>   He sees it in his joy;
> The Youth, who daily farther from the east
>   Must travel, still is Nature's Priest,
>   And by the vision splendid
>   Is on his way attended;
> At length the Man perceives it die away,
> And fade into the light of common day.[1]

[1] Ode. Intimations of Immortality from Recollections of Early Childhood, 58–76.

Nevertheless, the earth has its own pleasures and yearnings. She tries, with good purpose, to make her foster child forget, not only the glories of his former home, but even the home itself. The child soon begins to adjust himself to his new surroundings. He is possessed of fancy and imagination, and endeavors to realize his own mental creations — to devise some plan, " some fragment from his dream of human life"; to reproduce, after his own fashion, all phases of life, thus anticipating much of the actual experience which later years bring,

> As if his whole vocation
> Were endless imitation.[1]

But, why should he thus forecast and covet the earthly life? It will soon bring its weary burden to him. Why should he forsake the superior vision, and the blessedness of these early years, to live in imagination the conventional, burdensome life of the man? And what, according to Wordsworth, is the power of the soul in these early years, and what the blessedness of its hours? His answer gives an insight into his psychology of childhood. The small, feeble body of the child belies his soul's immensity. Not the man, but the child, is the best philosopher; who keeps his glorious heritage; who is the "eye among the blind." It is he who reads "the eternal deep," "haunted forever by the eternal mind." He is the prophet and seer who intuits those profound and vital truths which men toil a lifetime to find, lost in darkness — even the darkness of the grave. To the child immortality is an ever-present reality — brooding over him like the day. Stronger, too, is his grasp of fundamental truths than that of the full-grown man, and far superior, also, is his intellectual vision. Why, then, does he, so near to the radiant glory and truth of the past, look forward with the eye of imagination from the blessedness and freedom of these early years to a future, when the "inevitable yoke" of manhood will be placed upon his neck, and the weary burden of custom will weigh upon his soul?

[1] Ode. Intimations of Immortality from Recollections of Early Childhood, 106–107.

The thought of these years of childhood breeds in the Poet " perpetual benediction," and he raises the song of praise, not for the delight, freedom, and new-fledged hope which are so peculiar to these first years, but rather for the visionary dream which yields an ethereal world — for the trance that supplants the objective, corporeal world of sense with the subjective, unsubstantial and ideal world of soul — for those powerful intimations of a spiritual world behind the physical world ; those recollections of a prenatal day ; those intuitions of truths ; those visions of an Ideal, which, after all, is the truly Real.   The song of praise is raised

> for those obstinate questionings
> Of sense and outward things,
> Fallings from us, vanishings ;
> Blank misgivings of a Creature
> Moving about in worlds not realised,
> High instincts before which our mortal Nature
> Did tremble like a guilty Thing surprised :
> But for those first affections,
> Those shadowy recollections,
> Which, be they what they may,
> Are yet the fountain-light of all our day,
> Are yet a master-light of all our seeing ;
> Uphold us, cherish, and have power to make
> Our noisy years seem moments in the being
> Of the eternal Silence : truths that wake
> To perish never :
> Which neither listlessness, nor mad endeavour,
> Nor Man nor Boy,
> Nor all that is at enmity with joy,
> Can utterly abolish or destroy !
> Hence in a season of calm weather
> Though inland far we be,
> Our souls have sight of that immortal sea
> Which brought us hither,
> Can in a moment travel thither,
> And see the Children sport upon the shore,
> And hear the mighty waters rolling evermore.[1]

[1] Ode. Intimations of Immortality from Recollections of Early Childhood, 145-171.

These words must be carefully considered, as they are exceedingly significant in a study of Wordsworth as a poet of Nature and a poet of Man. Fortunately there are a number of recorded conversations which interpret them, although they do not embody a remarkably unique experience and view of Reality for the student of the history and psychology of religious or of philosophic and poetic mysticism, and the trance-vision so often intimately associated with it. We have already seen in his Fenwick note how, frequently, when going to school, Wordsworth had to grasp at a wall or a tree to recall himself from "this abyss of idealism to the reality." In a conversation with Reverend Robert Perceval Graves, of Windermere, he makes a similar statement. Mr. Graves, in a letter written in 1850 to Mr. Hawes Turner, editor of "Selections from Wordsworth," says : "I remember Mr. Wordsworth saying, that at a particular stage of his mental progress, he used to be frequently so rapt into an unreal transcendental world of ideas that the external world seemed no longer to exist in relation to him, and he *had to reconvince himself of its existence by clasping a tree, or something that happened to be near him.*" [1] Again, in a letter by Professor Bonamy Price to Mr. Turner, we find words of similar import. He says : "You will be glad, I am sure, to receive an interpretation, which chance enabled me to obtain from Wordsworth himself of a passage in the immortal 'Ode on Immortality.' . . . It happened one day that the poet, my wife, and I were taking a walk together by the side of Rydal Water. We were then by the sycamores under Nab Scar. The aged poet was in a most genial mood, and it suddenly occurred to me that I might, without unwarrantable presumption, seize the golden opportunity thus offered, and ask him to explain these mysterious words. So I addressed him with an apology, and begged him to explain, what my own feeble mother-wit was unable to unravel, and for which I had in vain sought the assistance of others, what were those 'fallings from us, vanishings,' for which, above all other things,

[1] Poems, edited by William Knight, VIII, 201 n.

he gave God thanks. The venerable old man raised his aged form erect, he was walking in the middle, and passed across me to a five-barred gate in the wall which bounded the road on the side of the lake. He clenched the top bar firmly with his right hand, pushed strongly against it, and then uttered these ever-memorable words : There was a time in my life when I had to push against something that resisted, to be sure that there was anything outside of me. I was sure of my own mind ; everything else fell away, and vanished into thought.' Thought, he was sure of ; matter for him, at the moment, was an unreality — nothing but a thought. Such natural spontaneous idealism has probably never been felt by any other man." [1]

It is evident from the foregoing that the words of Section IX of the ode refer to Wordsworth's trance-experience, which was a common occurrence with him when a boy — an experience in which his mind seemed to be submerged in a complete subjectivism, the objective world of sense falling away into unsubstantiality and unreality, leaving him merely the consciousness of his own mind, and its functioning in the form of thought, so-called matter itself being merely a form of thought.

But it will be noticed, also, in this ninth section, that not only do we have a revelation concerning the nature of being — an idealistic view of Reality — but also a revelation with respect to knowledge. Knowledge is *recollection*. We have " shadowy recollections " of Reality as viewed in the primal, prenatal state of the soul. These are "a master-light of all our seeing." Eternal, universal truths are awakened in us — truths that condition all our knowledge, that neither indifference, nor mad endeavor, nor all that is hostile to our happiness "can utterly abolish or destroy." They give us a profound sense of our nearness to God, so that the " noisy years " of our life seem but "moments in the being of the eternal Silence." They give us, also, a sense of our own eternity — a sight of an immortal sea on which we have sailed hither,

1 Poetical Works, edited by William Knight, VIII, 201-202 n.

whose ever-rolling waters are heard by the spirit of Man. In other words, the knowledge of the child consists largely of "shadowy recollections" of a previous state of existence. These remembrances grow more shadowy as we grow older; nevertheless, though far removed, we catch glimpses of that transcendent, supersensuous, preincarnate world which originally was, and, indeed, is still, our home. This childhood-vision is closely related to Wordsworth's poetic power, "the vision and the faculty divine" — to his mystical insight into things; hence its significance.

But the fading of childhood's vision does not depress the Poet. Rather will he rejoice. Its radiance and splendor are gone, but he will not grieve. Indeed, he will find strength

> in what remains behind;
> In the primal sympathy
> Which having been must ever be;
> In the soothing thoughts that spring
> Out of human suffering;
> In the faith that looks through death,
> In years that bring the philosophic mind.[1]

The vision that now rises before him has not the glory of the rosy vision of Man's dawn, but, through a mixture of lights and shades, it always has an atmosphere of hope. And concerning Nature, although she does not wear in maturer years the aspect of the "glory and the dream" of childhood, nevertheless her might is felt, and his love for her has grown stronger and richer. It has been humanized by "hearing oftentimes the still, sad music of humanity." To this he bears testimony in the last verse of the immortal ode:

> And O, ye Fountains, Meadows, Hills, and Groves,
> Forbode not any severing of our loves!
> Yet in my heart of hearts I feel your might;
> I only have relinquished one delight
> To live beneath your more habitual sway.
> I love the Brooks which down their channels fret,

[1] Ode. Intimations of Immortality from Recollections of Early Childhood, 184–190.

Even more than when I tripped lightly as they;
The innocent brightness of a new-born Day
    Is lovely yet;
The Clouds that gather round the setting sun
Do take a sober colouring from an eye
That hath kept watch o'er man's mortality;
Another race hath been, and other palms are won.
Thanks to the human heart by which we live,
Thanks to its tenderness, its joys, and fears,
To me the meanest flower that blows can give
Thoughts that do often lie too deep for tears.[1]

This supernormal experience of childhood seems intimately related to his poetic power, especially in its apprehension of Nature,
which is such a notable feature of his poetry, and it may be perti-
nently asked whether, indeed, it be not in a certain sense the gate-
way to a complete understanding of his ontology — his conception
of being. The conception of a universal spirit in Nature, emphasized by Wordsworth in such a manner as almost to cancel, at times,
the reality of a corporeal world, seems to have its roots in the
mysticism of his nature, which, not only in childhood, but later in
life, was often attended by these peculiar trance-experiences. In
them the bodily sense, through which we gain our vision of the
world of things, seems to be laid asleep, and the soul appears to be
plunged into the deeps of a subjective experience, with its ethereal
or dreamlike world, formed of materials of consciousness which
carry with them no extramental reference. In other words, what
we call the external, material world seems, in these trance-states,
as the Poet himself declares in the Fenwick note to the ode, to
have no reality. He says: " I was often unable to think of external things as having external existence, and I communed with all
that I saw as something not apart from, but inherent in, my own
immaterial nature."[2] And again, elsewhere in his conversation
with Mr. Graves, already referred to, he says that he was " frequently so rapt into an unreal transcendental world of ideas that the

[1] Ode. Intimations of Immortality from Recollections of Early Childhood,
191–207.   [2] Poetical Works, edited by William Knight, VIII, 189 n.

external world seemed no longer to exist in relation to him." [1]
Once more, he says to Mr. Price, as we have seen, that in these
experiences he was sure of his own mind; "everything else fell
away, and vanished into thought." [2]

Where such a conception attains to the dignity of a permanent
reasoned view of the external world, it is known in philosophy as
Subjective Idealism. However, up to this time it does not seem
to have been held by the Poet as a creed or permanent faith. It
is referred to in the ode only as an experience of childhood, and
in his Fenwick note, as well as in his remark to Mr. Graves
previously quoted, he shows that this was only a temporary experience, and that he put the trance-world to a test by clasping a wall
or a tree, or some other object, until he was convinced that an
objective world really existed. And in his remark to Mr. Price he
reveals the fact that he regarded the extramental world as, after
all, a *real world*. Only for the moment it was lost in a subjective
world of thought, which was the product of a mystical trance.

Nevertheless, he refers to it in such a way as to intimate that he
owes some sort of obligation to it. He rejoices in contemplating
the Past, and tells us why:

> O joy! that in our embers
> Is something that doth live,
> That nature yet remembers
> What was so fugitive!
> The thought of our past years in me doth breed
> Perpetual benediction. [3]

And he raises "the song of thanks and praise" for this thought of
past years, for this "something that doth live," for that which his
nature still remembers. And for what is he thankful? Not for
"the simple creed of Childhood" — delight and liberty — but for
the phenomena of that early trance-experience —

---

[1] Poetical Works, edited by William Knight, VIII, 201 n.   [2] Ibid., 202 n.
[3] Ode. Intimations of Immortality from Recollections of Early Childhood,
133–138.

> those obstinate questionings
> Of sense and outward things,
> Fallings from us, vanishings.[1]

An abiding impression seems to have been made — an impression concerning the ultimate nature of being, namely, that *matter* is not the true Reality. It seemed, indeed, to have no existence at all in these experiences. *Spirit* is the one great fact — the true and ultimately real thing. The corporeal world falls away at times; things vanish, but the thinking mind remains, and functions in such a way as to present to him a tremendously real world. Later in life this appears to have affected his views of the physical world, for his mysticism was with him many years. Dead, inert, material, or corporeal being is not the sum total of Nature. It had no claim to reality at all in those supreme moments of his childhood, and very shadowy claims, at best, in those " serene and blessed " moods of his soul of later years, when the bodily sense was laid asleep, and he was enabled to " see into the life of things." Nature is something more than lifeless substance ; it is matter endowed with Spirit.

It has been customary with certain critics to speak of Wordsworth's Platonism, especially in the doctrine of preëxistence, and much of this ode is cited as evidence. Plato presents this conception in a number of his works, but in the " Phædo "[2] it appears in its most interesting development. It is in the views as here presented that we specially find a similarity between his teachings and those of Wordsworth. The famous Greek philosopher represents Cebes, in a conversation with Socrates, as saying: "Your favorite doctrine, Socrates, that knowledge is simply recollection, if true, also necessarily implies a previous time in which we learned that which we now recollect. But this would be impossible unless our soul was in some place before existing in the human form."[3] Wordsworth's conception is, in some respects, the same. His doctrine of

---

[1] Ode. Intimations of Immortality from Recollections of Early Childhood, 145–147.   [2] 73–78 Stephanus.
[3] The Dialogues of Plato, translated by Jowett, I, 399

"shadowy recollections," which are "a master-light of all our seeing," is similar to Plato's view; but, with Wordsworth, these recollections grow dimmer as life advances; whereas Socrates, in Plato's "Phædo," seems to teach that the *recollection* of knowledge gained in a preëxistent state is a progressive process of our earthly life.

That Wordsworth was familiar with Plato's teachings on this point is evident from the Fenwick note already quoted. There, in defense of his own position, which seemed to have offended some "good and pious persons," he refers to the fact that a preëxistent state "is known as an ingredient in Platonic philosophy," as well as having "entered into the popular creeds of many nations." But this hardly warrants us in saying that he borrowed his doctrine from Plato. The roots of the Poet's conviction seem to have been imbedded in the subsoil of his trance-experiences of childhood, which gave him the consciousness of a world above, and more real than the natural world of sense. It is probable that this unique phenomenon of his mystical consciousness, in the presence of which he stood in great awe, constituted for him both a psychological and a philosophical problem, and that, in trying to interpret this experience to himself, and then to others, so far as it related to preëxistence, he found his conviction sanctioned by Plato. But the conviction itself appears *ultimately* to have had its origin in these unique experiences of childhood and youth, which were not only recalled, but repeated, in maturer years, although they did not then possess the vividness and splendor of the early trance. This explanation seems all the more probable because the consciousness of preëxistence is not unusual in the mystic's trance. Tennyson, for example, tells us that both preëxistence and immortality were present to consciousness in his trance-experiences as indubitable realities.[1]

Students of Wordsworth have also raised the question whether some of the thoughts in the ode may not have been inspired by those of Henry Vaughan, a seventeenth-century mystical poet. That

[1] Alfred, Lord Tennyson, A Memoir, by his Son, I, 320.

Wordsworth was acquainted with Vaughan's "Silex Scintillans" seems probable, as he owned a copy of it, and there is a similarity of thought in the two poets. Especially in the poem entitled "The Retreate" does Vaughan embody reflections to which those of Wordsworth's ode bear close resemblance. This will be manifest in comparing certain portions of the ode with Vaughan's poem:

> Happy those early dayes, when I
> Shin'd in my angell-infancy!
> Before I understood this place
> Appointed for my second race,
> Or taught my soul to fancy aught
> But a white, celestiall thought;
> When yet I had not walkt above
> A mile or two from my first love,
> And looking back, at that short space,
> Could see a glimpse of his bright face;
> When on some gilded cloud or flowre
> My gazing soul would dwell an houre,
> And in those weaker glories spy
> Some shadows of eternity;
> Before I taught my tongue to wound
> My conscience with a sinfull sound,
> Or had the black art to dispence
> A sev'rall sinne to ev'ry sence,
> But felt through all this fleshly dresse
> Bright shootes of everlastingnesse.
>   O how I long to travell back,
> And tread again that ancient track!
> That I might once more reach that plaine,
> Where first I left my glorious traine;
> From whence th' inlightned spirit sees
> That shady city of palme-trees.
> But ah! my soul with too much stay
> Is drunk, and staggers in the way!
> Some men a forward motion love,
> But I by backward steps would move;
> And when this dust falls to the urn,
> In that state I came — return.[1]

[1] The Sacred Poems and Private Ejaculations of Henry Vaughan, 86–87

We seem to be largely dependent upon internal evidence in trying to determine the relation between the two poets.[1] Wordsworth's thoughts are indeed similar to Vaughan's, but the similarity is not so striking as to warrant a positive statement that the later poet was influenced by the earlier. Both express apparent belief in the preëxistent state, and in the nearness of childhood to it; that we get farther away from its glory as we grow older; also, that certain things in this life give us hints of that previous life. Furthermore, both turn back with fond feelings to childhood, although Vaughan longs to go back and live it over again, while Wordsworth, in the ode, expresses no such desire. Both, too, express belief in immortality. However, in the case of beliefs so widely held as those of preëxistence and immortality, it must not be regarded as strange that such similarity should exist in the reflections of two poets, or as conclusive evidence that Wordsworth was familiar with Vaughan, especially since the external evidence bearing on the question is so feeble. If we are to be guided by internal evidence alone, we might, with equal justification, say that Wordsworth was influenced by Thomas Traherne, another seventeenth-century mystic. In some respects the ode resembles Traherne's poem "Wonder" more than any of Vaughan's. Especially is this so in the description of the world as it appears to the child-mind. To this must be added the similarity of views on preëxistence, and of views concerning changes that take place in the child's view of Nature as he advances in age. Thus Traherne exclaims:

> How like an angel came I down!
> How bright are all things here!
> When first among His works I did appear
> Oh how their Glory me did crown!
> The world resembled his *Eternity*,
> In which my soul did walk;
> And every thing that I did see
> Did with me talk.

[1] Wordsworth may have become acquainted with the English Neoplatonists while at Cambridge, or through Coleridge.

The skies in their magnificence,
　　The lively, lovely air,
Oh how divine, how soft, how sweet, how fair!
　　The stars did entertain my sense,
And all the works of God, so bright and pure,
　　So rich and great did seem,
　　As if they ever must endure
　　　　In my esteem.

.　　.　　.　　.　　.　　.　　.　　.　　.

The streets were paved with golden stones,
　　The boys and girls were mine,
Oh how did all their lovely faces shine!
　　The sons of men were holy ones,
In joy and beauty they appeared to me,
　　And every thing which here I found,
　　While like an angel I did see,
　　　　Adorned the ground.

Rich diamond and pearl and gold
　　In every place was seen;
Rare splendours, yellow, blue, red, white and green,
　　Mine eyes did everywhere behold.
Great Wonders clothed with glory did appear,
　　Amazement was my bliss,
　　That and my wealth was everywhere,
　　　　No joy to this!

Cursed and devised proprieties
　　With envy, avarice
And fraud, those fiends that spoil even Paradise,
　　Flew from the splendour of mine eyes.
And so did hedges, ditches, limits, bounds,
　　I dreamed not aught of those,
　　But wandered over all men's grounds,
　　　　And found repose.

Proprieties themselves were mine,
　　And hedges ornaments;
Walls, boxes, coffers, and their rich contents
Did not divide my joys, but all combine.

Clothes, ribbons, jewels, laces, I esteemed
    My joys by others worn:
For me they all to wear them seemed
    When I was born.[1]

In their views of childhood, also, Traherne and Wordsworth have
much in common. These views are the common property of mystical poets, and, in default of positive external evidence, it is the mark
of wisdom not to impose on Wordsworth an obligation to one or
more of the seventeenth-century poets which he may not owe. It
appears far more likely that his conceptions, as embodied in the
ode, had their genesis in his own mystical consciousness, and
especially in that unique form of its functioning which was present
with him in childhood, which seemed to transfigure the physical
world, and bring him into close contact with a transcendental world
of Spirit — which seemed to carry the mind back to a preincarnate
life; and that, if he was influenced at all by Vaughan and others,
it was only by way of confirmation of a belief which had already
grown out of his own personal experience.

The mystical mood of Wordsworth took on several forms. In its
exaggerated form it was a profound trance, in which the world of
material things is canceled, is superseded by a world that seems to
emanate from the depths of the soul's inner being — a transcendent, highly spiritualized world. This mood is often attended by
exalted states of feeling, even of rapture. The envisagement of
its content is so rich and intense that it carries with it a sublime
sense of its reality, and the world thus apprehended is so marvelous that the trance seems to be of the nature of an illumination
or revelation in which the very heart of Reality is unveiled. So
wonderful does it appear at times, that words fail in attempting to
describe it. It is ineffable. Wordsworth's trance-experience took
on this form more especially in childhood and youth. This mood,
which is not uncommon with philosophic and religious mystics, and

[1] The Poetical Works of Thomas Traherne, 1st edition, edited by Bertram
Dobell, 4–7.

occasionally with poetic mystics also, sometimes assumes a still
more extreme form, in which even the categories of thought appear
to be canceled, and the consciousness of self seems to be submerged
into a greater and more abstract consciousness. Among the philosophic mystics this may be seen in the Neoplatonists. Of the
religious mystics, it is not uncommon among Buddhists and Chris-
tians. Mystical poets, also, furnish striking illustrations of it, as
in the case of Tennyson.[1] Even Wordsworth, if we are to interpret
what is said of the Wanderer, in the first book of " The Excursion,"
as indicative of his own experience, was subject to this exaggerated
form. The vanishing of the so-called world of corporeal things was
not really the limit of the canceling power of his mysticism. In
his profoundest moods he seemed almost to lose his identity as a
self-conscious agent. The distinctions of thought were nearly oblit-
erated by the tremendous tide of rapturous feeling that sometimes
flooded his soul. This will be evident when we come to deal with
his description of the Wanderer's youth, in which the Poet is undoubtedly referring to his own personal experience.

The " saner " form of Wordsworth's mystical mood, however —
which, indeed, was the predominating one — did not abolish the
world of things, but enabled its subject to gain an insight into their
essential life. And this insight was attended by such a feeling of
reality that Nature, as possessed of Spirit, became with him an
abiding faith. It also brought him into such close, conscious relationship with this Spirit (apprehended as immanent not only in Nature,
but also in Man), that he seemed to divine its office as a fashioner,
guide, tutor, comforter, and moral preceptor to the soul. And the
apparent *realness* of his spiritual perception or intuition led him to
regard it as of the nature of a revelation. It was a spiritual illumination. So convinced was he of this, that he felt morally burdened
with a message which he had to speak to men. He felt that he
was to communicate not a mere fancy or dream, but a spiritual
vision or spiritual interpretation of the world. Probably the finest

---

[1] The Ancient Sage; see also Memoir, by his Son, I, 320, and II, 473.

description of this saner mysticism of the Poet, and the noblest expression of the faith to which it gave rise, is to be found in the "Lines composed a few miles above Tintern Abbey," where the mood is represented as

> that serene and blessed mood,
> In which the affections gently lead us on, —
> Until, the breath of this corporeal frame
> And even the motion of our human blood
> Almost suspended, we are laid asleep
> In body, and become a living soul:
> While with an eye made quiet by the power
> Of harmony, and the deep power of joy,
> We see into the life of things.[1]

In such a mood came the spiritual vision and intuition, with their sense of reality, and attended by, if not a rapturous, at least an exalted, joy:

> And I have felt
> A presence that disturbs me with the joy
> Of elevated thoughts; a sense sublime
> Of something far more deeply interfused,
> Whose dwelling is the light of setting suns,
> And the round ocean and the living air,
> And the blue sky, and in the mind of man:
> A motion and a spirit, that impels
> All thinking things, all objects of all thought,
> And rolls through all things.[2]

That this mystical apprehension becomes to him a working faith is manifest in the love of Nature which, according to his own confession, results in the recognition of her as the anchor of his purest thoughts, the nurse, guide, and guardian of his heart, and the very soul of his moral being;[3] so that it is unquestionably true that Wordsworth's Nature-faith, or his belief in the spiritual nature of corporeal being, had its rise in his mystical constitution and experience.

Psychologists differentiate between the sporadic moods of the mystic, which seem almost involuntarily produced, or flashed on or

---

[1] Lines composed a few miles above Tintern Abbey, 41–48.   [2] Ibid., 93–102.
[3] Ibid., 102–111.

through the normal consciousness, and those which are super-induced by methods of cultivation, as is often the case in religious mysticism. Sometimes the moods of Wordsworth, especially in the early years, belonged to the former class. At times, too, they seem to have been superinduced by his fixed and intense gaze on physical objects, as, for example, is revealed in the poem "To Joanna," where the various "delicious hues" fuse "in one impression" as the result of his fixed perception; that is, his mystical mood seems to be brought on by the fixedness of his gaze. Joanna notes the ravishment in his eyes, and laughs aloud, and then this mood, already present, impels the mind of the Poet to take up the voice, abstract it, and make it fill the very mountains. And so with the daffodils. He "gazed and gazed," little thinking what wealth the sight had brought him. The sense-impressions were so intense, and the memory images resulting were so vivid, that often, in vacant or pensive moods, they would flash on the inward eye. And so, again, in the case of the cuckoo. The "two-fold shout" arrests his attention, and, as he *listens*, the mood steals upon him, and soon the vale is full of sound; the earth is unsubstantialized, and becomes a fairy-world. Sometimes, too, it seems as though the mood were superinduced by his method of poetical composition. As we have seen, Wordsworth had a keen sense of sight and of sound, and was a close and intense observer of things. As a result, his sense impressions were strong. These impressions would often transcend sense-limits, and become an object of intense, imaginative contemplation. This contemplation was often suffused with either calm, or passionate, or rapturous feeling, which colored the object of the imagination. By some strange, peculiar, psychological mechanism, this process was transformed into poetic insight or intuition. He was thus enabled to "see into the life of things."

It may be, too, that at least his saner mysticism was not altogether unrelated to a kind of moral and spiritual preparation for his task. In a sense he, like other mystics, pursued a regimen in connection with his work. Believing, as he did, in a Spirit of Nature, and in its relation to Man, he would often seek inspiration. He would indulge himself in a "wise passiveness." He would put himself in a receptive mood, and thus prepare the way for the approach of the Spirit. Then the inspiration came, and the lessons were imparted. Indeed, this was so in a larger sense. Feeling the importance and sacredness of his vocation, he pursued it with a conscientious mind. He endured much, and sacrificed much, for his art. He felt himself to be the High Priest of Nature, and the bearer of her message, and, in devotion to his high calling, he abjured society, and sought solitude. There was a kind of asceticism connected with his life at Alfoxden and Grasmere. By preparation he put himself into a proper mental and moral attitude for inspiration or illumination, whatever that vague, mysterious, and ultimately inexplicable thing may be.

Such preparation or self-discipline, if not actually superinducing the mystic's mood, may at least have partly controlled or directed it. Throughout this prolific Grasmere period it may have been the trained mind and pure heart that helped him in no small measure in gaining a truer insight into Nature than was afforded by his extreme mystical moods, in which he was swamped by subjectivity. There are ethical momenta in knowledge. The normal man's moral development and moral attitude affect his perception of the truth. We see not only with the mind, but with the heart. A true science of knowledge recognizes this fact, and it is quite probable that the mystic's apprehension of truth and reality may be affected by this law. By his own confession Wordsworth felt himself to be the oracle of Nature, and he served before her altar with clean hands and a pure heart.

The profound trance of Wordsworth's early years, then, was not the predominating one with him, nor were its revelations those which most affected his views of Reality, although they undoubtedly contributed much to the spiritual conception of things which became his faith. It was the less profound, but much "saner," mood, in which the external world of things did not vanish, but had its inner nature revealed to the Poet's mystical soul as a Spiritual Life, that ultimately determined his ontological views, as well as his belief in the relations of Nature to Man. And this is the mood that seemed to prevail during these years in Grasmere, and its intuitions are embodied in much of his best poetry — poetry full of inspiration and power.

Emerson says that Wordsworth's "'Ode on Immortality' is the high-water mark which the intellect has reached in this age. New means were employed, and new realms were added to the empire of the muse, by his courage." [1] This, of course, is extravagant, but it may be said that in this poem we approach the high-water mark of Wordsworth's genius as a poet. Indeed, Professor Saintsbury thinks we reach " the summits of Wordsworth's poetry " in the " Lines composed a few miles above Tintern Abbey," and in this famous ode. He says that they are "poems of such astonishing magnificence that it is only more astonishing that any one should have read them and failed to see what a poet had come before the world." [2] So far as the content of the ode is concerned, it reveals him still to be the great lover and poet of Nature, beholding her with a mystical gaze, and seeing, with a penetrating vision, deep into her blessed life. It strongly hints, also, at the origin of "the vision and the faculty divine," and sheds further light on his refined conception of material Reality. And, concerning Man, Wordsworth may still be seen as the lover and poet of Man — to such a degree, indeed, that he continues to look on Nature as he did when he wrote " Lines composed a few miles above Tintern Abbey," hearing "the still, sad music of humanity"; and to such an extent that even

> the meanest flower that blows can give
> Thoughts that do often lie too deep for tears.[3]

[1] Emerson, English Traits, 282

[2] Saintsbury, A History of Nineteenth Century Literature, 54

[3] Ode. Intimations of Immortality from Recollections of Early Childhood, 206-207.

Before we close these chapters on the Grasmere period, several of the more conspicuous events in Wordsworth's life during his residence at Town-end ought to be mentioned, as they had a more or less direct influence on his life as a poet. These were, first, the publication of two new editions of the "Lyrical Ballads," respectively in 1802 and 1805, which shows that he was not without appreciative readers. This fact could not have failed to give him encouragement in the pursuit of his art, although the sale of his works was not large enough to yield much more than was required to defray the expense of publication.

Another event worthy of note was the death of the Earl of Lonsdale, in 1802. The Earl, as we have seen before, refused to pay a debt of £5000, due the Wordsworths. After his death his successor not only paid the original amount, but also accrued interest of £3500. Wordsworth's share of this amount was about £1800. This, of course, placed him in a more independent position in a pecuniary way, and enabled him to pursue his work with less anxiety concerning the future.

Still another event of importance was his marriage with Mary Hutchinson, his cousin, for many years an intimate friend of the Wordsworths. They were married October 4, 1802. Mrs. Wordsworth proved to be a quiet force in the Poet's life. This is evident from his references to her in "The Prelude"; also in the two sonnets "To a Painter," in the Dedication to "The White Doe of Rylstone," and in the poem entitled "She was a Phantom of delight." Here she is represented as

> A Being breathing thoughtful breath,
> A Traveller between life and death;
> The reason firm, the temperate will,
> Endurance, foresight, strength, and skill;
> A perfect Woman, nobly planned,
> To warn, to comfort, and command;
> And yet a Spirit still, and bright
> With something of angelic light.[1]

[1] She was a Phantom of delight, 23–30.

Five children were born of this marriage : John, June 18, 1803 ; Dora, August 16, 1804 ; Thomas, June 16, 1806 ; Catherine, September 6, 1808 ; and William, May 12, 1810. Three of these died during the Poet's lifetime.

During this period, as we have seen, another visit was made to France, in which he became keenly alive to the trend of political events, which, in turn, kindled his poetic fire and drew from him many of the noble sonnets " Dedicated to National Independence and Liberty."

The tour to Scotland with Dorothy and Coleridge must also be noted. It appealed to Wordsworth's poetic nature, and we have, as a result, a number of beautiful lyrical poems — " Ellen Irwin, or, the Braes of Kirtle," " To a Highland Girl," " Stepping Westward," " The Solitary Reaper," " Rob Roy's Grave," etc. Nature and the Poet were intimate friends on this tour. This is evident from the poems already considered, and also from Dorothy's Journal. The journey was undertaken because of their love for Nature, and resulted in furnishing suggestions and materials for many poems, some of which are regarded as among his most beautiful productions. It was further signalized by a visit to Walter Scott.

The death of his brother, Captain John Wordsworth, occurred during this period. This bereavement naturally impelled Wordsworth to serious reflection on death and the future life. He came to the conclusion that the destruction of " the thinking principle " in man by death would involve a greater love in man than in God. Such a conclusion seemed to him inevitable " except upon the supposition of another and a better world." [1] The death of his brother inspired " Elegiac Verses." It did much more than this however. It brought him into closer sympathy with his fellows, and fitted him all the more to be a poet of Man. Does he not say, and is there not evidence of it in his work,

A deep distress hath humanised my Soul?

[1] Myers, Wordsworth, 71.

Finally, an event worthy of note, was the visit of Walter Scott and his wife to Dove Cottage. At this time Wordsworth, in company with Scott and Sir Humphry Davy, all of them lovers of Nature, made an ascent of Helvellyn. This memorable excursion was referred to by Wordsworth, more than thirty years later, in " Musings near Aquapendente ":

> His spirit
> Had flown with mine to old Helvellyn's brow,
> Where once together, in his day of strength,
> We stood rejoicing, as if earth were free
> From sorrow, like the sky above our heads.[1]

In nearly all of these events we can perceive the direct influence of either the natural or the human environment on the unfolding of Wordsworth's genius. They stir his poetic imagination to activity, and furnish suggestions and material for his work. They were events that broke the more or less peaceful tenor of the Poet's meditation during these long and happy years at Town-end, in the beautiful Grasmere Vale.

Thus, in the tranquil life of Dove Cottage, and in the rambles among its surroundings, in fields and woods, over hills and mountains, and around the silver lake, Nature vouchsafed to Wordsworth beautiful visions, and spoke to him in a language full of inspiration and meaning, and burdened with a wholesome message, which he embodied in poetry of enduring worth. Here Nature is apprehended as in the Alfoxden days, and the Poet's communion and inspirations merely confirm and intensify his former beliefs.

Man, too, as he met him in these quiet haunts, occupying lowly stations, ministered to his spirit, and, as of old, he was led to exalt and idealize that which is fundamental in us. And ever and anon he lifted his eyes, and looked beyond the confines of the peaceful vale, to Man in higher stations, and in the great and stirring social and political movements of the time, sounding a note of warning, or a trumpet call in defense of his essential rights, and for the maintenance of those liberties which civilization had won through long years of struggle, and which, in the Poet's judgment, were to be preserved at all hazards. For this sacred cause he contended in verse, not merely as a lover of his own country, but as "a patriot of the world," and the sonnets inspired by these important events constitute one of the chief glories of Wordsworth's poetry. It was verse like this that led a fellow poet to say : " He was the heroic poet of his age : so long as there lives one man of English blood who has any sense of noble poetry, that blood will thrill and tingle in his veins at the very thought of the trumpet-notes of Wordsworth. . . . Those other poets of his day who dealt more immediately than he with martial matter had in them less of heroic thought and intelligence than the seemingly self-centered student of uninvaded solitudes. Scott could make men breathe the breath of battle. Byron could only make men smell the reek of carnage ; but Wordsworth alone could put into his verse the whole soul of a nation armed or arming for self-devoted self-defence ; could fill his meditation with the spirit of a whole people, that in the act of giving it a voice and an expression he might inform and renovate that spirit with the purity and sublimity of his own. Therefore, and on this account above all others, may his immortal words of sympathy find immortal application to himself : there is not a breathing of the common wind which blows over England that ever shall forget him ; his memory has great allies : he too has friends in the exultations and the agonies of his fellowmen, in their love of country, in the unconquerable mind of his race." [1]

[1] Swinburne, Miscellanies, Essay on Wordsworth and Byron.

CHAPTER XIV

COLEORTON. STOCKTON-ON-TEES. ALLAN BANK

After six years' residence at Town-end, Wordsworth moved to Coleorton. With a gradually increasing family the Poet and his household began to feel the accommodations of Dove Cottage to be inadequate. Sir George and Lady Beaumont were friends of the Wordsworths, and from time to time, between the years 1803 and 1806, visited the modest home in Grasmere. In 1806 the Beaumonts temporarily withdrew from their farmhouse adjoining Coleorton Hall, and offered it to their Grasmere friends, who occupied it during the winter of 1806–1807.

As in previous places of abode, so here Nature called forth the poetic activity of this unique man who was so peculiarly sensitive to her subtle power. Wordsworth found himself in a region remarkable for beauty and sublimity, and we have his own statement testifying to the fact that his genius was stimulated, and its productions colored, by his local surroundings. In the Epistle Dedicatory, inscribing to Sir George the first collected edition of his poems, published in 1815, Wordsworth writes : " My dear Sir George, — Accept my thanks for the permission given me to dedicate these Poems to you. In addition to a lively pleasure derived from general considerations, I feel a particular satisfaction ; for, by inscribing them with your name, I seem to myself in some degree to repay, by an appropriate honour, the great obligation which I owe to one part of the Collection — as having been the means of first making us personally known to each other. Upon much of the remainder, also, you have a peculiar claim, — for some of the best pieces were composed under the shade of your own groves, upon the classic ground of Coleorton ; where I was

animated by the recollection of those illustrious Poets of your Name
and Family, who were born in that neighbourhood; and, we may
be assured, did not wander with indifference by the dashing stream
of Grace Dieu, and among the rocks that diversify the forest of
Charnwood. Nor is there any one to whom such parts of this
Collection as have been inspired or coloured by the beautiful country
from which I now address you, could be presented with more propriety than to yourself — who have composed so many admirable
Pictures from the suggestions of the same scenery. Early in life,
the sublimity and beauty of this region excited your admiration;
and I know that you are bound to it in mind by a still strengthening attachment."[1] In another letter written to Sir George in
November, 1806, we find him rejoicing in the beauty of his surroundings.[2] Dorothy, too, writes enthusiastically to Lady Beaumont, and her letters tell of her brother's delight in Nature.[3]

However, of the poems composed here, there are no real Nature-
poems. The so-called Inscriptions to the Coleorton grounds
can hardly be called such, and, indeed, only a few of them were
written here. But there is a notable lyric, composed during these
winter months, entitled " Song at the Feast of Brougham Castle,
upon the Restoration of Lord Clifford, the Shepherd, to the
Estates and Honours of his Ancestors," which must be considered.
It celebrates the restoration of Lord Clifford to the ancestral honors
and estates of which he had been deprived for nearly a quarter of
a century, during which time he followed the life of a shepherd in
Yorkshire or Cumberland. It is one of Wordsworth's best lyrics,
and, according to some of his critics, one of the noblest in the
English language. Professor Reed, Wordsworth's American friend,
said : " Had the Poet never written another ode, this alone would
set him at the head of the lyric poets of England."

The poem, although not a poem of Nature, reveals Wordsworth's
continued belief in Nature's power over the human mind. The

---

[1] Knight, The Life of William Wordsworth, II, 55.   [2] Ibid., 76–79.
[3] Ibid., 79–81.

first part of the minstrel's song presents the forlorn condition of
the hero and his mother pursued by the slain father's foe. Next,
it presents him as a youth, leading the life of a shepherd, wandering from hill to hill, but enjoying and profiting by the loving
sympathy, and gladsome ministry, of Nature:

> — Again he wanders forth at will,
> And tends a flock from hill to hill:
> His garb is humble; ne'er was seen
> Such garb with such a noble mien;
> Among the shepherd-grooms no mate
> Hath he, a Child of strength and state!
> Yet lacks not friends for simple glee,
> Nor yet for higher sympathy.
> To his side the fallow-deer
> Came, and rested without fear;
> The eagle, lord of land and sea,
> Stooped down to pay him fealty;
> And both the undying fish that swim
> Through Bowscale-tarn did wait on him;
> The pair were servants of his eye
> In their immortality;
> And glancing, gleaming, dark or bright,
> Moved to and fro, for his delight.
> He knew the rocks which Angels haunt
> Upon the mountains visitant;
> He hath kenned them taking wing:
> And into caves where Faeries sing
> He hath entered; and been told
> By Voices how men lived of old.
> Among the heavens his eye can see
> The face of thing that is to be;
> And, if that men report him right,
> His tongue could whisper words of might.[1]

The minstrel's song next presents the dawn of another day —
the day of revenge — that calls on the young man to avenge his
father's death and his deposition from the honors and estates of
his ancestors. Wordsworth, however, makes a sudden turn in the

---

[1] Song at the Feast of Brougham Castle, 110–137.

poem. On the part of the youth we find no such response as the call of the song would lead us to expect. From Nature and misfortune he had learned a nobler lesson than revenge. The savage instincts of the race had died within him; so also had "all ferocious thoughts." The Poet is still preoccupied with his old and favorite theme of Nature's tutorial relation to the mind, and her ethical influence upon human life.

> Alas! the impassioned minstrel did not know
> How, by Heaven's grace, this Clifford's heart was framed:
> How he, long forced in humble walks to go,
> Was softened into feeling, soothed, and tamed.
>
> Love had he found in huts where poor men lie;
> His daily teachers had been woods and rills,
> The silence that is in the starry sky,
> The sleep that is among the lonely hills.
>
> In him the savage virtue of the Race,
> Revenge, and all ferocious thoughts were dead:
> Nor did he change; but kept in lofty place
> The wisdom which adversity had bred.
>
> Glad were the vales, and every cottage-hearth;
> The Shepherd-lord was honoured more and more;
> And, ages after he was laid in earth,
> "The good Lord Clifford" was the name he bore.[1]

As Sarah Coleridge says, in a note in her edition of her father's "Biographia Literaria": "The beautiful and impressive aspects of nature are brought into relationship with the spirit of him whose fortunes and character form the subject of the piece, and are represented as gladdening and exalting it, whilst they keep it *pure and unspotted from the world*."[2] In other words, here again Wordsworth is giving expression to his belief that Nature is a great moral teacher of the human heart.

If we turn, next, to an interesting piece of Wordsworth's prose in the form of a letter written during this brief stay at Coleorton,

[1] Song at the Feast of Brougham Castle, 157–172.
[2] Poetical Works, edited by William Knight, IV, 97 n.

describing plans for a winter-garden which Lady Beaumont had asked him to lay out, his careful observation of Nature is again noticeable. The detailed description to be found in this letter shows a minuteness of observation that is quite remarkable. It illustrates what was made evident in the letter written to Coleridge, describing the journey from Alfoxden to Grasmere Vale, that, while Wordsworth often viewed Nature with a peculiar insight into her essential life, and frequently apprehended her in her spiritual unity, he also studied her in detail — in her particularity, determining the æsthetic values of specific objects, and apprehending, as well as glorying in, her external form. It is noticeable, too, how he had studied the poets with reference to these peculiarities, for in this letter he refers to Chaucer, Thomson, Burns, and Grahame in illustration of some point in their appreciation of Nature which he himself emphasizes. In reading the works of his brother poets his eye seemed eager to note their attitude toward the natural world. The letter to Lady Beaumont is purely local in character, and can hardly be regarded as laying down general principles for landscape gardening. But it is of interest to us in throwing a sidelight on one aspect of Wordsworth's attitude toward Nature at this time. The poet, as well as the landscape artist, is seen in this epistle. In fact, the poet of Nature is really behind the landscape gardener.[1]

But, although quietly housed during these winter months, far away from the political strife of the times, and surrounded by the calm and peace of Nature in this delightful spot, Wordsworth did not lose sight of Man. He was alive to current events, and kept a steady eye on the ambitious movements of the French monarch. Several sonnets belonging to this brief period were inspired by the Poet's interest in the political movements of his time. One is entitled "A Prophecy." It was suggested by the action of Frederick Augustus, Elector of Saxony, who made a treaty with Napoleon, in which he showed himself to be in league with France. The sonnet

---

[1] Memoirs of Coleorton, edited by William Knight, I, 191-209

pronounces woe upon the "Bavarian" who was the "first open traitor
to the German name."

A better-known sonnet, and one, too, which Wordsworth regarded
as the best he had written up to this time, and which, according
to Crabb Robinson, he desired to become popular, is entitled
"Thought of a Briton on the Subjugation of Switzerland." Like
the preceding sonnet, it belongs to the poems "Dedicated to National Independence and Liberty." Napoleon, who by this time had
conquered practically the entire Continent, evidently continued to
be a source of anxiety to Wordsworth. In the sonnet the Poet calls
attention to the fruitless efforts of the Swiss in their fight against
the invader. But, though Liberty be driven from her memorable
mountain home, and be thus bereft of the mighty Voice of the
mountains — one of the two great Voices in which she has always
rejoiced — she is enjoined by the Poet to cleave to the mighty
Voice that still remains — the Voice of the sea.

> What sorrow would it be
> That Mountain floods should thunder as before,
> And Ocean bellow from his rocky shore,
> And neither awful Voice be heard by thee! [1]

The quiet life at Coleorton was, at times, pleasantly interrupted
by a visit of some distinguished friend. In 1806 Coleridge
returned to London from the Continent, and in December went
to Coleorton to see his friends. On this occasion "The Prelude"
was read to him by Wordsworth. "Lines to William Wordsworth,"
which Coleridge wrote in response, was "composed for the greater
part on the same night after the finishing of his recitation of the
Poem, in Thirteen Books, on the growth of his own mind," and
the last verse of this response records the deep impression Wordsworth's metrical autobiography made upon his brother-poet — an
impression so profound that when he had finished reading it he
found himself in prayer.

[1] Thought of a Briton on the Subjugation of Switzerland, 11-14.

In the spring of 1807 the Wordsworths were favored with another visit of Walter Scott, who joined Wordsworth and his wife at London and accompanied them to Coleorton. Nothing more of import relating to the life of our Poet at this countryseat remains to be recorded. He returned with his family to Grasmere early in the autumn of 1807. On the last day of November of the same year he left Grasmere for Stockton-on-Tees, to visit the Hutchinsons. Here he composed about one half of the poem entitled "The White Doe of Rylstone." He returned to Dove Cottage just before Christmas, 1807, where the first draft of it was completed in February, 1808. This unique poem is concerned with one of the most serious problems of Man — the problem of human suffering — and in it we see that "terrible strength" which is so often to be found in Wordsworth.

The poem relates the story of the fate of the Nortons in the insurrection resulting from Queen Elizabeth's action when she learned that certain Scottish and English nobles were secretly negotiating for the marriage of Mary Queen of Scots to the Duke of Norfolk. The conflict really represented an uprising of the Roman Catholics against the Government. Two of the Norton family (Emily and Francis) were Protestants, and were unwilling that their father and brother (who were Catholics) should identify themselves with the hostile movement, in which they finally lost their lives. Francis, too, was slain in attempting to carry out his father's last wish that he should try to regain the standard borne by the insurrectionists in the conflict, and, taking it to Bolton Priory, place it on Saint Mary's Shrine. According to the poem, having been warned of the inevitable by her brother Francis, poor Emily's duty throughout these times was

> to stand and wait;
> In resignation to abide
> The shock, and finally secure
> O'er pain and grief a triumph pure.[1]

[1] The White Doe of Rylstone, 1069–1072.

After the shock in all of its force had come, she was helped, in a measure, to endure it through the apparent sympathy and devotion of a white doe which became her life-companion. Suffering gradually did its perfect work. Emily was

> By sorrow lifted towards her God;
> Uplifted to the purest sky
> Of undisturbed mortality.[1]

In the poem Wordsworth aims at an ethical and spiritual interpretation of suffering. This is evident from the poem itself, as we have seen, and also from his own explanation of it. In the " Advertisement " Wordsworth explains wherein it differs from certain poems of Walter Scott with which it has been compared, both poets dealing with subjects taken from feudal times. He points out the spiritual significance of his own work. " Sir Walter," he says, "pursued the customary and very natural course of conducting an action, presenting various turns of fortune, to some outstanding point on which the mind might rest as a termination or catastrophe. The course I have attempted to pursue is entirely different. Everything that is attempted by the principal personages in " The White Doe " fails, so far as its object is external and substantial. So far as it is moral and spiritual it succeeds. The heroine of the poem knows that her duty is not to interfere with the current of events, either to forward or delay them, but

> to abide
> The shock, and finally secure
> O'er pain and grief a triumph pure.[2]

This she does in obedience to her brother's injunction, as most suitable to a mind and character that, under previous trials, has been proved to accord with his. She achieves this not without aid from the communication with the inferior Creature, which often leads her thoughts to revolve upon the past with a tender and humanising influence that exalts rather than depresses her. The anticipated beatification, if I may so say, of her mind, and the

---

[1] The White Doe of Rylstone   [2] Ibid., 1070-1072.

apotheosis of the companion of her solitude, are the points at which the Poem aims, and constitute its legitimate catastrophe, far too spiritual a one for instant or widely spread sympathy, but not, therefore, the less fitted to make a deep and permanent impression upon that class of minds who think and feel more independently, than the many do, of the surfaces of things and interests transitory, because belonging more to the outward and social forms of life than to its internal spirit. How insignificant a thing, for example, does personal prowess appear compared with the fortitude of patience and heroic martyrdom; in other words, with struggles for the sake of principle, in preference to victory gloried in for its own sake." [1]

This poem is really a remarkable portrayal of human patience and strength in the presence of an inexorable fate. Wordsworth, in his long years of struggle with the course of events during the French Revolution, in his anxiety about the seemingly inevitable outcome of the situation which the nations of Europe were confronting at the time this poem was written, in his personal struggles with Fortune, in his deep affliction caused by the death of his beloved brother, must have schooled his own spirit to an unusual degree of submission to the bald and unavoidable realism of life. Otherwise he never could have presented such a picture of sublime resignation. Lord Morley says that "Wordsworth had not rooted in him the sense of Fate — of the inexorable sequences of things, of the terrible chain that so often binds an awful end to some slight and trivial beginning." [2] Just the opposite, nevertheless, is sometimes seen in Wordsworth, despite his optimism. His optimism is not blind, and does not fail to reckon with things as they are, and with the inevitableness of the law of sequence, whether in Nature or in the human world. This is seen in poems like "Ruth," "The Ruined Cottage," "The Affliction of Margaret——," in certain

---

[1] Poetical Works, edited by William Knight, IV, 101-102 n.
[2] Morley, The Complete Poetical Works of William Wordsworth, p. lxvi.

portions of " The Excursion," and it is preëminently manifest in the poem under consideration.

Life, according to Wordsworth, grows strong by meeting just such situations as " The White Doe of Rylstone " describes. Calm, patient, heroic, lofty resignation is the lesson to be learned. Suffering plays its part in the human economy. It cannot be escaped. We are not to try to flee from it. It must be met, and met heroically. It makes for character if properly borne. To stand and wait, to abide, resignedly, the shock, and thus attain a pure triumph over grief and pain is our duty and privilege. But sorrow, the Poet teaches, may be a means not only of moral development, but also of spiritual elevation. By it the soul is brought nearer to God. This is the Poet's philosophy of suffering.[1]

But even in such sorrow Nature breathes her word of comfort. Even here, where Wordsworth is dealing with an intensely human picture of the inexorable in human suffering, he does not fail to bring in his favorite theme of the ministry of Nature to the soul. She does not forget poor Emily. Through the white doe Nature ministers to her.

This masterpiece of Wordsworth is of peculiar interest to his mental and spiritual biographer, for it reveals how the Poet was gradually changing his mental and spiritual attitude toward Nature. The stress of life, especially as revealed in human suffering, led him more and more to make Man, and especially Human Life, the object of his consideration. To work out a philosophy of Life seems to have been the problem preëminently before his mind at this time. This poem should be studied in connection with " The Excursion," which was also in process of composition during the three years covered by the writing of " The White Doe of Rylstone." And, of course, the problem of life, especially as it relates to human suffering, was one of the chief concerns of the Poet in " The Excursion." It is interesting, too, to note how, gradually, Wordsworth was drifting away from an apparent acceptance

[1] The White Doe of Rylstone, 1852–1853.

of the sufficiency of Nature, as manifested in his previous poetry, to a recognition of the necessity of religion. He recognizes the aid of Nature, but her ministry hardly seems sufficient. As a rational being Man needs some sort of an explanation of suffering; its meaning is demanded; and Wordsworth finds this meaning in the end which it subserves. It develops character, and lifts the soul nearer to God. This, however, he seems to gather from the religious consciousness of Man, rather than from Nature or from Reason. Religious faith solves the problem. This is emphasized not only in the lines quoted above, which tell how Emily was sanctified through suffering; how she was

> By sorrow lifted towards her God;
> Uplifted to the purest sky
> Of undisturbed mortality;[1]

but also, as we shall soon see, in "The Excursion," and in a sonnet composed a little later (probably in 1815), which precedes an extract from Lord Bacon, relating to those who "deny a God." This extract, with the sonnet, appeared in connection with "The White Doe of Rylstone" in the quarto edition of 1815.[2] The sonnet reads:

> "Weak is the will of Man, his judgment blind;
> Remembrance persecutes, and Hope betrays;
> Heavy is woe; — and joy, for human-kind,
> A mournful thing, so transient is the blaze!"
> Thus might *he* paint our lot of mortal days
> Who wants the glorious faculty assigned
> To elevate the more-than-reasoning Mind,
> And colour life's dark cloud with orient rays.
> Imagination is that sacred power,
> Imagination lofty and refined:
> 'T is hers to pluck the amaranthine flower
> Of Faith, and round the sufferer's temples bind
> Wreaths that endure affliction's heaviest shower,
> And do not shrink from sorrow's keenest wind.

[1] The White Doe of Rylstone, 1851–1853.
[2] See Poetical Works, edited by William Knight, IV, 105 n.

Man's mind is something more than rational intellect. It is imagination, and imagination, in the presence of "our lot of mortal
days," leads to Faith. Still later, in 1837, he quoted six lines concerning suffering (from "The Borderers," Act III, 1539–1544),
and added to them seven more, in which he again took the religious
attitude. These thirteen lines were attached to the Dedication of
"The White Doe of Rylstone" in 1837. The lines are as follows :

> " Action is transitory — a step, a blow,
> The motion of a muscle — this way or that —
> 'T is done ; and in the after-vacancy
> We wonder at ourselves like men betrayed :
> Suffering is permanent, obscure and dark,
> And has the nature of infinity.
> Yet through that darkness (infinite though it seem
> And irremoveable) gracious openings lie,
> By which the soul — with patient steps of thought
> Now toiling, wafted now on wings of prayer —
> May pass in hope, and, though from mortal bonds
> Yet undelivered, rise with sure ascent
> Even to the fountain-head of peace divine."

This change of attitude toward Nature, and this recognition of religious faith as the "one adequate support for the calamities of
mortal life," will be more manifest when we come to deal with
"The Excursion" in detail. It is an interesting and significant
fact in the mental and spiritual evolution of the Poet.

Wordsworth's movements between February and June, 1808,
are difficult to determine. They depended largely on Coleridge,
who was in wretched health. In March he visited London to see
his friend. The inadequate accommodations of Dove Cottage made
it necessary for the Wordsworths to find a new home, so they
moved from Town-end to Allan Bank in June, 1808. The years
spent there are very interesting, although they did not witness much
in the way of poetical composition. Wordsworth's mind was exceedingly active at this time, and both Nature and Man were the
subjects engaging his attention. But Man was preëminently the
object of interest, as we see in his correspondence and prose

compositions, as well as in several political sonnets belonging to this period. Owing largely to the conduct of the French, political conditions in England and on the Continent were such that Wordsworth became deeply engrossed in them.

This intense interest in the political welfare of Man lies at the basis of much of his poetical activity, as is evident from the " Poems dedicated to National Independence and Liberty," many of which were composed during the years spent at Allan Bank. How intense and absorbing it was at this time can be fully appreciated only through an examination of his essay "The Convention of Cintra," and his private letters written to the editor of *The Courier*, to Captain Pasley, Miss Fenwick, and others, besides the political sonnets composed here. Concerning the political tract just referred to, Professor Knight says : " A study of this essay — and it deserves to be studied, not only for the wisdom it contains, but for the splendour of its form — will dispel the notion that Wordsworth was a mere recluse student of Nature, little interested in human affairs and the aspirations of oppressed nationalities. It was from a certain vantage ground, as a dweller amid the mountains away from the strife of parties, that he was best able to judge of these things." [1] Furthermore, in a letter to Miss Fenwick, Wordsworth himself says : " It would not be easy to conceive with what a depth of feeling I entered into the struggle carried on by the Spaniards for their deliverance from the usurped power of the French. Many times have I gone from Allan Bank in Grasmere Vale, where we were then residing, to the Raise-Gap, as it is called, so late as two o'clock in the morning, to meet the carrier bringing the newspaper from Keswick. Imperfect traces of the state of mind in which I then was may be found in my tract on the Convention of Cintra, as well as in the ' Sonnets dedicated to Liberty.' " [2]

The Convention of Cintra was an agreement, signed at Cintra, in which the French, who were waging war in Spain and Portugal, and who had been defeated at Vimeiro by Sir Arthur Wellesley,

[1] Knight, The Life of William Wordsworth, II, 126.   [2] Memoirs, I, 383.

agreed to withdraw from Portugal to France, on condition that they should be permitted to retire without sacrifice of arms or other effects. The signing of this agreement by the British generals caused widespread indignation in England, and the Government was compelled to court-martial them. The trial, however, ended in their acquittal.[1] Wordsworth's essay, according to the "Advertisement" prefacing it, "originated in the opposition which was made by his Majesty's ministers to the expression in public meetings and otherwise, of the opinions and feelings concerning the Convention of Cintra."[2] It was written in November and December, 1808, but its printing and publication were delayed so that it did not appear before the latter part of May, 1809. It is an unusual tract, and ranks high as a piece of prose literature. Charles Lamb, writing to Coleridge, said : " Its power over me was like that which Milton's pamphlets must have had on his contemporaries, who were tuned to them. What a piece of prose !"[3] It is said that Canning thought it "the most eloquent production since the days of Burke."[4]

The elaborate title of the pamphlet indicates its content. It reads: "Concerning the Relation of Great Britain, Spain, and Portugal, to each other, and to the Common Enemy, at this crisis ; and specifically as affected by the Convention of Cintra : the whole brought to the test of those Principles, by which alone the Independence and Freedom of Nations can be Preserved and Recovered."[5] In the essay he traces the history of the English and the Spaniards in their alliance against the French (who were seeking, in the peninsular war, to subjugate Spain and Portugal), emphasizing specially the moral basis of the union, and the supremacy of moral over physical force, the tyranny of the French, and the humiliation and suffering of the Spanish and Portuguese. He then calls attention to the fact that when the British had defeated the French at Vimeiro, and were apparently in a position to put a speedy end to

---

[1] Knight, The Life of William Wordsworth, II, 127.
[2] Prose Works, edited by William Knight, I, 111.   [3] Memoirs, I, 404 n.
[4] Ibid., 403.   [5] Prose Works, edited by William Knight, I, 109.

Napoleon's aggressions, their generals entered into a treaty by which the French alone actually profited, and in which the Spanish and Portuguese received less consideration than the common enemy. He vigorously protests against the action of the generals, accuses them of having exceeded their authority, discourses on the feelings of sorrow and indignation which their conduct aroused in England, and remarks on the attitude of the Government against the people in their expression of sorrow and righteous anger. In all of this Wordsworth's soul seems to be on fire with the moral aspects of the case, and his language breathes a noble spirit. Virtually from the beginning he manifests a righteous indignation at what seems to him a great injustice both to England and to her allies involved in the treaty. The paper does, indeed, resemble, in spirit at least, Milton's vigorous pamphlets.

Wordsworth wrote several sonnets while he was writing this prose essay. One, written in 1808 and published in 1815, bears the long title "Composed while the Author was engaged in Writing a Tract —occasioned by the Convention of Cintra, 1808." Here he considers the fate of Spain in the light of Napoleon's ambitious program. Not in the midst of a slavish, selfish, human world, but in the sublime school of Nature, does he weigh "the hopes and fears of suffering Spain." He bears on his heart the wrong and injustice done to this oppressed people, and tries to determine, with a measure of hope, what Time may bring to them.

The second sonnet, also published in 1815, is entitled "Composed at the same Time and on the same Occasion." It refers to the fate of his political tract. He predicts that the world will manifest the same indifference to it that men asleep manifest toward a raging storm. Still, some anxious hearts will give heed to its hopeful prophecy, that out of the storm "bright calms" will ultimately emerge.

In 1809 Wordsworth wrote fourteen sonnets which belong to the class "dedicated to National Independence and Liberty." They indicate how intensely interested he was in the political situation of the time, and how anxiously his mind and heart were fixed on the liberties of those who were the victims of Napoleon's campaign of subjugation. We see in them a real lover of Man, and an uncompromising champion of universal justice. Six of these sonnets relate to the Tyrolese, and celebrate, for the most part, their resistance of the French. The first of them is addressed to Hofer, the principal leader of the Tyrolese, and memorializes the leadership of the "godlike warrior," and the bravery of his undaunted followers. The second, beginning "Advance — come forth from thy Tyrolean ground," is a spirited address to Liberty to advance and move through the long chain of the Alps. The third, "Feelings of the Tyrolese," exploits the firm conviction of these brave people that it is their duty, "with weapons grasped in fearless hands," to assert their virtue, and "to vindicate mankind." The fourth, beginning "Alas! what boots the long laborious quest," questions the value of knowledge "to elevate the will," and make the passions subservient to reason, in view of the fact that "sapient Germany," with all her great schools of learning, must lie depressed "beneath the brutal sword." In contrasting her action with that of the Tyrolese, he says:

> A few strong instincts and a few plain rules,
> Among the herdsmen of the Alps, have wrought
> More for mankind at this unhappy day
> Than all the pride of intellect and thought.[1]

The fifth sonnet, "On the Final Submission of the Tyrolese," is a fine tribute to the moral purpose which animated those brave shepherds in their struggle against the invader. In the last sonnet of this group, "The martial courage of a day is vain," the Poet reproaches Austria for her action in ceding the Tyrol to France.

The remaining sonnets, belonging to the year 1809, all deal with the political conditions of the time. Most of them laud heroes that would not yield to Napoleon, such as Palafox and his band, the heroic defenders of Saragossa; Schill, the brave Prussian,

---

[1] Alas! what boots the long laborious quest, 11-14.

who strove to liberate Germany from the power of the French;
also Gustavus IV, the Swede, who "never did to Fortune bend
the knee," and whose conduct in this respect is contrasted with
Napoleon's in still another sonnet, beginning "Look now on that
Adventurer who hath paid."

If we omit the epitaphs translated from Chiabrera (nine in
number), and the work done from time to time on "The Excursion," nearly all of Wordsworth's poetic activity in 1810 was
engaged with political sonnets. Like those of the previous year,
they relate almost entirely to political events on the Continent, and
the brave resistance of the Spaniards to Napoleon.

These sonnets, like all of those "dedicated to National Independence and Liberty," evince intense loyalty to Man as Man. There
is no partisanship here, no provincial patriotism, no circumscribed
love of freedom. Wordsworth loves liberty and justice not merely
as an Englishman, but as a man, and for all men. They belong
to men as men, and the Poet's soul is aflame with indignation
when men are ruthlessly stripped of them, whether they be his
compatriots or not.

If, in conclusion, we review these years spent at Coleorton,
Stockton-on-Tees, and Allan Bank, it may be said that they merely
repeat the old story of Wordsworth contemplating Nature, and
apprehending her, as heretofore, to be on intimate terms with
Man. Especially does he emphasize her moralizing influence. It
must be evident by this time, that Wordsworth does not conceive
of Nature as exercising a moral influence on the human soul merely
through natural laws, which somehow make for righteousness. His
conception is much more personal than this. There is a mighty
Spirit in things, akin to the spirit of Man, interested in his moral
life, ministering to it in admonition and love, and leading it into
righteousness and truth.

This, however, is a period in which Man is conspicuously supreme
in his heart. During these years he is just as ardently the " patriot
of the world " as in the early part of the French Revolution, if not,

indeed, more so. He watches the course of events in Europe with profound emotion and anxious thought. Man is dear to his soul, and the glorious principles of liberty and independence are conceived of as his essential birthright. They are his priceless possessions, and the Poet's soul is stirred with just and profound indignation as he notes them threatened by the aggressions of a mighty Power — a Power apparently bent on subjugating the civilized world ; hence the superb sonnets of this period, breathing love of liberty and love of Man, and hurling powerful denunciations at tyranny and the tyrant. The history of poetry abounds in names writ large and imperishable in the annals of Freedom, and these sonnets of Wordsworth entitle his name to a conspicuous place on this glorious roll of Immortals.

CHAPTER XV

THE EXCURSION

We have already seen that Wordsworth, while still living in Racedown and Alfoxden, had in mind the composition of an elaborate philosophical poem on " Man, Nature and Society." It was to be entitled " The Recluse." In our interpretation of " The Prelude " we noticed how this autobiographical poem was to constitute the first part of the work. It was to be a preparatory poem conducting " the history of the Author's mind to the point when he was emboldened to hope that his faculties were sufficiently matured for entering upon the arduous labour which he had proposed to himself; and the two Works have the same kind of relation to each other, if he may so express himself, as the ante-chapel has to the body of a Gothic church." [1] In the preface to " The Excursion " the author tells us that "his minor Pieces, which have been before the Public, when they shall be properly arranged, will be found by the attentive Reader to have such connection with the main Work as may give them claim to be likened to the little cells, oratories, and sepulchral recesses, ordinarily included in those edifices." [2] " The Recluse " itself was to consist of three parts. The first and third parts were to be composed " chiefly of meditations in the Author's own person." " The Excursion " was to constitute the second or intermediate part, the main features of which were to be the " intervention of characters speaking," and the adoption of " something of a dramatic form." [3]

" The Recluse," as thus planned, was never completed. As previously stated, the First Part of Book I was left in manuscript.

[1] The Poetical Works of William Wordsworth, edited by Thomas Hutchinson, 754.   [2] Ibid.   [3] Ibid.

The Second Part, "The Excursion," was completed. The Third Part was only planned; but, as Professor Knight says, "the materials of which it would have been formed have, however, been incorporated, for the most part, in the Author's other Publications, written subsequently to 'The Excursion.'"[1]

In the Preface to the edition of 1814 of "The Excursion" the author states the subject, or rather subjects, of the poem. He tells us that he does not intend "to formally announce a system," but he intimates that a system is latent in the poem, and leaves the reader to construct it for himself. It is really questionable whether Wordsworth, notwithstanding his undoubted mental power, could really have formulated a system. His was not a real philosophic mind. He was preëminently a poet, and, so far as we may call him a philosophic poet, preëminently an intuitionist. Up to this point we have seen that virtually all of his poetry, so far as it deals with basal conceptions, is intuitional in character. He seldom *reasons;* he *sees.*[2] He is a seer rather than a philosopher. Here, however, in "The Excursion," he reasons, but the reasoning is often disjointed, and frequently issues into mere musing. There is not a carefully, consecutively, and logically reasoned-out world-view, nor a real philosophy of life. The reasoning is often interrupted by narrative and description, and, indeed, not only interrupted, but sometimes almost lost.

In the Preface, after calling attention to the fact that it is not his purpose to announce a system, he proceeds to give us a "kind of Prospectus of the design and scope of the whole Poem," in the form of a quotation from the conclusion of the first book of "The Recluse," as follows :

> On Man, on Nature, and on Human Life,
> Musing in solitude, I oft perceive
> Fair trains of imagery before me rise,
> Accompanied by feelings of delight

---

[1] Poetical Works, edited by William Knight, III, 122 n.

[2] This is especially true in his poetry of Nature, although he does reason about Nature in his prose writings.

Pure, or with no unpleasing sadness mixed;
And I am conscious of affecting thoughts
And dear remembrances, whose presence soothes
Or elevates the Mind, intent to weigh
The good and evil of our mortal state.
— To these emotions, whencesoe'er they come,
Whether from breath of outward circumstance,
Or from the Soul — an impulse to herself —
I would give utterance in numerous verse.
Of Truth, of Grandeur, Beauty, Love, and Hope,
And melancholy Fear subdued by Faith;
Of blessed consolations in distress;
Of moral strength, and intellectual Power;
Of joy in widest commonalty spread;
Of the individual Mind that keeps her own
Inviolate retirement, subject there
To Conscience only, and the law supreme
Of that Intelligence which governs all —
I sing: — " fit audience let me find though few ! "[1]

This Prospectus itself in a measure illustrates what has been
said above. It does not present a number of concepts to be considered, on subjects in an orderly relation, such as would lead us
to expect the development of a *system* of thought, or of rational
belief. Indeed, the Prospectus itself properly characterizes the
nature of the mental process revealed in this poem. It is " musing
in solitude " on Man, Nature, and Human Life, rather than systematically reasoning concerning them. He is to weigh the good
and evil of life. He is to sing of truth, grandeur, beauty, love,
hope, melancholy fear subdued by faith, blessed consolations, moral
strength, intellectual power, widespread joy; of the individual mind
living in solitude, subject only to the laws of conscience and the law
of God. And when, a little farther on, he reveals the ethical aim
of his poem to be to

arouse the sensual from their sleep
Of Death, and win the vacant and the vain
To noble raptures,[2]

[1] The Recluse. The Poetical Works of William Wordsworth, edited by Thomas
Hutchinson, Prospectus, 1–23.   [2] Prospectus to The Excursion, 60–62.

he enlarges the scope of his work, for he immediately continues,

> while my voice proclaims
> How exquisitely the individual Mind
> (And the progressive powers perhaps no less
> Of the whole species) to the external World
> Is fitted : — and how exquisitely, too —
> Theme this but little heard of among men —
> The external World is fitted to the Mind ;
> And the creation (by no lower name
> Can it be called) which they with blended might
> Accomplish : — this is our high argument.[1]

These are splendid themes, and many of them are fundamental in character, but the order of their conception and presentation can hardly be regarded as a logical one, and is not thus carried out in the poem. It indicates what is really the fact about "The Excursion" — that the Poet *muses* rather than philosophizes. We have a series of musings or meditations on basal problems of the world and life, rather than a real philosophical poem.

After thus indicating the design and scope of the work, and declaring his moral aim or purpose in writing it, our Poet invokes the prophetic Spirit to descend upon, and inspire, illumine, and guide him, so that his song

> With star-like virtue in its place may shine,
> Shedding benignant influence, and secure,
> Itself, from all malevolent effect
> Of those mutations that extend their sway
> Throughout the nether sphere![2]

And, as if desirous of enlarging still more the scope of the poem, and in further need of the Spirit's aid, he adds :

> And if with this
> I mix more lowly matter ; with the thing
> Contemplated, describe the Mind and Man
> Contemplating ; and who, and what he was —
> The transitory Being that beheld
> This Vision ; when and where, and how he lived ; —

---

[1] Prospectus to The Excursion, 62–71.   [2] Ibid., 89–93.

Be not this labour useless. If such theme
May sort with highest objects, then — dread Power !
Whose gracious favour is the primal source
Of all illumination, — may my Life
Express the image of a better time,
More wise desires, and simpler manners ; — nurse
My Heart in genuine freedom : — all pure thoughts
Be with me ; — so shall thy unfailing love
Guide, and support, and cheer me to the end ! [1]

These are not merely formal words, placed here at the beginning
of a long work, which the Poet meant to be part of his *magnum
opus*, as a kind of professional introduction. They are in harmony
with his well-known ethical views of poetry, and his conviction
that the real poet speaks by inspiration — by illumination — his
message being an oracular utterance. For, with him, the prophetic
Spirit is specially near to the bard, possessing, indeed, "a metro-
politan temple in the hearts of mighty Poets." [2]

In a careful study of "The Excursion" we must, of course,
take into consideration the effect of physical environment on the
author's mind. In the case of less elaborate poems, written during
the years covered by its composition, we have seen that Wordsworth's mind was powerfully influenced by his natural surroundings. It is none the less true in regard to "The Excursion." All
through the poem it is evident that he is affected by local scenery,
and the effects of his intimacy with Nature are manifest in every
book. It was the natural beauty and grandeur of Racedown, Alfoxden, Grasmere, and Allan Bank that appealed to him, and furnished materials for description, as well as inspiration and insight.
Although Hazlitt, in a measure, overstates the facts, still, in the
main, what he says on this point is true : "The poem of 'The
Excursion' resembles that part of the country in which the scene
is laid. It has the same vastness and magnificence, with the same
nakedness and confusion. It has the same overwhelming, oppres-
sive power. It excites or recalls the same sensations which those

---

[1] Prospectus to The Excursion, 93-107.   [2] Ibid., 83-87.

who have traversed that wonderful scenery must have felt. We are surrounded with the constant sense and superstitious awe of the collective power of matter, of the gigantic and eternal forms of nature, on which, from the beginning of time, the hand of man has made no impression. Here are no dotted lines, no hedge-row beauties, no box-tree borders, no gravel walks, no square mechanic inclosures; all is left loose and irregular in the rude chaos of aboriginal nature. The boundaries of hill and valley are the poet's only geography, where we wander with him incessantly over deep beds of moss and waving fern, amidst the troops of red deer and wild animals. Such is the severe simplicity of Mr. Wordsworth's taste, that I doubt whether he would not reject a druidical temple, or time-hallowed ruin, as too modern and artificial for his purpose. He only familiarizes himself to his readers with a stone, covered with lichens, which has slept in the same spot of ground from the creation of the world, or with the rocky fissure between two mountains caused by thunder, or with a cavern scooped out by the sea. His mind is, as it were, coeval with the primary forms of things; his imagination holds immediately from nature, and 'owes no allegiance' but 'to the elements.'"[1]

What is true in regard to physical surroundings is true also with respect to social environment. The human nature and human life with which Wordsworth came in contact in these different places of abode constitute "Man" on whom he muses. Lowly, unconventionalized "Man" really furnishes the subject for his meditative song. Here, as elsewhere, he does not deal with human nature in its accidents, inequalities, individualities, and extremes. It is the universal elements of our nature that arrest his attention, and on which his mind is focused. Hence the lack of the really dramatic in this poem, as in his poetry in general, although he said "something of a dramatic form" had been adopted.

So far as the characters of "The Excursion" are concerned, in their views on fundamental questions, the Author, Wanderer, and

---

[1] Hazlitt, The English Poets, 343-344.

Pastor largely represent Wordsworth himself. However much they may differ on minor matters, on fundamentals their views are essentially the same. Even in the case of the Solitary, who, on the whole, represents the pessimistic view of life, Wordsworth is drawing largely on his own experience with the French Revolution, although, of course, the views of the Solitary are not, at the time of writing, those of the Poet.

Book First of "The Excursion" is entitled "The Wanderer." Its composition belongs to Racedown and Alfoxden, during the years 1795–1798. It tells of a meeting by appointment of the Author and Wanderer on a summer day near a ruined cottage. The Wanderer is a born poet — a poet "sown by Nature," possessing the gift of vision, yet without "the accomplishment of verse." He has had an interesting history, which the author relates, and in doing so Wordsworth is undoubtedly tracing his own personal experience. This history confirms, in a large measure, what has been said of the Poet's personal psychology, and adds further light on this interesting subject.

As a lad the Wanderer was a visionary, endowed with the mystic's consciousness, which affected his normal perception. So keen was his organic and emotional susceptibility that,

> While yet a child, and long before his time,
> Had he perceived the presence and the power
> Of greatness; and deep feelings had impressed
> So vividly great objects that they lay
> Upon his mind like substances, whose presence
> Perplexed the bodily sense.[1]

These impressions were so deep and lasting that, as he advanced in years, they constituted a kind of norm with which he compared his memories, thoughts, images, etc. Anything less vivid failed to satisfy him, so that he acquired the power of impressing these forms on his brain, and brooding on them to such an extent that they attained the vividness of dreams. He was fond of Nature.

[1] The Excursion, I, 133-139.

Even in childhood, both eye and ear were eager to feast upon the food which each season provided for sense, and, in later boyhood, Nature appealed to him in such a way as not only to arouse the senses, but to awaken imagination; for,

> many an hour in caves forlorn,
> And 'mid the hollow depths of naked crags
> He sate, and even in their fixed lineaments,
> Or from the power of a peculiar eye,
> Or by creative feeling overborne,
> Or by predominance of thought oppressed,
> Even in their fixed and steady lineaments
> He traced an ebbing and a flowing mind,
> Expression ever varying![1]

His imagination was chiefly nourished by tales of the mountains, and legends of the woods, which impelled the mind to apprehend the moral qualities and scope of things. Stories of martyrs, of giants, and fiends, also, stirred his imagination and feelings. This early fear was a prominent emotion, and seemed to furnish a kind of æsthetic pleasure — at least with him it was "a cherished visitant." Nature in her various aspects and forms had not as yet awakened in him the delight of love. Still he had felt her power, and the very intensity of his conceptions prepared him for her lesson of love. In all this we really see the Wordsworth of the first book of "The Prelude."

The youth, also, of the Wanderer was like the youth of the Poet, as described in his autobiographical work. Mysticism is very apparent, indeed, and reaches its height. As he beholds the great objects of Nature, he finds them full of gladness, and reads in the clouds "unutterable love." He is so overpowered by Nature as soon to be lost in a trance in which "sensation, soul and form" all melt into him. There is no sense of bodily life. Even thought expires in enjoyment. It is a visitation from God, and the soul is rapt in communion which transcends specific prayer and praise. The mind itself seems to be a thanksgiving, blessedness, and love.

[1] The Excursion, I, 154–162.

The self is almost lost in a supernormal experience. Not only the ordinary physical, but, indeed, almost the psychological, distinctions are canceled. His whole being is resolved into feeling-consciousness — a high, holy, transcendent emotional state. In short, the soul is submerged in the deeps of a trance-experience in which the intellectual limits of self practically vanish, and the feeling-self enters into a profound communion with the living God, rapt in an ecstasy of ineffable blessedness and love.[1]

And this mystical soul of the youth was intimately associated with Nature, being profoundly affected by her presence, for the experience just described was the result of beholding a sunrise from the top of a bold headland. Again, we are told that, as a herdsman in the mountains, he was so overcome by Nature as to be like one possessed. Here, in solitude, in the presence of the mighty forms of Nature, he was made to feel the truth of Revelation with reference to the " life which cannot die." Everything " breathed immortality." Things bordered on infinity. All little-ness disappeared. The soul mounted high, and spiritual vision dawned. There was no need of faith here, for he *saw*, and the ecstatic vision sanctified his nature. Low desires and thoughts vanished, and from the remembrance of these extreme moments he learned wisdom, patience, humility, and love.[2]

The descriptions of these accesses of mind peculiar to the Wan-derer are, of course, accounts of Wordsworth's own personal experiences. They tally with those to be found in " The Prelude," which record the history of his Hawkshead days, and his early life at Cambridge. It is evident from all this how profound a mystic Wordsworth was, and how much his poetic mind was indebted to this unique form of consciousness for its fine spiritual interpretation of the world.

As the history of the Wanderer continues, we read again the history of Wordsworth as we have learned it in " The Prelude." Poetry figures in his early education, Milton being especially

---

[1] The Excursion, I, 197–218.   [2] Ibid., I, 219–242.

mentioned. Then follows an account of his great love for Nature, which surpassed all other loves. He felt a wasting power in all things that weaned him from her influence. So fond of her was he that, when studying mathematics, the stars were his triangles, and he delighted to measure the altitude of " some tall crag that is the eagle's birth place," or some other impressive object of Nature. He made his abstract science concrete through his love of the natural world. Nature became more and more a factor in his life. Indeed, she almost overpowered him, so completely intoxicated by her joys was he, and so passionate was his love.

> And thus before his eighteenth year was told,
> Accumulated feelings pressed his heart
> With still increasing weight; he was o'erpowered
> By Nature; by the turbulence subdued
> Of his own mind; by mystery and hope,
> And the first virgin passion of a soul
> Communing with the glorious universe.
> Full often wished he that the winds might rage
> When they were silent: far more fondly now
> Than in his earlier season did he love
> Tempestuous nights — the conflict and the sounds
> That live in darkness. From his intellect
> And from the stillness of abstracted thought
> He asked repose; and, failing oft to win
> The peace required, he scanned the laws of light
> Amid the roar of torrents, where they send
> From hollow clefts up to the clearer air
> A cloud of mist, that smitten by the sun
> Varies its rainbow hues. But vainly thus,
> And vainly by all other means, he strove
> To mitigate the fever of his heart.[1]

We have met with all of this before in Wordsworth's account of his last days at Hawkshead, and his early life at Cambridge, to be found in " The Prelude." It is merely a reiteration of the story of Nature's strong hold on his affections in youth. We have here, also, the same Wordsworth whose ardent love for the sterner and

[1] The Excursion, I, 280–300.

more austere aspects of Nature had to be softened later by the gentle Dorothy. At this period Nature, with him, is a passion which he actively seeks to gratify.

But the history of the Wanderer continues. After he had reached later youth, he taught school for a maintenance, but found himself unfitted for the task, and soon adopted the vocation of a peddler. Thus moving from place to place, he saw much of men. Especially did he come in contact with rural folk, and saw

> Their manners, their enjoyments, and pursuits,
> Their passions and their feelings; chiefly those
> Essential and eternal in the heart,
> That, 'mid the simpler forms of rural life,
> Exist more simple in their elements,
> And speak a plainer language.[1]

Here, again, may be seen the Wordsworth of " The Prelude " and of the " Lyrical Ballads." [2] Of course, the detailed history of the Wanderer is not the history of Wordsworth. Our Poet never taught school, nor did he lead the life of a peddler, but he was strongly inclined to the latter vocation because of the charm afforded by moving through the country from place to place, and meeting simple folk. We see, in the words quoted above, what has been noticed so often in " The Prelude," as well as in the Preface to the " Lyrical Ballads," and in the ballads themselves, how Wordsworth felt that in these rustic folk are to be found the essential and eternal passions and feelings of the human heart existing more simply, and speaking a plainer language, than in more highly developed Man.

But the peddler's life also brought him in contact with Nature, and her influence was potently felt.

> In the woods,
> A lone Enthusiast, and among the fields,
> Itinerant in this labour, he had passed
> The better portion of his time; and there

---

[1] The Excursion, I, 342–347.   [2] Cf. Preface to the Lyrical Ballads.

Spontaneously had his affections thriven
Amid the bounties of the year, the peace
And liberty of nature; there he kept
In solitude and solitary thought
His mind in a just equipoise of love.[1]

Here, once more, is Wordsworth's familiar conception of Nature's ministry to the human soul. So familiar are we with such words by this time that it is impossible to doubt his position. The mind unfolds under the tutelage of Nature, and reflects in itself many of her own peculiar traits.

The Wanderer pursued his vocation until he had acquired sufficient means to retire and live at ease. He was a man healthy, hopeful, undepressed by the world and its care, "observant, studious, thoughtful," and religious (although his religion was more a matter of nature and reason than of inheritance and institution), kind-hearted, considerate, his entire form breathing intelligence, with a history that has just been narrated. This was the person whom the Author met lying on a bench near a deserted hut, and who constitutes the chief figure of "The Excursion." Soon after their meeting, the Wanderer told the history of the ruined cottage, located near the place where he was lying. It is a story of affliction, one of the most pathetic of all the sorrowful tales embodied in Wordsworth's verse — a story of misfortune overtaking a happy couple, causing desertion on the part of the husband, almost indescribable suffering on the part of the wife, and, finally, the death of both. It is a tale that shows Wordsworth to be an unusual poet of pathos and passion.

In the cottage near by, says the Wanderer, dwelt Margaret with her husband and child. She was a woman "of a steady mind, tender and deep in her excesses of love." Her companion was an affectionate, sober, and industrious man. In this modest home they had spent many peaceful days, but, alas, two blighting seasons came, and the fields yielded a meager harvest. To this was added

---

[1] The Excursion, I, 347-355.

the calamity of war. The land was sorely smitten. Business was depressed. Men were idle, and poverty was manifest on every hand. These sorry conditions entailed much self-denial on the part of this humble family. At length the husband was stricken with a dangerous and lingering fever. On recovering he found that his small earnings had been virtually exhausted. Another child was born. The good man was anxious because of their poverty, but tried to conceal his fears in various ways, often assuming a mock cheerfulness. But the strain soon became too great, and, made desperate by his misfortune, he resolved to quit his home secretly, not having sufficient courage to bid his wife farewell. Before leaving he wrapped a little money in a paper, and placed it in her chamber. Margaret found it, and, amid her fears and misgivings, soon learned, from a messenger sent by her husband, that he had joined a troop leaving for a distant land. Nine weary years she waited for his return. With a sorrowful spirit she lingered, now in hope, now in despair, waiting and watching, her heart wasting away with daily disappointment and grief. In the meantime

> her poor Hut
> Sank to decay; for he was gone, whose hand,
> At the first nipping of October frost,
> Closed up each chink, and with fresh bands of straw
> Chequered the green-grown thatch. And so she lived
> Through the long winter, reckless and alone;
> Until her house by frost, and thaw, and rain,
> Was sapped; and while she slept, the nightly damps
> Did chill her breast; and in the stormy day
> Her tattered clothes were ruffled by the wind,
> Even at the side of her own fire. Yet still
> She loved this wretched spot, nor would for worlds
> Have parted hence; and still that length of road,
> And this rude bench, one torturing hope endeared,
> Fast rooted at her heart: and here, my Friend, —
> In sickness she remained; and here she died;
> Last human tenant of these ruined walls! [1]

[1] The Excursion, I, 900–916.

"The Ruined Cottage" illustrates the fact that Wordsworth, as a
Nature-poet, is not only a poet of insight, but a descriptive poet as
well; and, as such, he not only deals with Nature in the large, but
scans her with a minute and accurate observation. His description of
the garden near the deserted hut,[1] and the Wanderer's description
of his return to Margaret's place, and the condition in which he
found it,[2] make this evident. Indeed, "The Excursion" furnishes
abundant proof of Wordsworth's descriptive power, and his careful observation of Nature's forms. This fact indicates that his was
"the practised eye" as well as "the watchful heart." It is somewhat remarkable that this detailed description should be so frequently met with in Wordsworth, for he was deeply interested
either in the larger and more majestic aspects of Nature, or in her
inner life and meaning, and her intimate relations to Man as teacher,
comforter, and guide. This, however, did not render him insensible
to her particularity — to the more modest and detailed forms of
her manifestation. This was doubtless due to a native and trained
organic sensitiveness, and to the influence of his sister Dorothy
in leading him to a more minute observation of things, as well as
to a more tender regard for the less austere aspects of the physical
world.

But in the story of the ruined cottage we again see the poet of
Man. It is with the human heart that Wordsworth is primarily
concerned here, and it is the fundamental passions that engage
his attention. Here he deals with the domestic affections. He sings
"a lofty song of lowly weal and dole." The weal is a fleeting note,
but the dole constitutes the protracted, melancholy theme of the
song. Here is pathos, tenderness, and profound passion — a picture of silent, though desperate, sorrow on the part of a man, and
of heart-wasting fidelity and love on the part of a woman; and
their only reward is death and the grave. One rises from reading
this poem feeling that he has been listening to a careful and sympathetic student of the human heart, who is acquainted with its

[1] The Excursion, I, 451–462.   [2] Ibid., 706–730.

profounder moods and passions, who has looked long and steadily into its depths, who has noted the great undercurrents of its life, and can tell with delicacy and power what he has seen. There is no mawkish sentimentality, but a dignified, yet deeply passionate portrayal of the tragic experience of the soul. In this Wordsworth excels, and the wonder of it all is that so many have found, in this sympathetic and penetrative student of the elemental affections, a poet devoid of passion. He does not, indeed, storm the soul with violent outbursts of feeling, but he lays bare the heart in all the intensity of its emotional life, in the deeper pulsations of its basal feelings, and in all the tragic bitterness of its spiritual agony. With this chapter in Life's book Wordsworth was thoroughly familiar, and he makes us feel with him as he tells us of its dark and mysterious contents.

CHAPTER XVI

THE EXCURSION (CONTINUED)

In the second book of "The Excursion" we are introduced to another personage — the Solitary — in whose experience with the French Revolution can be traced much of Wordsworth's own history as we have already become familiar with it. The joyful expectancy, the ardent love of and hopes for Man, the awful disappointment, and the depressing and almost ruinous effect upon his spirit to be found in the Solitary's career are, in a large measure, but a reproduction of the Poet's own experience. Indeed, in many respects "The Excursion" is as really, although not as minutely and literally, a mental autobiography of Wordsworth as is "The Prelude"; therefore it deserves careful interpretation in a study of the history of the Poet's inner life.

After relating the sorrowful tale of the ruined cottage, the Wanderer and Author journey together to the home of the Solitary. After their arrival the conversation soon leads up to a consideration of fundamental problems in relation to which the Solitary takes a skeptical attitude. He expresses himself as, on the whole, indifferent to Man's origin and destiny. As to the latter, he prefers annihilation to continuance of life. Pessimism is his creed. Night is preferable to day, sleep to waking, and death to sleep. Sweet is the quiet stillness of the grave after life's fitful storms. It was not always thus with him. Once he loved to think of Man and his future, and viewed the world with hope and joy. But experience has changed his view, and now life has little worth for him. In "bitter language of the heart" he gives his estimate:

> And yet, what worth? what good is given to men,
> More solid than the gilded clouds of heaven?
> What joy more lasting than a vernal flower? —

None! 'tis the general plaint of human kind
In solitude: and mutually addressed
From each to all, for wisdom's sake: — This truth
The priest announces from his holy seat:
And, crowned with garlands in the summer grove,
The poet fits it to his pensive lyre.
Yet, ere that final resting-place be gained,
Sharp contradictions may arise, by doom
Of this same life, compelling us to grieve
That the prosperities of love and joy
Should be permitted, ofttimes, to endure
So long, and be at once cast down for ever.
Oh! tremble, ye, to whom hath been assigned
A course of days composing happy months,
And they as happy years; the present still
So like the past, and both so firm a pledge
Of a congenial future, that the wheels
Of pleasure move without the aid of hope:
For Mutability is Nature's bane;
And slighted Hope *will* be avenged; and, when
Ye need her favours, ye shall find her not;
But in her stead — fear — doubt — and agony![1]

The Solitary then unfolds to them his history, which was really responsible for his pessimism. He tells them of his once happy domestic life, then of his terrible affliction in the death of his wife and children, the sorrowful depression that ensued, his reawakened interest in life through the French Revolution, his grievous disappointment and disgust at the outcome, his visit to the Western world, where he thought Man existed as primeval Nature's child, his failure to find " that pure archetype of human greatness," but, instead, a wretched creature, and, finally, of his return to his native land. And now in this retreat they find him, cherishing a hope that his particular current of life will soon " reach the unfathomable gulf, where all is still."

It can hardly be doubted that Wordsworth, in the Solitary's speech, is giving vent (possibly in an exaggerated form) to feelings

[1] The Excursion, III, 437-461.

which were very like his own during the later days of the French Revolution, and the period immediately following. For he was then in the depths of spiritual darkness and despair, from which, temporarily at least, there seemed to be no way of escape. He had lost his faith in men, in the veracity of moral reason, and, by implication at least, in the immortal destiny of a being whose moral nature seemed to be a contradiction. To such an one life held out little hope, and his estimate of its worth must have reached a minimum. It seems as though Wordsworth introduced the Solitary's gloomy philosophy here for very much the same reason as that which impelled him to introduce the philosophy of Godwin into "The Borderers" — to purge himself of it, and also to secure an opportunity to present the saner views of human life and destiny which, by this time, he had formed.

In the fourth book of "The Excursion" is presented the Wanderer's reply to the Solitary. In it may be found Wordsworth's views concerning a philosophy of life. He affirms that there is but "one adequate support for the calamities of mortal life," and that is an assured belief that man's life is ordered of God, who is infinitely benevolent and powerful, and whose eternal purposes convert all accidents to good; resignation to his will, and love for him, as well as dread of all things unworthy that might dishonor him. This is the only faith for men whose hearts have been torn, as was the Solitary's, by the loss of all that we hold most dear. God alone is Man's refuge and strength in such hours of trouble. He alone can sustain the sick heart, and restore the languid spirit.[1]

But there are other articles to his creed. As mortals we are frail, and therefore we sorrow. If we could only grasp firmly the reality of the immortal life, and its blessedness, which reason sanctions, and revelation insures, then sorrow for the dead were both selfish and senseless. Immortality is a fact. The dead are not dead. They live, and are glorified; or, if they sleep, they shall wake again, and dwell with God in everlasting love. Hope less

[1] The Excursion, IV, 10-31.

than this is inconsistent with belief in infinite mercy and perfect wisdom. In short, belief in an all-wise and beneficent God (who ordains all things for the best, whose loving providence extends to every soul, overruling things and events for its good), and belief in the life everlasting, to which death is the gate — these, and the reality of duty, are the fundamentals of the Wanderer's creed. For it he is not apprehensive. He fears not the worst that reason can urge in opposition. Man's difficulty lies in lack of zeal for the life of faith, and in his failure to live up to it. This is why he is drawn away by the temptations and vanities of the world, and the evil passions and tendencies of the human mind. What, then, is to be done ? He must look to those sources whence come his moral and spiritual strength. And what are they ? What but

> vows, renewed
> On the first motion of a holy thought;
> Vigils of contemplation; praise; and prayer —
> A stream, which, from the fountain of the heart
> Issuing, however feebly, nowhere flows
> Without access of unexpected strength.
> But, above all, the victory is most sure
> For him, who, seeking faith by virtue, strives
> To yield entire submission to the law
> Of conscience — conscience reverenced and obeyed,
> As God's most intimate presence in the soul,
> And his most perfect image in the world.
> — Endeavour thus to live; these rules regard;
> These helps solicit; and a steadfast seat
> Shall then be yours among the happy few
> Who dwell on earth, yet breathe empyreal air,
> Sons of the morning. For your nobler part,
> Ere disencumbered of her mortal chains,
> Doubt shall be quelled and trouble chased away;
> With only such degree of sadness left
> As may support longings of pure desire;
> And strengthen love, rejoicing secretly
> In the sublime attractions of the grave.[1]

[1] The Excursion, IV, 216–238.

But there is another "support" for Man in sorrow, or another source of peace. This is knowledge, especially of Nature in all her forms. Such knowledge is delight, and delight leads to love and adoration. Rural life and solitude furnish an opportunity for its increase. The Wanderer urges the Solitary to bodily activity and intercourse with Nature. She is full of resources, and brings refreshment and health to the sick soul.[1] To flee from Man and to fail to rejoice in Nature is, indeed, a pitiable lot. She speaks of God and eternity. She can regenerate the human soul. She can awaken love which casts out all morbidity, disquietude, vengeance, and hate. And this love, when once called forth, extends to our fellow-men. It softens feelings of aversion, and fills the entire frame with a holy tenderness. It clarifies the mind, and impels it to seek, and helps it to find, the good. The time will come when Man, by contemplating Nature's forms in their relation to Man, shall see a spiritual meaning in them, and they will impart important lessons of human suffering, joy, and duty. Then, too, general laws, as well as local accidents, shall tend to rouse and urge him, "and, with the will, confer the ability to spread the blessings wide of true philanthropy," and sense shall be dominated by moral purpose. Then shall Man's spirit no longer deplore the burden of life. Then, too, shall Science be "a precious visitant," and be worthy of her name. Her heart shall kindle, and her dull eye, no longer chained in slavery to her object, shall watch patiently "the processes of things, and serve the cause of order and distinctness," conscious of her noblest office to guide and support "the mind's *excursive* power." In short, the Wanderer's cure for pessimism, and the cynicism and misanthropy which it so often involves, is faith in God and his kind providence, faith in immortality, obedience to conscience, and love for, and communion with, Nature.

The day after the Wanderer's reply to the Solitary's dark views of life, they, with the Author, leave the valley, and journey to a

[1] The Excursion, IV, 466–504.

churchyard in the vale beyond. Here the Solitary returns to the conversation of the preceding day, and, still in a mood of dejection, continues his melancholy commentary on human life. Now Man himself, in all his weakness and moral impotency, comes in for his scorn and condemnation. He recalls the Wanderer's reference to Man's "sublime dependencies, and hopes of future states of being," but, as he stands there in the midst of the dead, he asks his companions to contrast the prospects of the soul with the sober facts of human life. Suppose every grave in their presence were as a book disclosing the history of the lives of their mute inhabitants, what a revelation would there be! — what an uncovering of human weakness and perversity! How contrary to the judgments of right reason, and the imperatives of conscience, would seem the deeds of those who lie there! So shocking would the disclosure be, that they would recoil from it with sorrow and shame. Nearly the whole course of life presents a melancholy moral picture. What can philosophy and religion show as their triumphs in the field of human morals? Man seems prone to evil. Each day records moral failure or perverseness in every life.

> If the heart
> Could be inspected to its inmost folds
> By sight undazzled with the glare of praise,
> Who shall be named — in the resplendent line
> Of sages, martyrs, confessors — the man
> Whom the best might of faith, wherever fixed,
> For one day's little compass, has preserved
> From painful and discreditable shocks
> Of contradiction, from some vague desire
> Culpably cherished, or corrupt relapse
> To some unsanctioned fear? [1]

The Solitary seems anxious to settle accounts with both Man and Life. In his judgment there is very little of good in either. Morbidly, but eloquently, he proceeds:

[1] The Excursion, V, 355-364.

> In the life of man,
> If to the poetry of common speech
> Faith may be given, we see as in a glass
> A true reflection of the circling year,
> With all its seasons. Grant that Spring is there,
> In spite of many a rough untoward blast,
> Hopeful and promising with buds and flowers;
> Yet where is glowing Summer's long rich day,
> That *ought* to follow faithfully expressed?
> And mellow Autumn, charged with bounteous fruit,
> Where is she imaged? in what favoured clime
> Her lavish pomp, and ripe magnificence?
> — Yet, while the better part is missed, the worse
> In man's autumnal season is set forth
> With a resemblance not to be denied,
> And that contents him; bowers that hear no more
> The voice of gladness, less and less supply
> Of outward sunshine and internal warmth;
> And, with this change, sharp air and falling leaves,
> Foretelling aged Winter's desolate sway.[1]

One might suppose that in this quiet mountain vale, remote from the populous centers, with their numerous and foul temptations, Man would present a more wholesome picture. But this is not the case:

> They escape,
> Perchance, the heavier woes of guilt; feel not
> The tedium of fantastic idleness:
> Yet life, as with the multitude, with them
> Is fashioned like an ill-constructed tale;
> That on the outset wastes its gay desires,
> Its fair adventures, its enlivening hopes,
> And pleasant interests — for the sequel leaving
> Old things repeated with diminished grace;
> And all the laboured novelties at best
> Imperfect substitutes, whose use and power
> Evince the want and weakness whence they spring.[2]

Wordsworth seems to introduce the views of the Solitary somewhat at length in order to bring out his own creed of life in

---

[1] The Excursion, V, 391–410.   [2] Ibid., V, 428–439.

opposition to them. With the feelings and convictions of this pessimist he was quite familiar, for they represent, in a fair measure, his
own state of mind during the last days of, and immediately following, the French Revolution. However, he has now recovered his
grip on life, and measures its worth, and the worth of Man himself, from a different angle. And in the views of the Wanderer
and Author, as well as in those of the Pastor — who is soon to
appear on the scenes — he opposes to the pessimist's creed a
different " philosophy," which is evidently an embodiment of his
own rational convictions. He means to be fair, and therefore
allows the Solitary to paint Life and Man in unusually dark colors.
However, after the advocate of this gospel of doubt and despair
has said his worst, the Poet seems to think that there is a saner,
more wholesome, more helpful, view of Life and Man — one more
true to the facts of human experience, and to their legitimate
interpretation.

As the Solitary closes his mournful commentary on human
character and life, another person approaches the little group —
the Pastor of the village church. The Wanderer advises him of
their serious discussion, which involved such momentous questions
as these : Does Man, as generations pass, really make progress ?
Does the individual reach a life-line, " ere his hairs be gray," at
which his progress ceases ? Does good predominate over evil in
Man ? Does the human will acknowledge the law of reason ? Is
virtue a living power, or merely a name, destined soon to pass
away, leaving only pain and misery, and wretched life — the goal of
which is dust ? And he appeals to the Pastor to give them the light
of his experience in regard to these grave questions, so that their
hearts may be cheered. To this appeal the Pastor responds, and
again we are introduced to Wordsworth's own philosophy of life :

Man as a rational being is subject to limitations. He suffers
from a constitutional impotency of mind so far as the solution of
fundamental speculative problems is concerned. Furthermore, his
intellectual vision is clouded by his passions. They blind him,

in a measure, in his efforts to attain the truth. However, so far as the general purposes of faith in a divine Providence, as the source of comfort and support in the hour of human need, are concerned, he who lives in accord with the laws of right reason is the man who gains the clearest perception of those truths which the unaided reason is unable fully to grasp. As in the Christian life, he that doeth His will shall know of the doctrine, so here, the man who obeys the law of his moral being will have the clearest apprehension of those things which lie beyond the unassisted powers of his rational nature. Wordsworth, in the Pastor's introductory words, is calling attention once more to the ethical momenta in human knowledge, and, in so doing, is undoubtedly on solid ground so far as epistemology is concerned, for the moral life is unquestionably a factor in cognition.

But, descending from these lofty heights to more common levels, the Pastor affirms that life is fair and tempting, grateful and refreshing, or forbidding and cheerless, according as we view or approach it. To this the Wanderer assents, and remarks once more on the limitations of human reason. Moral truth is not a hard-and-fast thing, to be determined mechanically by the logical processes of the intellect; there is an element of relativity in it. It is subject to circumstances. It has a certain fixedness or stability at its base, but on the surface admits of manifold applications and interpretations as circumstances vary.

But now the Pastor, in response to the Wanderer's appeal, testifies from his own experience with actual men and women living about them, and with those who lie moldering at their feet, concerning the worth of life, and the worth or frailty of human nature In this way, getting away from abstractions to *facts*, from disputes to *plain pictures*, from reasoning to life (and to life at close quarters), they

may learn

> *To prize the breath we share with human kind;*
> *And look upon the dust of man with awe !* [1]

[1] The Excursion, V, 655–657.

He briefly refers to men living, and then presents biographies of those buried in the churchyard. They are such as every country minister is familiar with — histories of joy and sorrow, success and failure, struggles and conquest, victory and defeat, generosity and meanness, fidelity and unfaithfulness, sin and repentance, good and evil, life and death. On the whole the record is a credit to Man. It shows that life is in many respects a tragedy. It is full of mystery. Suffering, however, plays its part in the human economy. It develops the virtues, and builds up character. And Man is not left to his own unaided efforts in the struggle; there are many resources at his command. The virtues themselves which suffering calls forth, and which life develops, become in turn means of support. Furthermore, Nature and solitude minister to human need; and Man's extremity, in the presence of life's mystery, becomes Faith's opportunity to show her might, and to prove her excellence.

In short, Wordsworth's solution of the problem of life, in response to his own questioning as represented in the Solitary's doubts concerning its worth, and the worth of Man, is essentially the solution furnished by Christian Theism. Life is worth living, and the " inner frame " of Man is good. But life must be grounded in faith in divine Providence, in immortality, and in those sublime virtues which alone confer value on the human soul. Suffering, however mysterious, is not an unmitigated evil, if, indeed, it be an evil at all. It calls to patience, perseverance, fidelity, resignation, hope, faith, and love, and, in the final analysis, makes for the upbuilding of Man if he be willing to profit by it. Indeed, these very virtues themselves, which suffering develops, constitute, in a large measure, the means by which he may triumph over it.[1]

It is worthy of note that, even here, when the Poet is dealing more primarily with the immediate problems of life, he does not fail to record his belief in Nature's ministry to Man. She is one of the helpful agencies in restoring the sick soul — one of the

[1] The Excursion, V, VI, and VII.

supports of the spirit when burdened with the weary weight of life's mysterious suffering. There is healing in her solitudes, and minis-try in her beauty. Even Heaven commits afflicted souls to her loving care. She

> doth commend their weakness and disease
> To Nature's care, assisted in her office
> By all the elements that round her wait
> To generate, to preserve, and to restore;
> And by her beautiful array of forms
> Shedding sweet influence from above; or pure
> Delight exhaling from the ground they tread.[1]

But it must be observed, also, that we have here a change of mental attitude in Wordsworth. Heretofore we have found very little in his teaching that commends the suffering soul to the love and support of Divine Providence. On the whole, Nature has been regarded by him as the comforter, teacher, guide, and physician of the soul. She, rather than God or Divine Providence, has been considered as the "one adequate support for the calamities of mortal life." To whom did he turn in those dark days when he was passing through the severe mental and moral crisis occasioned by his experience with the French Revolution? Was it not to Nature? It was to her "beauteous forms" that he owed,

> In hours of weariness, sensations sweet,
> Felt in the blood, and felt along the heart;
> And passing even into my [his] purer mind,
> With tranquil restoration.[2]

It was to her that he owed "another gift, of aspect more sublime,"

> that blessed mood,
> In which the burthen of the mystery,
> In which the heavy and the weary weight
> Of all this unintelligible world,
> Is lightened.[3]

---

[1] The Excursion, VI, 182–188.
[2] Lines composed a few miles above Tintern Abbey, 37–41.   [3] Ibid., 37–41.

He had felt the presence of a Spirit that " rolls through all things," and that "impels all thinking things"—that seemed to afford, somehow, a refuge to his soul, so that he was constrained to say :

> Therefore am I still
> A lover of the meadows and the woods,
> And mountains ; and of all that we behold
> From this green earth ; of all the mighty world
> Of eye, and ear, — both what they half create,
> And what perceive ; well pleased to recognise
> In nature and the language of the sense,
> The anchor of my purest thoughts, the nurse,
> The guide, the guardian of my heart, and soul
> Of all my moral being.[1]

His experience with Nature had been such that he affirmed :

> 'T is her privilege,
> Through all the years of this our life, to lead
> From joy to joy : for she can so inform
> The mind that is within us, so impress
> With quietness and beauty, and so feed
> With lofty thoughts, that neither evil tongues,
> Rash judgments, nor the sneers of selfish men,
> Nor greetings where no kindness is, nor all
> The dreary intercourse of daily life,
> Shall e'er prevail against us, or disturb
> Our cheerful faith, that all which we behold
> Is full of blessings.[2]

Our examination of Wordsworth's poetry, prior to the consideration of " The Excursion," revealed this to have been his mental attitude generally. Nature was considered as Man's counselor and guide — his refuge and strength. But it seems as though the Poet had gradually, under the stress of human experience, been led to emphasize the religious, and especially the Christian, conception of God more than his poetic conception, although the two are in no respects opposed to each other. For example, this change is indicated in the words of the Wanderer :

[1] Lines composed a few miles above Tintern Abbey, 102–111.
[2] Ibid., 123–134.

                  One adequate support
For the calamities of mortal life
Exists — one only; an assured belief
That the procession of our fate, howe'er
Sad or disturbed, is ordered by a Being
Of infinite benevolence and power,
Whose everlasting purposes embrace
All accidents, converting them to good.
— The darts of anguish *fix* not where the seat
Of suffering hath been thoroughly fortified
By acquiescence in the Will supreme
For time and for eternity; by faith,
Faith absolute in God, including hope,
And the defence that lies in boundless love
Of his perfections; with habitual dread
Of aught unworthily conceived, endured
Impatiently, ill-done, or left undone,
To the dishonour of his holy name.
Soul of all Souls, and safeguard of the world!
Sustain, thou only canst, the sick of heart;
Restore their languid spirits, and recall
Their lost affections unto thee and thine.[1]

Here religious faith, and especially the functioning and the content
of Christian faith, seem to take the place of poetic intuition, with
its apprehension of a Spirit pervading all things, and in close relations to the spirit of Man. However, the Poet does not by any
means abandon the latter in " The Excursion," for, much as he
exalts the office of religious faith, and much as he interprets life
and the world from this standpoint, nevertheless, as we have seen
above, his favorite conceptions of Nature, and of her relations to
Man, still obtain, and even in the last book of " The Excursion "
we find these words :

    To every Form of being is assigned,
    Thus calmly spake the venerable Sage,
    An *active* Principle: — howe'er removed
    From sense and observation, it subsists
    In all things, in all natures; in the stars
    Of azure heaven, the unenduring clouds,

[1] The Excursion, IV, 10–31.

In flower and tree, in every pebbly stone
That paves the brooks, the stationary rocks,
The moving waters, and the invisible air,
Whate'er exists hath properties that spread
Beyond itself, communicating good,
A simple blessing, or with evil mixed;
Spirit that knows no insulated spot,
No chasm, no solitude; from link to link
It circulates, the Soul of all the worlds.
This is the freedom of the universe;
Unfolded still the more, more visible,
The more we know; and yet is reverenced least,
And least respected in the human Mind,
Its most apparent home.[1]

As previously stated, the conceptions and beliefs of religious faith, and the poetic intuitions, in Wordsworth's poetry, are not mutually opposed. In both cases they are essentially Theistic. However, in the latter instance he seems to apprehend Reality by means of a mystical mental process, whereas, in the former, he apprehends the content of his faith by means of the rational and religious consciousness, possibly aided by his æsthetic nature, as he mused or meditated on the mysterious problems which life especially presented to his mind. In later years he seemed to take the religious rather than the earlier poetic attitude, as is manifest in the "Ecclesiastical Sonnets." Whether this was due to a conscious recognition of the inadequacy of the poetic attitude, or to that singular loss of mystical insight into Nature which he experienced about the time of the completion of "The Excursion," to which reference will be made in the final chapter, it is impossible to say. But it is evident that, whatever may have been the reason, we have a more thoroughly religious mode of apprehending God, and his relations to Man, than in his earlier poetry, and therefore a more *human* mode — more human because it is far more *common* to Man himself than the other. In short, in "The Excursion," and in the later poetry of Wordsworth, the *content* of the Poet's

[1] The Excursion, IX, 1-20.

faith is essentially the same as in his earlier poetry, but the *way of approach to it,* or the *mode of apprehending it,* is different. In Wordsworth's early poetry we have mystical vision and intuition ; in the later we have rational and religious meditation and belief. In the former we have immediate apprehension of Reality ; in the latter, mediate. The object of the former is the Spirit of Nature ; the object of the latter is a personal God. Therefore, in a sense, God figures more conspicuously than Nature in " The Excursion " and " Ecclesiastical Sonnets."

CHAPTER XVII

THE EXCURSION (CONCLUDED)

In the eighth and ninth books of " The Excursion " Wordsworth introduces the reader to some of his views on society, or the social order. After discussing the subjects of the worth of Man and the worth of Life, the Wanderer, in response to a little playful rally on the part of the Solitary concerning his humble calling, takes occasion to direct attention to the condition of Britain to-day as compared with that in earlier days, when he traveled about as a peddler. This change is specially marked in the industrial order, and he calls attention to its baneful effects on Nature and Man :

> I have lived to mark
> A new and unforeseen creation rise
> From out the labours of a peaceful Land
> Wielding her potent enginery to frame
> And to produce, with appetite as keen
> As that of war, which rests not night or day,
> Industrious to destroy ![1]

Practically all of the elements have been utilized to bring about this change. The result, of course, has been to make Britain one of the great marts of the world, and a power to be respected and feared. But all this progress has been made at frightful expense — the spoliation of Nature, and the bodily and moral welfare of the people. On all sides forests have been laid bare, streams polluted, and the beauty of Nature outraged. But more than this, it has resulted in much demoralization of the people. It dwarfs the bodily nature of the child, and lays the sure foundations of disease. It aims a blow, also, at the home. Parents and children work in

---

[1] The Excursion, VIII, 89-95.

factories, and domestic duty and happiness must of necessity suffer. It strikes at virtue in bringing the sexes together in unguarded fashion. It destroys the charm and peacefulness of country life — the simplicity and sobriety, the respect for old institutions and customs, both moral and religious — which heretofore proved a refuge from the busy world. These are the fruits of the manufacturing spirit, and Wordsworth, in the words of the Wanderer, deplores them. He rejoices in the Nation's progress, and in the sovereignty of Man over Nature, but the physical enfeeblement of the child, and the social and moral degeneration which result from the industrial order, make him look upon this advance with grave misgiving and condemnation. To him the old life of toil, close to the heart of Nature, seems best for rural people.

What hope rises from the new order of things? "We live by hope," continues the Wanderer, "and by desire." Without them we languish and die. 'T is so with boyhood, with youth, and with manhood. Age looks back on childhood — the rising period of hope — with fondness. The good and wise will never be separated from hope, even in old age, which is forbidding, but which has an inviting aspect also, for it is as one seated on an eminence, far away from the busy noises of life, where, in its solitude, it can exercise the finer activities of sense and soul. And, indeed, may there not be a further purpose in the isolation or solitude of old age? It affords

> Fresh power to commune with the invisible world,
> And hear the mighty stream of tendency
> Uttering, for elevation of our thought,
> A clear sonorous voice,[1]

which cannot be heard by those who are busy with the world.

But if old age may aspire to such hopes, they will be possible only to those whose minds have not been starved by neglect, and whose bodies have not been crushed by incessant toil. Nature loves Man, and if she be allowed to have her way with him, and

[1] The Excursion, IX, 86–89.

Reason be permitted to rule, then the country, society, and time, through the grace of a beneficent God, make for his good, for, under such circumstances, all these forces partake

> Of one maternal spirit, bringing forth
> And cherishing with ever-constant love,
> That tires not, nor betrays.[1]

But life is turned from her true course when Man is converted into a mere tool or implement — a means for the realization of an end, there being no acknowledgment of his common right in the end itself. This weakens his power for good, and strengthens his power for evil. Man was not born for such issues as these. However, on the other hand, when he is not thus degraded and restrained, the very powers which, under such restraint, make for evil, become forces for good.

Of course, the Wanderer is here aiming his shafts at the social and industrial order referred to above — an order which seemed to him to starve the mind and crush the body, and to override the inherent claims of human personality. There is, indeed, a difference, continues the Wanderer, between the victims of this order, and the unfortunate peasant class referred to by the Solitary in disparaging Nature's assistance to Man. The latter class are slaves of ignorance and want, but they are " lineal heirs " of this vassalage; their ancestors bequeathed this unhappy legacy to them. But no one delights in such oppression, nor are any proud of it. It is a vice indigenous to every country. But the industrial evil is of a different character. It is a slavery that wears the aspect of good. It is a case in which a thing in itself beneficent has been carried to an extreme, and its very victims, as well as those responsible for them, are self-deceived, believing an evil to be a good. Even the wise have been misled, and think that these newer methods of industry make for the betterment of society. This is a grave delusion, and the Wanderer mourns for these children of rural England, whom he has seen corrupted, whose innocence and love circumstance

[1] The Excursion, IX, 111–113.

and Nature would have sheltered and cherished — children who might have lived in health and strength, and in tranquillity of mind, but for the intrusion of these unjust industrial conditions. How man differs from man! And he himself is responsible for it. He has established a social order that gives us the oppressor and the oppressed, the wise and the ignorant, the rich and the poor. This is not Nature's method. There is a natural equality that belongs to men. It is fundamental. The common joys of Nature exist for all. All possess the same noble gifts of reason and imagination, will and conscience. All must taste death, but all, too, can conceive an immortality for him who proves worthy of it.

> Strange, then, nor less than monstrous, might be deemed
> The failure, if the Almighty, to this point
> Liberal and undistinguishing, should hide
> The excellence of moral qualities
> From common understanding; leaving truth
> And virtue, difficult, abstruse, and dark;
> Hard to be won, and only by a few;
> Strange, should He deal herein with nice respects,
> And frustrate all the rest! Believe it not:
> The primal duties shine aloft — like stars;
> The charities that soothe, and heal, and bless,
> Are scattered at the feet of Man — like flowers.
> The generous inclination, the just rule,
> Kind wishes, and good actions, and pure thoughts —
> No mystery is here! Here is no boon
> For high — yet not for low; for proudly graced —
> Yet not for meek of heart. The smoke ascends
> To heaven as lightly from the cottage-hearth
> As from the haughtiest palace. He, whose soul
> Ponders this true equality, may walk
> The fields of earth with gratitude and hope;
> Yet, in that meditation, will he find
> Motive to sadder grief, as we have found;
> Lamenting ancient virtues overthrown,
> And for the injustice grieving, that hath made
> So wide a difference between man and man.[1]

[1] The Excursion, IX, 229–254.

An order of society that thus differentiates man from man, that creates such marked moral distinctions, that permits some men to prosper at the frightful expense of others, that builds up material interests by wasting the bodies and impoverishing the souls of many — such an order is against the will of Nature, who accords equal moral rights and gifts to all. And the Wanderer expresses a hope that England will soon bind herself by statute to secure for all her children elementary education, and training in moral and religious truth,

> so that none,
> However destitute, be left to droop
> By timely culture unsustained; or run
> Into a wild disorder; or be forced
> To drudge through a weary life without the help
> Of intellectual implements and tools;
> A savage horde among the civilised,
> A servile band among the lordly free![1]

This, he holds, is their essential right. Furthermore, ignorance breeds discontent and strife. England needs the "discipline of virtue":

> Order else
> Cannot subsist, nor confidence, nor peace.
> Thus, duties rising out of good possest,
> And prudent caution needful to avert
> Impending evil, equally require
> That the whole people should be taught and trained.
> So shall licentiousness and black resolve
> Be rooted out, and virtuous habits take
> Their place; and genuine piety descend,
> Like an inheritance, from age to age.[2]

If this be done, Britain need not fear an increase of population. It will not constitute a menace. Rather may she rejoice in it. Thus prepared for life, she can send her people forth to establish new communities wherever conditions favor hope, and can promise to perseverance and skill a just reward.

[1] The Excursion, IX, 303-310.   [2] Ibid., IX, 353-362.

Of course it is Wordsworth who speaks here through the Wanderer. However, in this protest against social conditions, it must not be inferred that we have a would-be reformer ranting against class distinctions and industrial progress. He is not a fanatic, nor an unreasoning and unreasonable observer of the social order. What he is inveighing against is material progress which involves a sacrifice of the health and strength of the people, as well as of their intellectual and moral welfare. Especially is he impressed by the moral aspects of the spread of the manufacturing spirit. He feels that the methods of industry are degrading. The people are being corrupted by them. The home, the very fountain-head of virtue, is being broken up. There is a gradual weakening of parental and filial relations. He thinks, too, that the sexes are thrown into unnatural and unsafe relations, and modesty and virtue are therefore threatened. He feels that respect for ancient social, moral, and religious institutions is disappearing, and that society is pervaded by a general moral laxity. Furthermore, he believes this system to be responsible for the dwarfed bodies of children, because of their premature introduction to factory life, and that this bodily deterioration weakens their moral power. He speaks as a lover of Man, and as a lover of his country, ambitious for her true welfare. It is the man, and the poet of Man, lifting up his voice against that which seems to him a great social and *moral* wrong. He emphasizes the sound ethical principle, that no person can be used merely as a means — as a mere tool or instrument for the realization of an end in which he has no inherent interest. Man is an ethical being, and he must be regarded and treated as such — not as a *means*, but as an *end in himself*, as Kant says. Progress cannot be justified from any point of view that overlooks this fact, and no social order should be tolerated that makes against, rather than for, Man's moral development. A Nation's greatness rests upon the moral worth of its people, and its prime duty is to secure to all born upon its soil the opportunities for at least an elementary education, and training in morality and religion.

"The Excursion" closes with this discussion of the industrial order. It is a long and, to some persons, a tedious poem. One can understand, although he may not sympathize with, Jeffrey's famous criticism, "It will not do." One can also understand how a man of Byron's temperament should speak of "a drowsy, frowzy poem, call'd 'The Excursion.'" On the other hand, one can also appreciate such praise as men like Hazlitt, H. Crabb Robinson, Southey, Charles Lamb, and others, bestowed upon it. Hazlitt opened his review in the *Examiner* by saying: "In power of intellect, in lofty conception, in the depth of feeling at once simple and sublime, which pervades every part of it, and which gives to every object an almost preternatural and preterhuman interest, this work has seldom been surpassed."[1] Robinson could place it "among the noblest works of the human intellect," and to him it was also "one of the most delightful." Southey, after reading it, was sure that "it is by the side of Milton that Wordsworth will have his station awarded him by posterity." Charles Lamb said, "It is the noblest conversational poem I ever read — a day in Heaven."

And so it has been since Wordsworth's day; critics have condemned and admired it. Unquestionably it has both merit and demerit. That it is gravely serious, sometimes gloomy, and more or less prosaic, frequently prolix, and, of course, without dramatic action, is evident. On the other hand, that it is full of noble sentiment, lofty conception, profound and tender feeling, beautiful description, eloquent apostrophe, sound teaching, and wise observation, is also evident to him who carefully peruses it. Of immediate interest to us, however, are the views of Nature, Man, and Human Life, which the author embodies in this didactic poem, and which must be summarized before the poem is dismissed.

Concerning the Poet's attitude toward Nature, as expressed in "The Excursion," it may be said that it is virtually the same as in his other works already considered, with the qualifications noted

[1] Hazlitt, The English Poets, p. 343.

in the previous chapter. All through this elaborate poem there is manifest that ardent love of Nature so conspicuous in the poems of the " Lyrical Ballads," and of the Grasmere period. Every book bears testimony to this fact. And the same peculiarities of the Nature-poet that have been revealed to us in the large body of verse already interpreted are evident here also. We see both the landscape artist and the poet of insight. He views Nature in her external features, enchanted by the variety and beauty of her forms, but he sees also deep into her inner life. Indeed, in " The Excursion," more than elsewhere, Wordsworth seems to be a descriptive poet, and often paints for us superb pictures of the face of Nature. What Professor Masson has said of Wordsworth as a descriptive poet is specially confirmed in " The Excursion " : " It was one of his most valued claims, therefore, that he should be considered a genuine English descriptive poet. And certainly this is a claim that even those who think most humbly of his attainments cannot deny him. There would be a propriety, we think, in remembering Wordsworth as a descriptive poet along with Chaucer and Thomson, thus distinguishing him both from such poets as Burns and Tennyson, on the one hand, and from such poets as Keats on the other. In such poets as Burns and Tennyson, the element of what may be called *human reference* is always so decided that, though no poets describe Nature more beautifully when they have occasion, it would still be improper to speak of them specially as descriptive poets. To borrow a distinction from the sister art, it may be said that, if Burns and Tennyson are more properly classed with the figure-painters, notwithstanding the extreme beauty and finish of their natural background, so, on the same principle, Wordsworth, whose skill in delineating the human subject is also admitted, may yet not erroneously be classed with the landscape-painters. On the other hand, he differs from poets like Keats in this, that, being a native of the country, and accustomed therefore to the appearances of rural nature in all seasons, he does not confound Nature with Vegetation. In the poetry of

Keats, as all must feel, there is an excess of merely botanical imagery; in reading his descriptions we seem either to breathe the air of a hothouse, heavy with the moist odors of great-leafed exotics, or to lie full-stretched at noon in some shady nook in a wood, rank underneath with the pipy hemlock, and kindred plants of strange overgrowth. In Wordsworth, as we have seen, there is no such unhealthy lusciousness. He has his spots of thick herbage, and his banks of florid richness too; but what he delights in is the broad, clear expanse, the placid lake, the pure pellucid air, the quiet outline of the mountain." [1]

But "The Excursion" also reveals the poet of insight — the mystical intuitionalist — possessed of "the vision and the faculty divine," whose mind transcends the limits of sense and ordinary poetic imagination, and sees into the inner life of Reality. As a result we find, as elsewhere, a rich spiritual conception of the physical world. Book I, which records the history of the Wanderer, is saturated with this spiritual conception of corporeal things, and in Book IX we find the Poet affirming an *active* Principle in "every form of being" — "the Soul of all the worlds" — uniting all things into a spiritual brotherhood.[2]

Furthermore, this Spirit of Nature ministers to human need. She brings consolation in distress, and comfort and healing to the sick soul. She is Man's counselor and friend, his teacher in moral and spiritual things, inciting him to high and holy purpose, and granting him wisdom, inspiration, and peace. Of all the fine passages in the numerous poems previously considered, in which our Poet speaks of Nature's relations to Man, it is questionable whether any of them can equal the eloquent description of Nature's ministry to Man presented in Book IV of "The Excursion." Indeed, it may be questioned whether, in the history of Nature-poetry, anything can be found to surpass it. Wordsworth here proclaims, in lofty verse, and with fervent spirit, the power of Nature to tranquilize, heal, dignify, inspire, teach, and bless the human soul.

[1] Masson's Wordsworth, Shelley, Keats, 45-46.   [2] The Excursion, IX, 1-20.

Still another point evident from " The Excursion," which is in harmony with what we have previously seen, is that Wordsworth's spiritual conception of Nature is rooted in his early mystical experience, and especially in the more pronounced forms of it as manifested in the trance-consciousness of his boyhood and youth. The mental history of the Wanderer, recorded in Book I, which is essentially the mental history of the Poet, proves this. It was in these " high hours " that the corporeal world seemed to have but a shadowy existence at best, and that Spirit appeared to be the great Reality. This gradually ripened into an abiding faith, which is the very soul of his earlier poetry, and, in a sense, the essence of his religion, for he soon conceived of this Spirit as not only the heart of all things, but as sustaining relations to, yes, as having its abode in, the mind of Man, and performing a most sacred office for him. So convinced was he of the truth of all this that he regarded it as a heavenly illumination, and believed himself called to be the oracle through which this spiritual revelation was to be made known to men.

One thing more ought to be noted here, and that is the Poet's attitude toward Science in her methods of dealing with Nature. Wordsworth is sometimes represented as being hostile to Science, and his severe condemnation of her in " The Excursion," unless carefully examined, might furnish grounds for such a conception. In the Wanderer's conversation with the Solitary he takes occasion to rebuke modern Science for losing the Soul of things in her methods of dealing with the world. He compares our " Great Discoverers " with the devotees of heathen religions, who see a spirit in things, and then exclaims : Shall they obtain

> From sense and reason less than these obtained,
> Though far misled? Shall men for whom our age
> Unbaffled powers of vision hath prepared,
> To explore the world without and world within,
> Be joyless as the blind? Ambitious spirits —
> Whom earth, at this late season, hath produced
> To regulate the moving spheres, and weigh

The planets in the hollow of their hand;
And they who rather dive than soar, whose pains
Have solved the elements, or analysed
The thinking principle — shall they in fact
Prove a degraded Race? and what avails
Renown, if their presumption make them such?
Oh! there is laughter at their work in heaven!
Enquire of ancient Wisdom; go, demand
Of mighty Nature, if 't was ever meant
That we should pry far off yet be unraised;
That we should pore, and dwindle as we pore,
Viewing all objects unremittingly
In disconnection dead and spiritless;
And still dividing, and dividing still,
Break down all grandeur, still unsatisfied
With the perverse attempt, while littleness
May yet become more little; waging thus
An impious warfare with the very life
Of our own souls![1]

But this does not end Wordsworth's condemnation of the attitude of Science. He protests against her arrogance and irreverence. There is no spiritual uplift in her methods, and her motives and ends evince a haughty self-love. Nature herself is offended by all this:

And if indeed there be
An all-pervading Spirit, upon whom
Our dark foundations rest, could he design
That this magnificent effect of power,
The earth we tread, the sky that we behold
By day, and all the pomp which night reveals;
That these — and that superior mystery
Our vital frame, so fearfully devised,
And the dread soul within it — should exist
Only to be examined, pondered, searched,
Probed, vexed, and criticised? — Accuse me not
Of arrogance, unknown Wanderer as I am,
If, having walked with Nature threescore years,
And offered, far as frailty would allow,
My heart a daily sacrifice to Truth,

[1] The Excursion, IV, 943-968.

I now affirm of Nature and of Truth,
Whom I have served, that their DIVINITY
Revolts, offended at the ways of men
Swayed by such motives, to such ends employed;
Philosophers, who, though the human soul
Be of a thousand faculties composed,
And twice ten thousand interests, do yet prize
This soul, and the transcendent universe,
No more than as a mirror that reflects
To proud Self-love her own intelligence;
That one, poor, finite object, in the abyss
Of infinite Being, twinkling restlessly![1]

It might be inferred from this that Wordsworth was really hostile
to scientific investigation, especially when the above protest is read
in connection with similar ones uttered in other parts of "The Excursion," and in "The Tables Turned," "A Poet's Epitaph," and
"Stanzas suggested in a Steamboat off St. Bees' Heads." However natural this inference, it is contrary to the real facts in the
case. Not infrequently does Wordsworth pay his tribute to Science,
acknowledging especially her beneficent work in the practical application of her results. What the Poet objects to is her "brutish
slavery" to the object, her subjection to sense (her votaries often
having no mind "but the mind of their own eyes"), her contempt
for imagination, her indifference to beauty, her arrogance and
irreverence, her heartless methods, her blindness to the Soul of
things, her general materialism and lack of spiritual insight. There
is much more in Nature than Science sees, or can see, with her
purely intellectual methods. She seems lost to the higher meaning
of things, and especially to their meaning for Man. She fails to
perceive the lofty offices of Nature — her moral, æsthetic, aye,
and even her religious ministry. To all this Science seems blind,
and she often affronts Nature herself by her pride and self-love.
It is against this that Wordsworth inveighs, and his protest is
the earnest protest of one who has walked daily with Nature,
recognizing and communing with her Spirit, learning with "the

[1] The Excursion, IV, 968–994.

practised eye," "the inevitable ear," and "the watchful heart" the
lessons that she had to impart. To him Nature had a voice, and
she spake of God and things eternal, of high and holy truths, of
consolation and spiritual healing, of wisdom and moral strength.
For him, too, she had visions and illuminations that disclosed her
inner being. When this is remembered, we can understand how
his poetic soul at times became impatient with him "whose mind
is but the mind of his own eyes"; whose irreverence permits him
to "peep and botanize upon his mother's grave"; whose "meddling
intellect" misshapes "the beauteous forms of things," and "murders
to dissect"; whose mind can "pry far off yet be unraised," or
"pore and dwindle as it pores"; and whose soul ruthlessly un-
souls the universe. For such a mind Wordsworth had little sympathy; but for the studious, reverent, far-seeing man of science,
who sees the life of things behind their external forms — the unity
of Nature beyond her manifold shapes — and tries to learn the high
ends which she subserves, the Poet had a welcome hand and a
sympathetic heart. He recognized the fact that there is no necessary antagonism between the Poet who looks at Nature with the
eye of sense, and with the eye of imagination, and the Scientist
who views her form through sense and reason. Indeed, he has
left on record an admirable statement of his views of the relations
between Poetry and Science. In it there is not the slightest
evidence of a feeling that mutual hostility necessarily exists between them. Rather, in many respects, does he think the Poet
and Scientist have the same end in view — to give pleasure —
and that only cordial relations naturally exist between their respective disciplines. In fact, Science is, in a sense, the help-meet of
Poetry, and Poetry is a supplement to Science. In the Preface to
the "Lyrical Ballads" it is stated that the Poet "considers man
and nature as essentially adapted to each other, and the mind of
man as naturally the mirror of the fairest and most interesting
qualities of nature. And thus the Poet, prompted by this feeling
of pleasure which accompanies him through the whole course of

his studies, converses with general nature, with affections akin to those, which, through labour and length of time, the man of science has raised up in himself, by conversing with those particular parts of nature which are the objects of his studies. The knowledge both of the Poet and the man of science is pleasure ; but the knowledge of the one cleaves to us as a necessary part of our existence, our natural and inalienable inheritance ; the other is a personal and individual acquisition, slow to come to us, and by no habitual and direct sympathy connecting us with our fellow-beings. The man of science seeks truth as a remote and unknown benefactor ; he cherishes and loves it as his solitude : the Poet, singing a song in which all human beings join with him, rejoices in the presence of truth as our visible friend and hourly companion. Poetry is the breath and finer spirit of all knowledge ; it is the impassioned expression which is in the countenance of all Science." [1] It is evident from all this that Wordsworth is not hostile to scientific investigation when it is carried on in the right spirit.

And now, passing from Wordsworth's treatment of Nature in " The Excursion," to summarize his views on Man as contained therein, we find that he takes the same attitude toward Man, and expresses the same sentiments concerning him, to be found in the rest of his verse. Here he is the lover of Man just as truly as in the " Lyrical Ballads," and in other poems. Men as they commend themselves for consideration are men in their elemental passions and feelings —

> chiefly those
> Essential and eternal in the heart,
> That, 'mid the simpler forms of rural life,
> Exist more simple in their elements,
> And speak a plainer language. [2]

All through " The Excursion " he deals with simple characters — persons who move in the humbler walks of life. He takes as his subjects chiefly the dalesmen of Grasmere Vale. In the very

[1] Prose Works, edited by William Knight, I, 61–62.
[2] The Excursion, I, 343–347.

beginning of this elaborate poem we see him influenced by the same conviction respecting men as he expresses in Book XIII of "The Prelude," and in the Preface to the "Lyrical Ballads," and as he illustrates in the ballads themselves. In the story of the ruined cottage he tells a pathetic tale of domestic sorrow. The narratives told by the Pastor in the churchyard, as we have seen, are those of village characters — a story of simple lives. And when he takes up the cause of Man, in Books VIII and IX, it is the cause of the plain rural folk whose bodily, intellectual, and moral welfare is threatened by modern industrial life. His heart is with these lowly people, and he regards them as the corner-stone of the Nation. Briefly, "The Excursion" reveals the poet of Man, with a heart full of love for him, and a mind solicitous for his welfare. It reveals, also, that this poet sees Man at his best among the unconventionalized rural folk who occupy the modest and obscure stations of human life.

In regard to Man's essential being, Wordsworth, in "The Excursion," represents him as endowed with a rational, moral, and religious nature — with capacities for self-determination and self-guidance in the light of lofty ideals. His nature is godlike, and he can commune with God. He is a creature of faith, hope, and love, and holds membership in a kingdom of eternal worths. His " inner frame " is good, and in it are the promise and potency of immortal life. And, concerning Human Life, the Poet's interpretation is essentially Christian, especially his interpretation of mental, moral, and physical suffering — " the good and evil of our mortal state." The faith that subdues " melancholy fear "— which brings " blessed consolations in distress," and the moral strength needed for the soul's support — is, in the final analysis, really the faith of the Gospels.

It must not be inferred, however, that Wordsworth was merely giving utterance to an inherited traditional faith. We have seen how he was lost in the mazes of skepticism, and in the darkness of despair, and how gradually he had worked his way out into the light. Undoubtedly much of the teaching of "The Excursion" represents his own independent thinking as he sought light on these profound problems which his bitter experience had brought most conspicuously before him. As he meditated on them, he gradually came to the conclusion that the faiths which condition the real worth of life are those which are fundamentally Christian; and he accepted them, not because they are Christian, but because they, above all else, impart a rational meaning to human experience. It is not, therefore, a blind faith which the Poet sings, but one that is the result of mature meditation as he labored under what often seemed to him "the heavy and the weary weight of all this unintelligible world."

CHAPTER XVIII

THE PERIOD OF WORDSWORTH'S BEST WORK. SUMMARY. WORDSWORTH'S CONTRIBUTION TO POETRY

It is a difficult and highly uncertain task to determine when in a poet's development he reaches the height of his power. It is probably a still more uncertain task to indicate the limits beyond which his poetic activity becomes worth while. This is due to the fact that genius itself is uncertain. In spite of its peculiarity, however, it is, in a measure, subject to the laws of development which obtain in the biological and psychological realms. It grows, develops, matures, and decays. But it seems more fitful and freakish than ordinary mentality. With poets like Tennyson, it holds out well to the end. In other instances it is subject to a comparatively early decay. In the case of Wordsworth it is not such a difficult undertaking to determine, approximately at least, the period in which he did his best work, and when he reached the climax of his power as a poet. Matthew Arnold, in his Preface to " The Poems of Wordsworth," says, " Wordsworth composed verses during a space of some sixty years ; and it is no exaggeration to say that within one single decade of these years, between 1799 and 1808, almost all his really first-rate work was produced." [1] This statement is not justified by the facts. A considerable body of excellent verse was written by him later. Principal Shairp's chart, which is accepted also by Professor Dowden, as mapping out " in a broad and general way " the chronology of Wordsworth, is more nearly correct. He says : " There were three epochs in Wordsworth's poetry, though these shade so insensibly the one into the other, that any attempt exactly to define them must be somewhat arbitrary. . . . The spring-time of his

[1] Arnold, Essays in Criticism, Second Series, 136

genius would reach from his first settling at Racedown, or at any rate his going to Alfoxden in 1797, till his leaving Grasmere Town-End in 1808. The second epoch, or full midsummer of his poetry, would include his time at Allan Bank and his first years at Rydal Mount, as far as 1818 or 1820. This was the time when 'The Excursion,' 'Laodamia,' 'Dion,' and the 'Duddon Sonnets' were composed. The third epoch, or the sober autumn, reaching from about 1820 till he ceased from the work of composition, is the time of the ecclesiastical and other sonnets, of 'Yarrow Revisited,' and the Scottish poems of 1833; and lastly, of the memorials of his Italian tour in 1837." [1] Although statements of this kind are more or less arbitrary, the body of his poetry written before the end of the year 1813 — the year that witnessed the completion of "The Excursion"—constitutes the limit of our study. This seems to be a safe limit, so far as our special purpose is concerned, for it can hardly be questioned that, were the study of Wordsworth as a poet of Nature and a poet of Man to be pursued beyond this boundary, it would yield comparatively meager results. It was during these years that his genius as a Nature-poet seemed to glow with an almost heavenly radiance—when he was literally possessed of "the vision and the faculty divine." It was during these years that, in his relations to the natural world, he was enabled "to see into the life of things"—that he was Nature's high priest, and was attended by "the vision splendid." But it is a singular and pathetic fact that this mystical insight, which was such a notable feature of his poetic genius, seemed to vanish at about the close of this period. It appeared to die away, "and fade into the light of common day," and with its fading, Wordsworth was shorn of much of his remarkable power as a poet of Nature. He himself was conscious of this fact, and he turned to other sources for inspiration, as is manifest, for example, in his excellent poems "Laodamia" and "Dion," and in the "Ecclesiastical Sonnets." True, he wrote Nature-poems

---

[1] The Poetical Works of William Wordsworth, edited by Edward Dowden, I, p. lxxii.

later than 1813, and some, too, of admirable character. For instance, the beautiful ode " Composed upon an Evening of extraordinary Splendour and Beauty," in which the radiant mystical vision appears, for a moment, to have been "by miracle restored," [1] "The River Duddon" (a series of sonnets), "Yarrow Visited," " Yarrow Revisited," and "The Primrose of the Rock " are poems of a fairly high order. But, meritorious as they and others of similar character are, they partake chiefly of the nature of descriptive poetry. Usually they are wanting in that peculiar mystical insight which dominates much of the Nature-poetry belonging to the years that witnessed Wordsworth at his best as a poet. In these later years he is still a lover of Nature ; both his poetry and his prose works indicate this. But he is not the poet of rare spiritual intuition, seeing deep into the inner life of material Reality, and apprehending Nature's meaning for Man. The vision revealing the Soul of things has vanished, and, as a rule, he gazes merely upon their external form. There is, too, in his later poetry, an almost unconscious change in his attitude toward Nature as a refuge for the soul. The grief caused by the death of his brother, the chastening experiences of life, the discipline of sorrow, "the burthen of the mystery" of a world that human reason often finds impossible to understand, seemed gradually to lead him to a dependence on Christian faith much more than on his Nature-faith for power to comfort and sustain the human soul. This was noted in the last chapter. How marked this change was may be seen in the " Ecclesiastical Sonnets." In this large body of verse the word " Nature " does not occur half a dozen times. Here his poetry enshrines his Christian belief rather than his earlier Nature-faith. Of course this would naturally be expected from the subject with which the Poet is dealing, but the very fact that he selects such a subject reveals how different his mental and spiritual attitude is from that of his earlier years. The vision and the gleam have departed. He sees now with the eye of Christian faith, and with the

[1] Composed upon an Evening of extraordinary Splendour and Beauty, 76.

eye of reason, rather than with the eye of mystical intuition. Still, it is interesting to note in these sonnets, as Professor Dowden points out, that here, too, Wordsworth evidently "found the Divine Presence abroad in nature and in the spirit of man, and refused to narrow it to a paddock, Anglican or other." [1]

Wordsworth's interest in Man, also, continued beyond this period. Political sonnets appear from time to time, revealing the Poet's keen interest in the course of events. They show him still zealous for the liberties and welfare of the people. The sonnets of 1816 furnish an interesting example. The "Ecclesiastical Sonnets," also, deal with a great human institution and, therefore, with Man. But here, also, there is a gradual falling off in power. Human nature, as it engrossed him in the "Lyrical Ballads," and in many of the short poems written at Grasmere, as well as in his two elaborate poems — "The Prelude" and "The Excursion" — does not occupy the place in his mind and heart that it once filled. There is comparatively little interpretation and exaltation of the primary feelings and passions, or exploiting of the fundamental virtues, as they are to be found in men living close to Nature — whose lives show the fashioning of her hand. Man thus considered no longer constitutes the Poet's prime source of inspiration. When, therefore, the year that witnessed the completion of "The Excursion" is set as the limit of our study of Wordsworth's development as a poet of Nature and a poet of Man, this does not seem to be purely arbitrary, but rather a line fixed, in a sense, by Nature herself. Regarding this, then, as the end of our journey, and reviewing "our long labour," we can say, in the words of him whose mental and spiritual evolution as a poet of Nature and a poet of Man we have been studying:

> We have traced the stream
> From the blind cavern whence is faintly heard
> Its natal murmur; followed it to light
> And open day; accompanied its course

[1] Dowden, The Poetical Works of William Wordsworth, I, p. lxi.

Among the ways of Nature, for a time
Lost sight of it bewildered and engulphed;
Then given it greeting as it rose once more
In strength, reflecting from its placid breast
The works of man and face of human life;
And lastly, from its progress have we drawn
Faith in life endless, the sustaining thought
Of human Being, Eternity, and God.[1]

But we have endeavored to trace the stream in more of its tributaries and branches, in more of its currents and undercurrents, and farther in its progress than did our Poet in "The Prelude," and it might be well, before bringing our study to a close, to look back and gather up our most important observations with reference to the content of Wordsworth's faith concerning Nature and Man.

First, it was found that, from childhood up to the close of the period of our study, Wordsworth's mind was possessed of the belief that Nature is something more than inert, insensate brute-matter — that she is endowed with conscious life. It was found that his conception of this Spirit in things varies. Sometimes he conceives of things and places as possessing souls of their own. Again, he seems to regard all things as permeated by one universal Spiritual Presence. The latter conception dominates his poetry. Furthermore, he does not say what matter, or corporeal reality, in itself is. He does not determine for us whether it is a mode of spiritual activity, or something *sui generis*. Nor does he deal with the metaphysical problem of the ultimate relation of material being to the Soul of things. He seems to conceive their relation as similar to that which exists between mind and body.

Secondly, it was seen also that, as Wordsworth gained more insight into Nature, he conceived of joyousness as being a part of her essential life. It became his faith "that every flower enjoys the air it breathes," and not only every flower, but trees and birds, and, indeed, even so-called inanimate objects. The heart of Nature is a joyous heart. Her whole being throbs with pleasure.

[1] The Prelude, XIV, 194–205.

Thirdly, Nature's life is a life of love also. Love pervades all things. It lies at the very core of all that is. It governs the relations of things with things, of things with men, and of men with men. Man and Nature are bound together in a kingdom in which love constitutes the omnipresent bond of Reality.

Fourthly, the Spirit of Nature is an ethical spirit, also, and morality is a part of her essential life. A moral Spirit lives in all things. Indeed, they are bound together by moral relations and laws. The order of the universe, to which the stars in their courses, as well as the minutest objects, are subject, is a moral order.

Fifthly, the Spirit of Nature is also a spirit of Wisdom. This is preëminently manifest in the offices which she performs in her relations to Man. She is in possession of resources that qualify her to perform a service which makes for his real welfare, and Wordsworth, at least by implication, seems to regard Wisdom as part of her fundamental life.

Turning from Wordsworth's conception of Nature's essential life to her functioning, we have found that Wordsworth conceives of Nature as sustaining the following important relations to Man :

First, from the very dawn of Man's existence she is in close relation to him, building and fashioning his soul. She builds and shapes human personality by operating especially through Man's emotional nature, and preëminently through the moral emotions.

Secondly, one of her principal offices is that of a moral teacher and guide to Man. From his childhood she performs this ministry, disciplining by her interventions — by her visitations of soft alarm, or by a ministry more palpable. She counsels, inspires, and impels to right living. She teaches and exemplifies the virtues, and warns against the vices. From her we learn more concerning good and evil than from all human teachers. Indeed, she serves as an ideal or pattern for Man. From her he can frame the measure of his own soul. However, under some circumstances, she incites to evil. One may be so constituted that, through sensitiveness to her voluptuous beauty, she may minister to the sensual within him, or he may so frequently violate the laws of his moral being, that her wilder moods may intensify his passions, and increase his spiritual callousness.

Thirdly, Nature may inform the mind along other than purely moral lines. The mighty sum of things has a voice, and speaks a message to the receptive and reverent mind. Nature can and does reveal truths to the intellect, and also to the higher spiritual nature of Man. She grants insight into the life of things, vouchsafing a much more profound conception of Reality than is to be gained by the analytical methods of science. She discloses her inner life or spirit to the reverent inquirer. Indeed, to the communing, sympathetic mind she furnishes a still deeper revelation to the soul — visions of God, and of the Spirit's eternal destiny.

Fourthly, Nature is a comforter and physician to Man. She brings consolations in distress, calm in anxiety and fret, support in weariness, healing in sickness, hope in despair, ministering to Man through her beauteous forms and through her manifestations of sympathy and love.

In short, we have found Wordsworth's faith to be, that there is a spiritual Presence dwelling in all things, and in the mind of Man. It is the quickening Power of both. As the Soul of things, it ministers in divers manners to the bodily, intellectual, æsthetic, moral, and even religious nature of Man. It is his builder, fashioner, counselor, physician, teacher, and friend. Instead of a crass materialism, or a naïve realism, the Poet gives us a spiritual interpretation of all Reality. Instead of a crude Deism, with merely a transcendent God, he gives us a world alive with the quickening power of an all-pervading Spirit. Instead of an all-engulfing Pantheism he teaches the transcendence of God, while, at the same time, predicating his immanence — preserving, however, the reality and individuality of God, things, and finite spirits, affirming their intimate relationship in a spiritual kingdom, and the gracious and beneficent ministry of the Spirit in things to the Spirit of Man. His is the Theist's faith in a spiritual universe, which our Poet affirms with his whole mind and heart, and with which his poetry of Nature throbs.

There was one aspect of Nature which failed to receive Wordsworth's serious attention, namely, her apparent cruelty. In the light of modern biological science a reflective poet of Nature cannot overlook the terrible struggle for existence in the animal world. Its trail of blood runs far back into the ages. Even a robust, optimistic faith, such as that of our Poet, would almost of necessity have wavered at times in contemplating this awful fact. It was this painful and bloody struggle, with the destruction and waste of living things, that at times almost overwhelmed his brother-poet, Tennyson. Cantos LIV, LV, and LVI of "In Memoriam" reveal to us how earnestly and carefully he had considered these things, and their bearing on faith in the goodness and love of God. Looking merely at Nature, he could find no ethical solution of the problem of suffering. For him Nature was "red in tooth and claw," and "with ravine, shriek'd against his creed" of faith in a God of love. He wrote to a friend, "If we look at Nature alone, full of perfection and imperfection, she tells us that God is disease, murder and rapine." [1] If Tennyson had been compelled to abide by the facts which Nature alone presented, he would never have been able to contemplate or interpret her in the optimistic fashion of Wordsworth. Rather would he have regarded her as a monster of iniquity. But his religious consciousness came to his aid when he was overwhelmed by the cruelty of Nature. He stretched "lame hands of faith" to what he felt was "Lord of all." He struggled with these ugly facts of Nature, and escaped the melancholy conclusions of the logical intellect, only by taking refuge in religious hope and trust.

Now Wordsworth seems as a rule to have closed his eyes to these phenomena. And it is difficult to determine the reason why. The fact that this great problem of biological evolution did not engross the scientific world during the period when Wordsworth

[1] Alfred, Lord Tennyson, A Memoir, by his Son, I, 314, New York, 1897.

wrote most of his poetry of Nature is hardly sufficient to account for it. A scientific elaboration of the fact of the struggle for existence, and the part which it plays in the evolution of the fittest types, is not necessary to make a man conscious of the terrible suffering that prevails, and has prevailed, in the animal world. As Professor Bradley remarks : " We need no theory to tell us that spiders eat flies and stoats kill rabbits, and yet Wordsworth almost entirely ignores such facts. A poet doubtless is at liberty to do so, and to confine himself to singing of the beauty and happiness of Nature. But then Wordsworth, unlike most poets, preached a *gospel* of Nature ; and, as a preacher, he was bound to face the phenomena that seem to throw doubt on his gospel, and to make us feel that after all they are consistent with it. I do not say that he could not have done this ; but he did not attempt it, and when he did not ignore the facts in question he showed an inclination to flinch from them.[1] He was here, it seems likely, still somewhat under the influence of Rousseau, which elsewhere he had shaken off. Just as Burns, in his address ' To a Field-mouse,' regrets that

> Man's dominion
> Has broken Nature's social union ;

just as Cowper declares that

> God made the country, and man made the town ;

so Wordsworth yields here and there too much to a tendency to contrast the happiness, innocence, and harmony of Nature with the unrest, misery, and sin of man." [2]

It is undoubtedly a fact that Wordsworth, in his attitude toward Nature, was primarily occupied with apprehending her as good and beneficent in her offices, and to a very large extent he ignored her cruelty, which often seemed to seriously perplex the faith of the spirit of Man. It may be that, in the revelations of the heart of

[1] See, for example, The Redbreast and the Butterfly.
[2] Professor Bradley, English Poetry and German Philosophy in the] Age of Wordsworth, 24–25.

Nature that came to him through his mystical intuition, she was apprehended as so essentially good in herself, and so essentially kind and ethical in her relations to Man and to the animal kingdom, that there was hardly room in Wordsworth's mind and heart for a less worthy conception. It may be, also, that, in his close relationship with Nature, he had gained such an insight into her real life that he apprehended even her warnings, penalties, and cruelties as beneficent ministries — as means toward worthy ends. Whether this be so or not, certain it is that Wordsworth's mind was dominated by an optimistic conception of Nature to such an extent that he seemed to be almost entirely oblivious of the awful facts that make against his faith. Such facts cannot properly be ignored by any one who proclaims a " gospel of Nature." Their bearing on faith in this gospel ought to be duly considered.

If we turn next to a summary of Wordsworth's views concerning Man, it will be recalled that he holds the following beliefs :

First, that Man may be found at his best where his life is most simple — where the conventionalities, customs, and institutions of society have not rendered it artificial and complex, and where he pursues his vocation close to Nature's heart. That is, among rural folk we may find human nature in its essential, universal, elemental life, better than elsewhere. And when we thus read it, despite all of the mental, moral, and spiritual infirmity disclosed, we find that fundamentally our humanity has worth. The inner nature is good ; and Man's potentialities are such that, under proper conditions, they will unfold to his credit, and he will achieve a worthy destiny under God.

Secondly, men are not isolated personal units. They exist as members of a spiritual kingdom, all possessed of moral natures, and subject to the same moral law. In this lies the fundamental oneness of the race, and the ultimate ground of the obligations of Man's humanity to Man. And, since Man is a moral being, no order of society is permissible that treats him as a tool — a mere means to an end. There is a native equality belonging to him by virtue of his essential constitution as moral, and this must be preserved at all hazards. Any violation of this moral obligation will not only entail serious consequences on the individual, but also on society and the nation. Again, Man as organized under government must rule in righteousness. Tyranny and injustice must be overthrown, and the essential rights of men must be zealously guarded. A nation's greatness does not lie in its material possessions, nor in its conquests, but in its moral ideals, in its righteous rule, in the lofty character of its statesmen, and in its moral achievements or progress.

Thirdly, Wordsworth holds that life is worth living. Despite its manifold evils, life itself is a good. The evils themselves may prove stepping-stones to good. Suffering is a means to an ethical end. Through it virtues are developed which strengthen and adorn the soul. Furthermore, Man is not alone in the world, nor alone in his sufferings. The resources of Divine Providence are at the command of the human soul in every condition of human need. Faith in God, in duty, and in a glorious destiny for the worthy, is the key to the solution of the problem of our earthly life, with its varied vicissitudes, and its large portion of physical and mental suffering.

This is the creed of the Poet of Nature and Man, which an extended study of his mental and spiritual development reveals. It is a creed full of lofty spiritualism, moral idealism, and sane optimism. Sometimes it is embodied in simple verse, and again, in noble and eloquent song — all of which breathes a pure spirit, and is colored by fervent sympathy and love.

Were we tracing the evolution of Wordsworth as a literary artist, we should, of course, find that he was under obligations to his English predecessors. He was undoubtedly indebted to Chaucer, Spenser, Shakespeare, Milton, and Burns. His obligations extend even beyond the boundaries of English poetry, for he owed a literary debt to ancient classical authors, especially to Vergil and Theocritus. But so far as his mental and spiritual attitude toward

Nature was concerned, his indebtedness to his predecessors was really not very large. He was probably influenced in this respect by Vergil among the ancients, and by Burns, Wither, and Lady Winchelsea among English poets. He was also influenced by Rousseau and the *Zeit-Geist*. The age was one in which the desirability of a return to Nature was proclaimed as a gospel. The atmosphere was more or less charged with it, and Wordsworth was undoubtedly affected by it — all the more because it was in harmony with his own predispositions and likings. But, after all, Wordsworth's profound interest in Nature, and his fundamental faiths concerning her, were largely due to his own mystical endowment, and to his personal relations with her during many years in a physical environment remarkable for its beauty and grandeur. He spoke out of his own rich experience. His poetry embodies convictions born of this unique experience, which, down to 1813, had covered half a lifetime and more. How far it differs from that of his predecessors in English Nature-poetry will be evident by a brief glance at their contributions. Much of Wordsworth's verse represents a reaction against the artificiality of preceding English poetry relating to Nature. Wordsworth affirms that from Milton to Thomson no new contributions had been made to nature-images. The same stereotyped pictures, and their verbal symbols, were used by successive poets. Such poetry indicates really no direct contact with, or love of, Nature. Its knowledge is not first-hand, and its emotion is really an affectation. According to Wordsworth, conventionalism, or artificiality, characterizes the poetic treatment of Nature during this period.

However, throughout the eighteenth century there was a strong feeling for Nature, and a careful study of the poets of this period reveals a foreshadowing of all the Wordsworthian conceptions concerning her. Not only was his idea of Nature as pervaded by a universal Spirit anticipated, but nearly all his views of the various relations which she sustains to Man were pointed out by more or less obscure poets. Concerning the presence of a Spirit in things, it is true that the dominant conception of God's relation to Nature prevailing at this time was of His transcendence rather than of His immanence. He is the creator, fashioner, and governor of the world. Still, we have God's immanence taught also. It may be found in minor poets, like Hamilton, Parnell, Mallet, Akenside, Beattie, and Lady Winchelsea (to whom Wordsworth was more or less indebted), although it does not appear as a powerful inspiring vision and faith dominating the art and life of the poet, as in the case of Wordsworth. We find the same teaching in Thomson's elaborate poem "The Seasons," and in Cowper's poem entitled "The Task." In Thomson's poem the heavens and the earth are filled with the Divine Presence. Even the seasons are manifestations of Him. But this does not represent Thomson's ruling conception. It is not for him a fervent, inspiring faith, a rich communion supporting the spirit, and controlling the conduct of the poet, as it is with Wordsworth.

Cowper, too, affirms :

> The Lord of all, himself through all diffused,
> Sustains and is the life of all that lives.[1]

But, although Cowper had a real love and passion for natural objects, as Wordsworth himself observes, what he says of a soul that lives and works in all things seems more like religious conviction than mystical intuition. It seems like a poetic expression of religious faith. It was different with Wordsworth. With him it was an overpowering spiritual vision which seemed to develop almost into a religion. He did not apprehend this spiritual Presence in Nature from the standpoint of a previously formed Theistic faith, but his Theistic faith, so far as it relates to Nature, seemed to be the natural result of his intuition.

Again, in Young's "Night Thoughts" we read :

> All-knowing! — all unknown! — and yet well-known!
> Near, though remote! and, though unfathom'd, felt!
> And, though invisible, forever seen!

[1] Cowper, The Task, VI, 221–222.

And seen in all! the great and the minute:
Each globe above, with its gigantic race,
Each flower, each leaf, with its small people swarm'd,
(Those puny vouchers of Omnipotence!)
To the first thought, that asks, " From whence?" declare
Their common source. Thou Fountain, running o'er
In rivers of communicated joy!
Who gavest us speech for far, far humbler themes!
Say, by what name shall I presume to call
Him I see burning in these countless suns,
As Moses, in the bush?[1]

But here, too, we have not a sublime spiritual intuition. Virtually throughout his elaborate poem Young is merely using poetry as a means to overthrow infidelity, and to give expression to a defense of his Theistic and Christian faith. It is a case of Apologetics in poetry. With Young, God in all things is not a mystical intuition, but rather a philosophical or theological conception expressed in verse.

Even Pope, writing prior to Cowper and Young, despite the Deistic influence to which he was subject in his relations to Bolingbroke, gives a richer conception of God's presence in Nature than they — one, also, that approaches more nearly to Wordsworth's. In his "Essay on Man" he says:

All are but parts of one stupendous whole,
Whose body nature is, and God the soul;
That, changed through all, and yet in all the same,
Great in the earth, as in th' ethereal frame,
Warms in the sun, refreshes in the breeze,
Glows in the stars, and blossoms in the trees,
Lives thro' all life, extends through all extent,
Spreads undivided, operates unspent.[2]

Fine as this undoubtedly is, yet how devoid of richness, color, and *subjectivity* it seems compared with Wordsworth's conception and belief as found in "Lines written in Early Spring," "To my Sister," "Expostulation and Reply," "The Tables Turned," "Lines

[1] Young, Night Thoughts, Night Ninth, 2199–2212.
[2] Pope, Essay on Man, Epistle I, 267–274.

composed a few miles above Tintern Abbey," and portions of
"The Prelude" and "The Excursion." How *objective* and *impersonal* it seems! With the exception of a few lines, how like a
philosophical or theological proposition, either inherited or ration-
ally inferred, and embodied in verse! It does not bear the marks
of real poetic inspiration and mystical insight. It does not seem to
be a real birth of spiritual imagination, nor does it throb with the
intense personal life of the author, as do the poems of the Grasmere
poet.

Wordsworth was, indeed, anticipated or foreshadowed by eighteenth century poets, so far as a feeling for Nature is concerned,
and also in his conceptions of the Spirit of Nature, and of her
relations to Man. But there is a marked difference in the attitude
of these poets and that of Wordsworth. With none of them was
Nature, as pervaded by a Spirit-life, such a profound *experience*
as she was with Wordsworth. From childhood he had felt her presence warning him, leading him, fashioning him, calling him to be
her high priest, counseling him, consoling him, refreshing him,
instructing him, vouchsafing visions to him, and acquainting him
with her inner life. He communed with her, reverenced her,
loved her. She was for many years an intense passion with him.
He was so charmed by, and engrossed with, her that he became
a reverent and affectionate worshiper at her shrine. Through his
mystical nature he gained an insight into the very Soul of things.
He *saw*, and then believed, and what he saw became a living
power in his life both as a poet and as a man. Much of his poetry
is the outgrowth of his vision and its attendant belief. What he *saw*
— with its meaning for Man — was for him a tremendous reality,
and he felt morally commissioned to speak the vision through his
art. It is in this sense that we must understand Wordsworth's apprehension of Nature as possessed of Spirit. It was not a mere series
of hints, suggestions, illuminating gleams, mild feelings, and pensive and more or less penetrating imaginations, as seems to be the
case with the minor poets referred to. With Wordsworth it was

rapturous vision, profound intuition, intense and sublime passion, deep ethical conviction, reverent and affectionate communion, heavenly illumination, and " woe is me if I preach not the message." It was not merely an intellectual proposition to be subscribed to, nor a conviction born of logical processes in reflecting upon Nature, nor even a religious conviction as such, but it was a powerful experience, the chief elements of which were vision, intuition, belief, communion, inspiration, love, and moral resolve. His poetry pulsates with this unusual sense of nearness to the life of Nature. He feels himself called of the Spirit, dedicated and commissioned by the Spirit, to speak no dream, but things oracular. And it is thus he speaks. His genius is aglow with the living warmth and radiance of the visions and illuminations vouchsafed, and is burdened with their vital ethical import for Man. And his metrical language is not merely a vehicle for the communication of the vision and inspiration, but it, too, constitutes, in a measure, the gift of the Spirit of Nature ; so that, in the richness and variety of their experience, in the penetration and profundity of their insight, in the quality and suggestiveness of their inspirations, in the sublimity of their apprehension of the moral import of Nature's relation to Man, the humbler poets, who foreshadowed Wordsworth, are far removed from him. He is immeasurably their superior. As a Nature-poet he is in a class by himself among English bards. His song is unmatched, voicing, in an almost incomparable manner, the exquisite melody of Nature's external life, and the beautiful, profound, and mystical harmony of her inner Spirit.

As a poet of Man, also, he was in a measure unique. There is something individual in the way in which he was led through love of Nature to love of Man — in the gradual subordination of the former, and in the exaltation of the latter, which, as we have seen, had a far-reaching influence on his art. There was something unique, also, in his method of approach to the observation and contemplation of Man, and in the results thereof. On the part of his critics this constituted a ground of objection to him as a poet. They accused him of degrading his art in the selection of his subjects. They also accused him of seeing far more in human nature as manifest in peasants, vagrants, and humble folk generally than may actually be found there. But we have seen that Wordsworth was a realist in this respect, firmly determined to find out what essential human nature is. He was a keen psychologist, endeavoring to discover what Man is when stripped of the artificiality due to the conventions and institutions of society — what the "feelings and passions" are which constitute his fundamental life. And it was among these simple folk that he believed the essentials of our common nature are to be found; therefore he trained his powers of observation and insight on such as these. "The lonely roads were open schools" in which he daily read

> With most delight the passions of mankind,
> Whether by words, looks, sighs, or tears, revealed;
> There saw into the depths of human souls,
> Souls that appear to have no depth at all
> To careless eyes.[1]

Here he heard

> From mouths of men obscure and lowly, truths
> Replete with honour; sounds in unison
> With loftiest promises of good and fair.[2]

This method of approach to the study of Man is refreshing and, in some respects, original. It lies at the basis of much of his optimism, for by its use he soon discovered that our "inner frame" is good. It was the "important lessons of mankind," learned in this way, that he embodied in verse, singing a lofty song in honor of essential human nature thus revealed, and as manifest in the fundamental relations which Man sustains.

There was something wholesome and refreshing, also, and in some respects unusual, in the genuine sympathy and love for Man which inspired much of his poetry, as well as in the democracy

---

[1] The Prelude, XIII, 163-168.   [2] Ibid, 183-185.

which lies at the foundation of it. He was a lover of the poor and lowly, and a champion of their rights and interests. He sympathized with them in their suffering, and did honor to their fidelity and spirit of endurance, their patience and resignation, under it. And the poems which are the outcome of this love are a genuine contribution to English verse. For tenderness and pathos, for sympathy and genuine passion, they are unsurpassed in the history of English poetry. Their author has sounded the depths of the human heart, and seems to appreciate and understand nearly every phase of human woe. He discerns the virtues it calls forth, and the meaning of suffering in the Divine economy.

Furthermore, he guards the moral claims of these lowly folk against the evils of the social order. He makes an earnest protest against an industrial system that destroys the *moral* equality of men. Nature has established this equality, and no order of Man ought to interfere with it. Men cannot be regarded as tools or instruments — as means to ends. They must be treated as ends in themselves. And Wordsworth, in his poetry, makes not only an earnest protest against interference with this moral equality, but an eloquent appeal for its preservation by statute. This, of course, is not a new doctrine, but it was so earnestly felt by the Poet that it would be difficult to find verse throbbing with a more ardent plea for recognition of this truth, and for action in accordance with it.

Again, originality is manifest in his apprehension of Man in the city. His was a unique method of forming an ideal in boyhood, based on the heroic figure and mien of the shepherd of his native hills. It was unique, also, to look at Man from the standpoint of this ideal when he beheld his physical and moral degradation in the great city by the Thames, and have his faith in human nature not only confirmed but strengthened thereby. There is poetic originality, too, in his mystical apprehension of the unity of the race under moral law, despite the diversity of human nature presented here; and also in his poetic intuition of Man's glorious destiny under God. It reveals the character of the optimism which underlies so much of his poetry, and also how his genius was pre-eminently genius of insight. It was genius that *saw* rather than inferred, believing only on the basis of inference. And this peculiar mark of his poetic power is stamped on his art.

Again, within the sphere of politics, he exhibits unusual qualities as a poet of Man. His patriotic poems — especially the political sonnets — reveal this. He is comparatively free from blind partisanship, and a purely emotional patriotism. There is sanity in his political fervor. A rich ethical vein runs through this part of his nature, and it manifests itself in his verse. Moral ideals dominate his views and feeling. A profound love of country is tempered by a sublime sense of duty, which makes him bold to rebuke his own Nation for shortcomings and failures. A government's power does not lie in might, but in right. Like the prophets of old he lifts up his voice against wickedness in high places. Neither is his patriotism provincial. In this respect he is a citizen of the world. All men are loved as brothers. National limits do not constitute limits to his love. Early he became " a patriot of the world," and remained such. Despising injustice and tyranny wherever found, he was champion and defender of the rights of men regardless of nationality. The " Poems dedicated to National Independence and Liberty " are a genuine contribution to English verse. They will bear comparison with the noblest productions of a literature rich in political poetry and prose. Mr. Myers truly says that they " are worthy of comparison with the noblest passages of patriotic verse or prose which all our history has inspired — the passages where Shakespeare brings his rays to focus on ' this earth, this realm, this England ' — or where the dread of national dishonour has kindled Chatham to an iron glow — or where Milton rises from the polemic into the prophet, and Burke from the partisan into the philosopher. The armoury of Wordsworth, indeed, was not forged with the same fire as that of these ' invincible knights of old.' He had not swayed senates, nor directed policies, nor gathered into one ardent bosom all the spirit of a heroic age. But he had deeply felt what it is that makes the greatness of nations; in that extremity no man was more staunch than he; no man more unwaveringly disdained unrighteous empire, or kept the might of moral forces more steadfastly in view. Not Stein could place a manlier reliance on 'a few strong instincts and a few plain rules'; not Fichte could invoke more convincingly the 'great allies' which work with 'Man's unconquerable mind.' " [1]

Finally, if, as a poet of Man, in dealing with the subject of Human Life, especially in " The Excursion," Wordsworth did not produce a carefully reasoned system, or a real philosophy of life, nor present anything especially new or striking in his musing on the profound problems which such a subject involves, he at least thinks for himself; his conclusions, involving a recognition of the Christian solution of these problems, are independently reached. His conviction that the " one adequate support for the calamities of mortal life " is belief in a beneficent God, who overrules all things for good, in the reality of virtue, and in the soul's imperishable worth, was not a blind adoption of traditional or generally accepted views, but a conviction born of serious meditation on the more mysterious aspects of human life. And in his meditations there is a rare frankness in his concessions to Pessimism. He freely grants all that can be truthfully said concerning the dark side of human experience. There is no flinching here. He recognizes the facts of pain and misery — of physical pain, and of mental and moral misery. In his poetry of Man the tragedy of life is most pathetically dwelt upon — to such an extent, indeed, and in such a manner that it would be difficult to find, in all poetical literature, Wordsworth's equal as a poet of pathos. He sounded the profound depths of human suffering. He was acquainted with many of its forms. He brooded over its mystery, and there is something unusual and inspiring in his unconquerable will to see light in darkness, and good in the midst of physical, mental, and moral evil. He anticipates Browning in this respect. He recognizes that

[1] Myers, Wordsworth, 78.

life has resources sufficient for life, and that these may be found in Nature and in Man himself, in faith in Divine Providence, in belief in duty, and conformity to it, and in the soul's firm conviction of her immortal destiny.

Such were the faiths and convictions which Wordsworth embodied in his poetry of Nature and of Man. After freely conceding all limitations and defects which a just criticism finds in this portion of his work, it would seem, in the light of our study, that we must see him as Coleridge saw him, when listening to "The Prelude," "ere yet the last strain dying awed the air," as "a great Bard," and "in the choir of ever-enduring men." By virtue of the rare quality of his genius, by the intrinsic worth of its creations, and by its illuminating and inspiring visions, intuitions, and meditations, with their profound significance for human life, Wordsworth has won for himself an exalted place among the Immortals.

INDEX

Admonition, 175
Advance — come forth from thy Tyrolean ground, 246
Affliction of Margaret——, The, 71, 101, 177, 187–189, 239
Akenside, 307
Alas! what boots the long laborious quest, 246
Alice Fell; or, Poverty, 184
Ancient Mariner, The, 90
Anticipation (October, 1803), 192
Arnold, Matthew, 295
At the Grave of Burns, 167
Autobiographical Memoranda, 2

Bacon, 241
Beattie, 42, 307
Beaumont, 171, 172, 231, 232
Beaumont, Lady, 173, 190, 231, 232, 235
Beaupuy, 77
Beloved Vale! I said, when I shall con, 175
Birkett, Mrs. Anne, 10
Böhme, Jakob, 90
Bolingbroke, 308
Borderers, The, 80, 88, 242
Bradley, 303
Brook! whose society the Poet seeks, 175
Brothers, The, 71, 93, 96, 101, 177, 178, 179, 181, 183, 189
Browning, 163, 314
Burke, 244, 313
Burns, 161, 163, 168, 235, 286, 303, 305, 306
Byron, 70, 100, 285

Caird, Edward, 137
Canning, 244
Carlyle, 132
Character of the Happy Warrior, 194, 201–203
Chatham, 313
Chaucer, 35, 235, 286, 305
Childless Father, The, 177

Clarkson, 184
Clifford, Lord, 232
Coleridge, Samuel Taylor, 31, 37, 54, 66, 73, 77, 86–91, 96, 104, 122, 123, 124, 135 n., 136, 145, 147, 148, 155, 164, 167, 168, 183, 195, 197, 219, 228, 235, 236, 242, 244, 315
Coleridge, Sarah, 234
Collins, 42
Complaint of a Forsaken Indian Woman, The, 93, 96, 101, 122
Composed at the same Time and on the same Occasion, 245
Composed upon an Evening of extraordinary Splendour and Beauty, 297
Convention of Cintra, The (Essay on), 243, 244
Convention of Cintra, The (Sonnet on), 245
Cottle, 73, 88, 124, 125
Courthope, 98 n.
Cowper, 51, 303, 307, 308
Crackanthorpe, Richard, 2

Dante, 70
Davy, 229
De Quincey, 74, 77, 78 n.
Descriptive Sketches, 43, 44, 46, 88
De Vere, 98
Dion, 296
Dobell, 221 n.
Dowden, 295, 296 n., 298
Duddon Sonnets, 296

Earl of Lonsdale, 227
Ecclesiastical Sonnets, 277, 278, 296, 297
Eillbanks, 10
Elector of Saxony, The, 203, 235
Elegiac Stanzas, 170
Elegiac Verses, 169, 170, 228
Ellen Irwin, or, the Braes of Kirtle, 228
Emerson, 226
England! the time is come when thou shouldst wean, 192

Evening Voluntaries, 130
Evening Walk, An, 42
Excursion, The, 11, 70, 71, 88, 147, 149,
    189, 195, 196, 197, 207, 222, 240, 241,
    242, 247, 249–294, 296, 298, 309, 314
Expostulation and Reply, 107, 108, 308

Feelings of the Tyrolese, 246
Fenwick, Miss, 205, 243
Fichte, 201, 314
Fielding, 30
Fountain, The, 93, 96, 101, 144, 189
Fox, Charles James, 90, 179, 180, 183,
    192, 203

Gay, 50
Godwin, William, 66, 67, 68, 77, 80, 81,
    84, 183, 266
Goethe, 70
Graham, 184
Grahame, 235
Graves, 211, 214, 215
Gray, 42
Green Linnet, The, 167
Guide to the Lakes, 151
Gustavus IV, 247

Hamilton, 307
Hart-leap Well, 156, 157, 184
Hazlitt, 100, 122, 123, 253, 254, 285
Her Eyes are Wild, 101
Hofer, 246
Home at Grasmere, 151 n.
Hudson, 190 n.
Hutchinson, Mary, 41, 160, 227
Hutchinson, Thomas, 196 n., 197 n.,
    249 n., 251 n.

I wandered lonely as a cloud, 115, 167,
    169
Idiot Boy, The, 93, 96, 101
In the Pass of Killicranky (1803), 192
Influence of Natural Objects, etc., 137
It is a beauteous Evening, calm and
    free, 167
It is not to be thought of that the Flood,
    191
It was an April morning: fresh and
    clear, 158, 159

Jeffrey, 135 n., 285
Johnson, 50
Jones, 42, 125, 138
Jowett, 216 n.
Juvenal, 50, 80

Kant, 284
Keats, 286, 287
Kitten and Falling Leaves, The, 167,
    171
Knight, 4 n., 41 n., 74 n., 78 n., 79 n.,
    91 n., 104 n., 116 n., 117 n., 124 n.,
    125 n., 136 n., 137 n., 139 n., 147,
    152 n., 153 n., 154 n., 155 n., 158 n.,
    163, 164 n., 182 n., 183 n., 184 n.,
    188 n., 192, 195 n., 197 n., 202 n.,
    206 n., 211 n., 212 n., 214 n., 215 n.,
    232 n., 234 n., 235 n., 239 n., 241 n.,
    243, 244 n., 250, 292 n.

Lamb, Charles, 66, 156, 160, 184, 244, 285
Laodamia, 296
Last of the Flock, The, 96, 101
Legouis, 2, 7, 42, 46, 50, 51, 52, 81
Lines (September, 1806), 192
Lines composed a few miles above
    Tintern Abbey, 124–135, 184, 200,
    201, 223, 226, 274, 275, 308
Lines on the Expected Invasion (1803),
    192
Lines written in Early Spring, 103, 104,
    105, 308
Look now on that Adventurer who hath
    paid, 247
Losh, James, 194
Lyrical Ballads, 70, 86–135, 180, 183,
    227, 259, 278, 286, 291, 292, 293,
    298

Mad Mother, The, 93, 96, 122
Mallet, 307
Marshall, Mrs., 79
Martial courage of a day is vain, The,
    246
Masson, 70, 71, 286, 287 n.
Matthews, 3
Michael, 71, 101, 177, 178, 179, 181,
    183, 189
Milton, 10, 35, 51, 182, 191, 244, 245,
    257, 285, 305, 306, 313
Milton! thou shouldst be living at this
    hour, 191
Morley, 110, 115, 165, 239
Musings near Aquapendente, 229
My heart leaps up when I behold, 167
Myers, 125, 170, 202, 228, 313, 314

Napoleon, 191, 192, 203, 235, 236, 245,
    246, 247
Narrow Girdle of rough stones and
    crags, A, 158, 160

Nature, Man, and Society, 194
Nelson, 201, 202, 203
Newton, 35
November (1806), 193
Nutting, 139, 140, 141

O Friend! I know not which way I
    must look, 191
October (1803), 192, 203
Ode. Intimations of Immortality, 6,
    137, 163, 184, 194, 204-229
Ode to Duty, 184, 194, 199, 200
Old Cumberland Beggar, The, 101, 116,
    117
Old Man Travelling, The, 93
Oldham, 50
On the Final Submission of the Tyro-
    lese, 246

Palafox, 246
Parnell, 307
Pasley, 243
Paul, 183 n.
Peter Bell, 117, 118-121, 145
Plato, 90, 216, 217
Plotinus, 90
Poems dedicated to National Independ-
    ence and Liberty, 70, 192, 193, 203,
    228, 236, 243, 245, 247, 313
Poems on the Naming of Places, 158
Poet's Epitaph, A, 109, 141, 142, 290
Poole, 124
Poole, Mrs., 147
Pope, 308
Prelude, The, 6, 9, 10, 11, 12, 13, 16,
    17, 18, 19, 20, 21, 22, 23, 24, 25, 27,
    28, 29, 30, 32, 33, 35, 36, 38, 43, 44,
    45, 46, 47, 49, 50, 52, 53, 54, 55, 57,
    59, 60, 61, 62, 63, 64, 65, 68, 72, 75,
    76, 82, 83, 84, 85, 89, 91, 94, 95, 102,
    110, 111, 112, 113, 114, 116, 120, 121,
    136, 138, 139, 140, 141, 147, 149, 167,
    171, 183, 186, 187, 194-199, 206, 227,
    236, 249, 256, 257, 258, 259, 264, 293,
    298, 299, 309, 311, 315
Price, 211, 215
Primrose of the Rock, The, 297
Prophecy, A, 235

Quillinan, Edward, 184

Raleigh, 71, 96, 167, 187, 189
Raymond, 43
Recluse, The, 88, 147, 148, 149, 151-
    156, 177, 195, 196, 249, 250, 251

Redbreast chasing the Butterfly, The,
    167, 303 n.
Reed, 2 n., 10 n., 232
Resolution and Independence, 177, 184,
    185
River Duddon, The, 297
Rob Roy's Grave, 228
Robinson, 171, 236, 285
Rose, Rev. Hugh James, 10
Rousseau, 10, 43, 56, 66, 303, 306
Ruined Cottage, The, 88, 239, 262
Ruth, 71, 101, 119, 144, 145, 146, 183,
    189, 239

Saintsbury, 226
Schelling, 90
Schill, 246
Scott, 228, 229, 237, 238
Shairp, 295
Shakespeare, 10, 28, 70, 305, 313
She was a Phantom of delight, 227
Shelley, 66
Simon Lee, 96, 101
Simplon Pass, The, 138, 139
Small Celandine, The, 167
Socrates, 216
Solitary Reaper, The, 167, 168, 228
Song at the Feast of Brougham Castle,
    232, 233, 234
Southey, 285
Sparrow's Nest, The, 4, 75, 167
Spenser, 10, 28, 35, 182, 305
Stanzas suggested in a Steamboat off
    St. Bees' Heads, 290
Stein, 314
Stepping Westward, 228
Sun has long been set, The, 167
Swift, 30, 50
Synesius, 90

Tables Turned, The, 108, 109, 290,
    308
Talleyrand, 192
Taylor, 90
Tennyson, 26, 163, 182, 204, 217, 222,
    286, 295, 302
Theocritus, 305
There is a bondage worse, far worse,
    to bear, 192
There is an Eminence, — of these our
    hills, 158, 160
There is a little unpretending Rill,
    175
There was a Boy, 136, 137, 164
Thomson, 235, 286, 306, 307

Thorn, The, 101, 122
Thought of a Briton on the Subjugation of Switzerland, 236
Thoughts suggested the Day following, on the Banks of Nith, etc., 167, 169
Three years she grew in sun and shower, 115, 142, 143, 184
'T is said, that some have died for love, 161, 162
To a Butterfly, 167
To the Cuckoo, 164
To the Daisy, 115, 165, 166
To a Highland Girl, 167, 228
To Joanna, 158, 160, 224
To M. H., 158, 160, 161
To the Men of Kent (October 1803), 192
To my Sister, 105, 106, 308
To a Painter, 227
To the Same Flower, 167
To a Sky-Lark, 167
To the Small Celandine, 167
Traherne, 219, 220, 221
Turner, 211
Two April Mornings, The, 93, 96, 101, 144, 162, 189
Two Thieves, The, 93
Tylor, 18 n.

Vaughan, 217, 218, 219
Veitch, 4
Vergil, 305, 306

We are Seven, 90, 93, 96
Wellesley, Sir Arthur, 243
When I have borne in memory what has tamed, 191
White Doe of Rylstone, The, 71, 227, 237-242
Winchelsea, Lady, 306, 307
With how sad steps, O Moon, thou climb'st the sky, 175
Wither, 306
Wordsworth, Captain John, 4, 147, 148, 155, 169, 202, 228
Wordsworth, Catherine, 228
Wordsworth, Christopher, 2, 195
Wordsworth, Dora, 171, 228
Wordsworth, Dorothy, 4, 41, 43, 69, 73-79, 86, 87, 90, 136, 147, 148, 151, 152, 153, 156, 168, 195, 228, 232, 259
Wordsworth, John, 228
Wordsworth, Mrs., 41, 169, 188, 227
Wordsworth, Richard, 15
Wordsworth, Thomas, 228
Wordsworth, William, 228
World is too much with us; late and soon, The, 175
Wrangham, 80

Yarrow Revisited, 296, 297
Yarrow Unvisited, 167
Yarrow Visited, 297
Yes, it was the mountain Echo, 174
Yew-Trees, 167
Young, 307, 308

DATE DUE